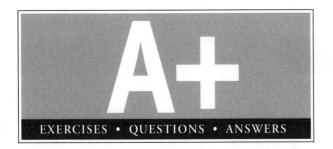

EXERCISES • QUESTIONS • ANSWERS

D1488942

# A+® Certification Press
# Lab Manual

# ABOUT THE AUTHORS

**Jane and Charles Holcombe** are consultants, trainers, and authors with decades of experience. They now write technical books and creative non-fiction as a team.

Jane has been developing computer courses and teaching classes in computer technology at an advanced level since 1984. She teaches both basic and advanced computer networking and operating system topics. Jane was a pioneer in PC support training in the mid-'80s when she co-founded a successful national training company and authored numerous technical-training courses and taught them coast-to-coast. She has been a Microsoft Certified Trainer (MCT) for a number of years and she has earned the Microsoft Certified Systems Engineer (MCSE) certification for Windows NT 3.51, Windows NT 4.0 and Windows 2000. She also holds A+, Network+ and CTT+ certifications. Her current training and consulting focus is on the Windows 2000 and Windows XP operating systems.

Chuck was a pioneering computer programmer, sales analyst, salesman, sales manager, and computer-based training product manager for a super-computer manufacturer. For the past 23 years he has been an independent trainer and management consultant during which time he authored and delivered training courses worldwide. His focus has been on human interaction: sales, customer relations, negotiation, and teaching interpersonal skills to technical people. He is now returning to his first love, computer technology.

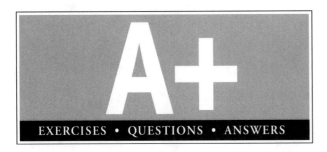

EXERCISES • QUESTIONS • ANSWERS

# A+® Certification Press
# Lab Manual

Jane Holcombe
Charles Holcombe

**McGraw-Hill**/Osborne
New York Chicago San Francisco
Lisbon London Madrid Mexico City Milan
New Delhi San Juan Seoul Singapore Sydney Toronto

**McGraw-Hill/Osborne**
2600 Tenth Street
Berkeley, California 94710
U.S.A.

To arrange bulk purchase discounts for sales promotions, premiums, or fund-raisers, please contact McGraw-Hill/Osborne at the above address. For information on translations or book distributors outside the U.S.A., please see the International Contact Information page immediately following the index of this book.

**A+® Certification Press Lab Manual**

1234567890 DOC DOC 01987654321

ISBN 0-07-219569-X

| | | |
|---|---|---|
| **Publisher** | **Senior Project Editor** | **Production and Editorial** |
| Brandon A. Nordin | Betsy Manini | **Services** |
| | | Anzai!, Inc. |
| **Vice President & Associate** | **Acquisitions Coordinator** | |
| **Publisher** | Athena Honore | **Series Designer** |
| Scott Rogers | | Roberta Steele |
| | **Technical Editor** | |
| **Acquisitions Editor** | Tina Rankin | **Series Cover Designer** |
| Chris Johnson | | Greg Scott |

This book was composed with Corel VENTURA™ Publisher.

We fondly dedicate this book to those who share our lives
and keep us honest, busy, amused, involved and broke:
Rex, Jade, Sunny, and Angel

# CONTENTS

# ACKNOWLEDGMENTS

We greatly appreciate the help and contributions of the following people:

- Neil Salkind of Studio B, who brought this project to our attention.
- The people at McGraw-Hill/Osborne who originated and managed this project. They include Chris Johnson, Athena Honore, and Betsy Manini among many others we met through our countless e-mails.
- Our technical editor, Tina Rankin, who made significant and valuable suggestions that sent us off to test and revise. More than once she kept us from being embarrassed.
- Our unofficial (stealth?) technical editors, Bob Krone, a true hardware wizard, and Fred Shimmin.
- Tom Anzai and his entire Anzai! Inc. team, who all took a greater interest in this project than their assigned tasks required. We especially thank Lee Musick, who went far beyond copy editing by making valuable suggestions about the content.

# INTRODUCTION

Welcome to the *A+ Certification Press Lab Manual*. This manual contains 59 lab exercises designed to give you hands-on, practical experience in your preparation for the CompTIA A+ Certification exams. Use the exercises in this lab manual to reinforce the concepts you learn in a comprehensive reference manual, such as the Global Knowledge Certification Press *A+ Certification Study Guide*.

The lab exercises are presented in the context of real-world situations to prepare you for on-the-job experiences. Learning objectives align with the exam topics of both the hardware and operating system A+ exams. Because technology does not stand still, several lab exercises point you to resources on the Web, where you research recent developments, and simultaneously learn web-based research skills for your future career. The labs have grown out of nearly two decades of field and classroom experience with the topics.

You have a great deal of flexibility in how you use these labs, because each individual lab lists the materials and setup required. We have also worked to avoid dependencies between the labs. There are a few, but in general you can pick and choose labs in the areas in which you need to study.

In each lab, you are presented with a scenario that you might encounter on-the-job. It may be a task that must be accomplished or a problem that must be solved. You will then go through the steps to accomplish the task or solve the problem.

The exercises teach the concepts and skills needed without providing each mouse click of instruction. To that end, the lab exercises guide you through the tasks step-by-step rather than click-by-click. In some labs we provide more detail, only because we judged that someone preparing for their A+ exams might not have the experience to perform the task without such detail.

You will find these lab exercises engaging, with a variety of activities. In a single lab exercise you may be asked to do research on the Web, dismantle a computer, and answer questions about your research and experience in the lab.

In addition to the lab exercises, each chapter includes the following sections:

- **Lab Analysis Test** which contains essay questions
- **Key Term Quiz** which builds vocabulary and gives you the confidence to "talk the talk"

- **Lab Solutions,** found at the end of each chapter, which provide answers to the Lab Analysis Test and Key Term Quiz and explain both the expected outcome of the lab exercises and why the outcome occurred
- **Hint** icons that assist students through sticky spots
- **Warning** icons that draw attention to irreversible pitfalls
- **Cross-reference** icons that direct students to relevant information in the corresponding textbook

A+ instructors are often looking for additional hands-on labs for their students. While this lab manual was designed to complement the *A+ Certification Study Guide*, instructors and students will find it valuable regardless of the text they are following in class.

We have enjoyed creating this book. It involves working with a skill set we recognized as being needed in the mid-80's. We wrote and taught courses for supporting PC hardware and software at that time, and updated it monthly as technology changed. In the 90's many individuals and organizations recognized that this is the foundation knowledge for a variety of computer support-related careers, and CompTIA developed their A+ Certification exams. Our hope is that this lab manual will help you gain the skills and knowledge needed in the computer support field, and pass the A+ exams as many computer professional have done before you. We hope this certification will be your stepping stone to a long and rewarding career.

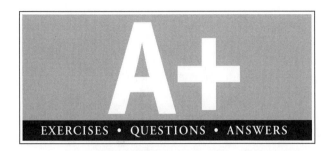

# A+® Certification Press
# Lab Manual

EXERCISES • QUESTIONS • ANSWERS

# 1

# Identifying, Adding, and Removing System Components

## LAB EXERCISES

A ssume that it's your first day on the job as an Information Services Technician, and your boss gives you an important assignment. The finance department on the fifth floor is upgrading the accounting software on all the PCs in the department. Before the upgrade can be done, you must upgrade the memory in each computer to at least 128 megabytes and add network interface cards to several computers.

Or perhaps you are working in an Information Technology department that has just received a shipment of new PCs. Your job is to add the appropriate devices (internal and external) to the PCs before another technician installs all the necessary software. To do this, you must be familiar with the motherboard of a PC and where and how components are connected, plus you must know how to connect external components to the PC.

Are you ready for these tasks? Have you sufficiently mastered the concepts and skills needed to do the job? Do you understand the terms, concepts, and functions of the parts of a computer system, and how they work? Can you perform the basic procedures for adding and removing field-replaceable units (FRUs) in desktop and laptop systems?

**lab**
**Hint**

*The term **Field-Replaceable Unit** is more accepted in the industry than field-replaceable modules, and is an important term to remember. Watch for the term FRU in documentation, training materials, and exams.*

Do you know the common IRQ assignments? Have you mastered the differences between DMA channels and I/O addresses? Do hexadecimal addresses cause your palms to sweat? Are you able to identify common peripheral ports, associated cabling, and connectors?

Before you add or remove components in a computer, you must be able to identify each part, understand what it does, and know where it belongs in the system. This chapter gives you practice in identifying, adding, and removing components, both inside and outside the computer, and in understanding system resources. The exercises help you to build the skills needed in the corporate environment.

**cross**
**Reference**

*The following labs are designed to help you to tie together what you learned in Chapter 1 of the **A+ Certification Study Guide** and to think of these skills within the context of on-the-job experiences.*

## LAB EXERCISE 1.01

# Identifying System Components

**I Hour**

You were hired as a hardware service technician for Nerd Matrix, a company that supplies technicians to install hardware and software for client companies in a large metropolitan area. It's your first day on the job and, for your first assignment, you and your boss are to go to Pico's Place of Precious Pets. Phillip, the manager of the store, wants his computer upgraded. You'll be installing a new, larger hard drive; adding memory; installing a network interface card; and removing a modem card that is no longer needed. Your first task is to identify and remove the components from the computer.

## Learning Objectives

Before you upgrade or fix a computer, you need to be familiar with all its parts. After you've completed this lab, you will be able to:

- Recognize and identify key hardware components in a personal computer

## Lab Materials and Setup

The materials you need for this lab are:

- An assortment of personal computer hardware components
- A personal computer (optional)
- A screwdriver (optional)

cross
**Reference**

***To learn more about where to find system components in a computer, check out the color photographs in the middle of the A+ Certification Study Guide.***

## Getting Down to Business

In this lab you will view several photos and identify components shown on some of the photos from the *A+ Certification Study Guide*, reproduced below for convenience. Optionally, you will identify actual hardware components in your classroom lab.

Refer to the six photographs shown in the following pages. Within each photo are numbers on or next to various system components. Enter the number of the component in the Identifier # column next to the correct name for the component in the table provided for that photo.

Use Figure 1-1 and the Table 1-1 to identify various components of a typical motherboard.

**FIGURE 1-1**

A typical
motherboard

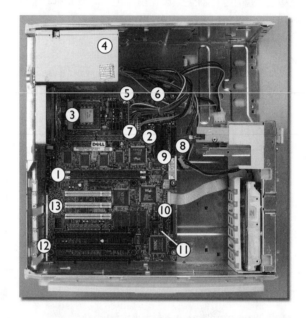

**TABLE 1-1**

Components
of a typical
motherboard

| Component | Identifier # |
|---|---|
| 3.3V power input connector | |
| PCI expansion card connectors | |
| DIMM memory sockets | |
| Power supply | |
| System board jumpers | |
| Primary IDE/EIDE channel connector | |
| Secondary IDE/EIDE channel connector | |
| ISA expansion card connectors | |
| Microprocessor | |
| Floppy disk drive interface connector | |

| TABLE 1-1 | Component | Identifier # |
|---|---|---|
| Components of a typical motherboard (continued) | Control panel connector (for power and drive lights on front of computer case) | |
| | Power input connector | |
| | Battery socket | |

Use Figure 1-2 and the Table 1-2 to identify various components visible when an open case is viewed from the back.

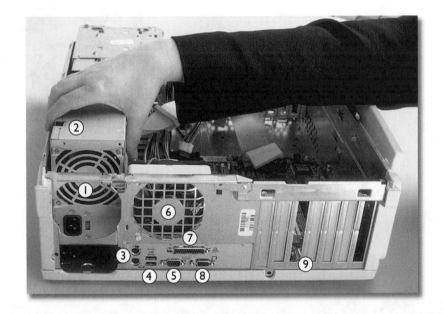

| FIGURE 1-2 |
|---|
| Open PC viewed from the back |

| TABLE 1-2 | Component | Identifier # |
|---|---|---|
| Components visible from the back | Serial port (9-pin male) | |
| | Slot covers | |
| | Power supply cooling fan | |
| | USB (Universal Serial Bus) port | |
| | Cooling fan | |

| TABLE 1-2 | Component | Identifier # |
|---|---|---|
| Components visible from the back *(continued)* | Power supply | |
| | Monitor port (15-pin female) | |
| | Keyboard and PS/2 mouse connectors | |
| | Parallel port | |

Use Figure 1-3 and the Table 1-3 to identify various components located near the processor on a motherboard.

| FIGURE 1-3 |
|---|
| Interior view of a PC |

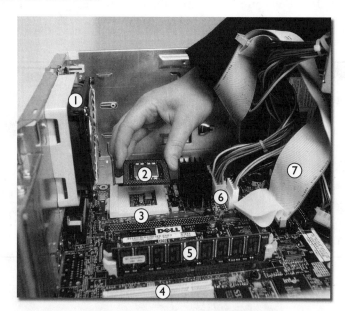

| TABLE 1-3 | Component | Identifier # |
|---|---|---|
| Components located near the procesor | Power supply connectors | |
| | Cooling fan | |
| | PCI expansion slot | |
| | IDE/EIDE flat data ribbon cable | |
| | CPU (processor; central processing unit) | |

| TABLE 1-3 | Component | Identifier # |
|---|---|---|
| | 168-Pin DIMM memory | |
| | Processor socket | |

Components
located near the
procesor
*(continued)*

Use Figure 1-4 and the following table to identify components in the front of an open PC.

FIGURE 1-4

Front view of
an open PC

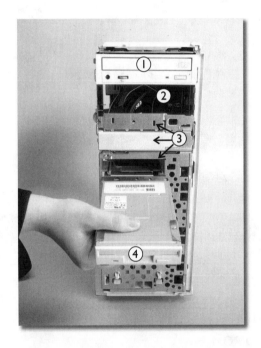

| Component | Identifier # |
|---|---|
| Floppy disk drive bays (3.5-inch size) | |
| CD-ROM drive | |
| Floppy disk drive | |
| Additional CD-ROM or tape drive bay (5.25-inch size) | |

Use Figure 1-5 and the following table to identify various components visible in an open PC.

| Component | Identifier # |
|---|---|
| Additional CD-ROM or tape drive bays (5.25-inch size) | |
| Power cable | |
| CMOS battery | |
| Master/slave jumpers | |
| CD-ROM drive | |
| Additional connector for another IDE/EIDE device | |
| Sound card connector | |
| IDE/EIDE cable | |
| Power supply connectors | |

Use Figure 1-6 and the following table to identify components used when configuring a floppy disk drive.

FIGURE 1-6

View of a small portion of a motherboard

| Component | Identifier # |
|---|---|
| Jumper configuration settings | |
| Configuration jumpers | |
| Floppy disk drive cable | |

lab
ⓗint

*Were some of the components in the pictures difficult to identify? It is very important to see these components in the flesh (or silicon and metal), which you will do in the next step, using whatever equipment is available to you.*

Use Table 1-4 to identify components in the sample equipment provided in the classroom or that you have assembled on your own. Identify each component in the list and place a check mark in the verification column for that component. (Note: There may be items in this list that were not shown in the photos, and it is possible that the sample equipment may not contain all the components listed. There also may be equipment shown that is not included in the list, in which case, simply add the equipment to the table. There are blank rows for this purpose.)

| TABLE 1-4 | Component | Verified |
| --- | --- | --- |
| Components in the sample equipment | 168-pin DIMM memory | |
| | Additional CD-ROM or tape drive bay (5.25-inch size) | |
| | Additional connector for another IDE/EIDE device | |
| | CD-ROM drive | |
| | CMOS battery | |
| | Configuration jumpers | |
| | Control panel connector (for power and drive lights on front of computer case) | |
| | Cooling fan | |
| | CPU (processor; central processing unit) | |
| | DIMM memory sockets | |
| | Floppy disk drive interface connector on drive | |
| | Floppy disk drive connector on motherboard | |
| | Floppy disk drive | |
| | Floppy disk drive bays (3.5-inch size) | |
| | Floppy disk drive cable | |
| | IDE/EIDE flat data ribbon cable | |
| | ISA expansion card connectors | |
| | Jumper configuration settings | |
| | Keyboard and PS/2 mouse connectors | |
| | Master/slave jumpers | |
| | Microprocessor | |
| | Monitor port | |
| | Parallel port | |
| | PCI expansion slot | |
| | PCI expansion card connectors | |

| TABLE 1-4 | Component | Verified |
|---|---|---|
| Components in the sample equipment (*continued*) | Power cable | |
| | Power input connector | |
| | Power supply | |
| | Power supply cooling fan | |
| | Primary EIDE channel connector | |
| | Processor socket | |
| | Secondary EIDE channel connector | |
| | Serial port | |
| | Slot covers | |
| | Sound card connector | |
| | System board jumpers | |
| | USB port | |
| | | |
| | | |
| | | |
| | | |
| | | |

## LAB EXERCISE 1.02

# Adding and Removing Components

**1.5 Hours**

Remember that you are preparing to go along with your new boss at Nerd Matrix to Pico's Palace of Precious Pets to upgrade store manager Phillip's computer. You've now shown that you can recognize the major components and correctly identify them. But Phillip specifically wants to install new software, which will require you to install a new hard drive, additional memory, and a network interface card. You will also need to remove the unneeded modem card. It's now time to review how to install and remove these components.

## Learning Objectives

In this lab, you practice adding and removing hard drives, memory, and network interface and modem cards for desktop and portable systems. By the end of this lab, you'll be able to:

- Remove memory, drives, and other system components from a desktop or laptop computer

- Add memory, network interface cards, or hard drives to a desktop or laptop computer

## Lab Materials and Setup

For this lab, you need the following tools and components:

- One working desktop computer with a hard drive and internal modem (or another card that can be removed)

- A large, open workspace with an anti-static mat (if possible)

- A Phillips screwdriver or appropriate nut driver

- One or more containers in which to place and organize screws and other small parts

- A notepad on which to take notes and make sketches of the computer and components

- The user manual for the computer (more than just a "nice-to-have")

- A laptop computer (optional)

Optionally, try performing this lab using a laptop computer, if you have one available. You will find that the components you can safely remove will vary by manufacturer. Usually, you would not actually remove the keyboard, processors, memory modules, or screen in a laptop computer, because doing so may void the warranty on the computer or cause serious damage. Can you hear the voice of experience here? Memory modules are often the exception to this rule. Read the manual before making any hardware changes to a laptop.

# Getting Down to Business

The following steps provide general instructions to guide you through adding and removing hard drives, memory, and network interface and modem cards for desktop and portable systems. Don't be a maverick! Always be sure the actions you perform on these computers are within those endorsed by the manufacturer. Where do you find out about all this? From the documentation for the computer. If you do not have it in paper form, try to find it on the manufacturer's web site.

*If you are unsure of the safe procedures to follow, read ahead in the A+ Certification Study Guide, beginning with the section titled "Personal Safety Procedures" in Chapter 4, stopping at Exercise 4-2.*

**Step 1.** This is a precautionary step which you may already know from previous experience. Before beginning disassembly, power up the computer and go into the BIOS setup program. Each BIOS manufacturer has a different procedure for this. Watch for an instruction on your screen during the BIOS bootup—the earliest stages of system bootup when the BIOS loads its programs and runs the Power on Self Test (POST). Usually you must press a key, such as DELETE, or a key combination such as CTRL-S to get into the setup program. After you press the appropriate key combination, the BIOS screen will appear. Write down all the settings (there are usually several screens), and then exit from the BIOS program without making and/or saving any changes. This provides you with cheap insurance against the possibility that the battery powering the CMOS RAM is disconnected and you lose the setup information that is saved there. If that should happen you will have to restore the settings, and having the correct data available will save your day.

*Don't want to get writer's cramp? If there is a printer attached to your computers parallel port, power it up and do a screen print on each screen. With page printers, like laser jet and ink jet printers, you will need to push the form feed button on the printer after each screen or two. We find that we can usually fit two screens per page. It won't be pretty, but it is an easy way to accurately capture the BIOS setup settings.*

**Step 2.** Power down the computer and all attached peripherals. Unplug the computer from the wall outlet. Disconnect all external cables connected to the computer, including the monitor, mouse, and keyboard connection. Move the monitor, mouse, and keyboard to a safe place while you work on the computer. Place the computer in the workspace and ensure that you have followed proper procedure regarding electrostatic discharge.

lab
**Warning**

*Never open a power supply or a monitor. Both contain potentially dangerous (even lethal) voltage charges, even after being unplugged! You must follow safe procedures when working on computers! Pay special attention to electrostatic discharge (ESD) and its possible effect on delicate components.*

**Step 3.** Remove the case cover by following the manufacturer's instructions in the user manual for the computer, or by following your instructor's directions. Be very careful not to disturb cables inside the system unit as you remove the cover. Place any screws or other attachment hardware in a container so that they don't disappear. Once the case is open, you will see the interior, which varies from model to model. Stop now and draw a rough sketch, identifying the components and their locations, and make any notes that will aid you when you reassemble the computer.

cross
**Reference**

*The following sections in Chapter 1 of the A+ Certification Study Guide provide information on removing most FRUs: Exercise 1-2, "Removing a Hard Drive;" Exercise 1-4, "Removing a PGA Processor;" SEC/Slot 1, Memory, SIMM Memory, and DIMM Memory.*

**Step 4.** Remove the following components: memory modules, hard and floppy drive(s), and one or more circuit boards (network interface card, modem, and so on). If you are unsure of how to remove a component, review the sections of the book listed in the cross-reference. For components for which actual removal procedures are not described, refer to the user manual for the hardware and/or to your instructor.

lab
**Hint**

*When you disconnect a plug, be sure to firmly grasp the plug, not the cable. Pull the plug straight out, being careful not to bend any pins or to damage the connectors in any way. Do not apply excessive force. If a component cannot be disconnected, skip it. Use your own discretion, because, like a medical professional, a service technician first must do no harm!*

**Step 5.** By now you should have a workspace just chock full of computer pieces. Check your notes and plan how you will reassemble the computer, securing all components with the screws or other fasteners that originally held them in place. Begin the reassembly with the internal components. As you reinstall drives and interface cards, be sure to reconnect all appropriate cables. Close the computer case, being careful not to disturb any of the cables inside the computer. Fasten the case with the fasteners you removed from it. Check to ensure that there are no spare parts lying about. If all appears neat and tidy, plug the power cable into a wall outlet and power on the computer.

**lab**
**ⓦarning**

*Do not remove the CMOS battery because that will cause the setup information to be lost. More on CMOS in Chapter 2. Again: Do not remove the CMOS battery!*

**Step 6.** If the computer powers up normally—go celebrate. If it does not power up properly, turn it off, disconnect it from the wall outlet, and regroup. You must go over every aspect of assembling the computer, checking your notes, the user manual (if available), and any other reference or resources that will help you successfully reassemble the computer. Don't despair—everyone has days like this!

**Step 7.** Optionally, perform a similar set of steps on a laptop computer, removing only the components that you are sure you can safely remove. You say you weren't born knowing which ones they are? Well, if you are in a classroom situation, ask the instructor. If you are using this lab manual for self-study, check the laptop's user manual. In general, all you should remove and reinstall in a laptop are the battery, a PCMCIA card (PC Card), and, just maybe, the drives—floppy, hard, and CD-ROM/ DVD. Remember to remove components only if you have explicit instructions on the proper way to remove them and to reinstall them. After the laptop is reassembled, power it up. If it does not power up, you have to troubleshoot it, using the suggestions provided earlier for the desktop computer.

**LAB EXERCISE 1.03**

# Understanding System Resources

I Hour

Alice's Auto Repair called you to install an internal modem in Alice's personal computer. The computer is running Windows 2000, a plug-and-play operating system, and the computer has a plug-and-play BIOS. (Plug-and-play is often called PnP.) You do not expect to have a problem with this installation because the modem is also PnP. However, before you install it, you want to check out what resources are in use. In particular, you are curious to see the COM port settings because you know that there is also a scanner connected to a serial port on the computer that is configured as COM2.

Remember that PC hardware resources are very limited. There are only 16 IRQs, 8 DMA channels, and 64KB of available I/O addresses. The PnP standard was introduced to PCs in 1993, although most of us were not aware of it until the advent of Windows 95, the first version of Windows to support PnP. PnP is designed to make the allocation of these resources automatic, even to the point of resolving potential conflicts. However, to truly work, this standard depends on the BIOS, the operating system, and the hardware all being PnP-compliant. Hardware that must be PnP-compliant includes the system bus (the PCI bus is PnP) and peripherals. Manufacturers of motherboards include both PCI slots and the older ISA slots, but many now make the ISA slots PnP-capable by linking them to the PnP circuitry of the motherboard. However, you will certainly run into non-PnP systems somewhere in your career.

**lab**
**Hint**

*Learning how to resolve resource conflicts may make you a hero! Although it is tempting to move on to more interesting topics in the belief that PnP will solve these problems for you, you never know what awaits you on the job. Perhaps a company has many computers that depend on a specialized interface card, but this special card has such a small market that the manufacturer is continuing to produce it as a non-PnP device. Also, although it may seem to be the norm for organizations to update their computers on a regular schedule, many continue to use older systems and/or older peripherals (scanners, printer, etc.) until they actually completely fail. Therefore, technicians need to be prepared to recognize the typical settings for IRQs, I/O addresses, and DMA channels.*

## Learning Objectives

In this lab, you are preparing to install a modem into a computer and need to check out its resource usage. Because the I/O port addresses are shown in hexadecimal, you will brush up your hexadecimal math skills. Then you will identify the resource usage in your lab computers and prepare to install a non-PnP device in a computer. By the end of this exercise, you'll be able to:

■ Identify and translate hexadecimal addresses

■ Identify the IRQ, DMA, and I/O address usage on a computer

■ Identify steps to resolve IRQ conflicts

## Lab Materials and Setup

To complete this lab you will need:

■ A computer running Windows 95 or a newer version of Windows

■ The user manual for the computer (optional)

■ The Calculator program that comes standard with Windows

This lab is in two parts. Steps 1 & 2 are the first part, which is a primer on understanding the hexadecimal numbering system, which is very useful when viewing system resources. From here on we'll use the shortened name of "hex." If you are already very comfortable with hex, you may skip this first part.

Steps 3–6 make up the second part of the lab, in which you view and record the system resource usage on a computer. Then, you practice the actions needed to resolve an IRQ conflict on a lab computer.

## Getting Down to Business

When viewing I/O addresses, you will typically see them represented as four hex digits. In binary, that would be 16 binary digits (or bits). Therefore, an I/O address can be as large as the largest number that you can represent with 16 binary digits, which is 65,636, or 64 kilobytes (KB). Two different conventions are commonly used to clue you to the fact that the number you are looking at is a hex number. It may be preceded with "0x" as in 0x0A79, or it may be terminated with an "h" as in

0279h. But often you simply have to guess. If, for example, the number is 022B, it is obviously hex because it contains an alphabetic character. But how would you know that 0170 is hex? This can be a real problem. To resolve it, consider the context: are you seeing this notation when you look at I/O addresses in Device Manager? If yes, then it is a hex value. The leading zeros are also a clue. In the Windows 2000 version of Device Manager, the I/O addresses are shown as eight-place hex numbers—with lots of leading zeros.

Furthermore, I/O addresses will be shown as a range of addresses. For instance the I/O address range for LPT1 begins at 378h and ends at 37Fh. Depending on the program you are using to view I/O addresses, the range in hex will be shown as 0x0378-0x037F, or 378-37Fh, or 0378-037F. This is a range that includes 8 bytes because it includes the starting and ending addresses.

lab
ⓗint

*The I/O ranges for LPT1 (0378-037F) and for the COM ports are very important ranges to remember for practical and testing purposes! We have provided one, but you have to research the others in this lab. Be sure to memorize them!*

**Step 1.** Use your Internet browser to go to www.webopedia.com or to a similar online encyclopedia. At this site, search on the word "hexadecimal" or "hexidecimal" (it accepts either spelling). They make the point that the value of an 8-bit byte, which is represented by eight places when written in binary, is represented by only two places in hex notation. Therefore, one character in hex notation can represent the same value as four characters in a binary number. While you are visiting Webopedia, try searching on a related term—kilobyte—and write the definitions below:

_____

_____

cross
**⌐eference**

*Look at Table 1-2 on in Chapter One in your A+ Certification Study Guide and note that the hexadecimal column shows a single character, while the binary column uses four characters, and the decimal column uses one or two characters to represent the same value.*

**Step 2.**   You want to practice calculating ranges of addresses in hex. Open the Calculator program, change the view to scientific, calculate the size of the following range of addresses, and write the value in the space provided. To do this, you first click on the Hex radio button to work in Hex, and then enter the ending address in the range (02FF in the first problem). You then click on the minus sign and enter the beginning address in the range (02F8). Click on the equal sign, and the result will appear. To this result, you will add one byte, because the range includes the beginning address as well as the ending address.

1.  02F8-02FF = _____

2.  0330-0331 = _____

3.  0376-0376 = _____

4.  03F2-03F5 = _____

5.  03F8-03FF = _____

**Step 3.**   View the I/O address usage on your classroom computer. There are several methods for viewing resource usage on a computer. On a Windows 95 or Windows 98 computer you can follow the steps provided in Exercise 1-7 in Chapter 1 of the *A+ Certification Study Guide.* You vary these steps slightly on a Windows 2000 computer because there is no longer a Device Manager tab in the System Properties dialog box. Instead you must click the Hardware tab, then the Device Manager button. This brings up the Device Manager Console, where you can select View| Resources by Type.

lab
(i)int   *Another way to view resource usage on a Windows NT or Windows 2000 computer is to run the WINMSD.EXE program from the Run command in the Start menu. The Windows NT version of this program is the Windows NT Diagnostics program, while the Windows 2000 version opens the System Information console.*

Depending on the version of Windows on your computer, use one of the tools described above to view the IRQ usage on your computer. Enter the device names next to the IRQ number in the following table. If an IRQ is not shown as being in use by a device, leave it blank in the table. If an IRQ is being used by more than one device, indicate all devices in the space provided.

| IRQ# | Device |
|------|--------|
| 0 | |
| 1 | |
| 2 | |
| 3 | |
| 4 | |
| 5 | |
| 6 | |
| 7 | |
| 8 | |
| 9 | |
| 10 | |
| 11 | |
| 12 | |
| 13 | |
| 14 | |
| 15 | |

lab
ⓗint

*Read (or re-read) the reference in the **A+ Certification Study Guide** on maskable interrupts (the type listed above) versus nonmaskable interrupts (NMIs). If you do not have the **A+ Certification Study Guide**, search Microsoft's Technet site at www.microsoft.com/technet to learn more about the distinction between these two types of interrupts.*

**Step 4.** Use the same program that you used to find the IRQ settings to find the DMA settings for your computer and enter them in the following table. It is important for you to remember that DMA Channel 2 is assigned to the floppy disk drive controller because it is the standard assignment, cannot be shared by another device, and it could appear on a test.

| DMA Chanel | Device |
|---|---|
|  |  |
|  |  |
|  |  |
|  |  |

**Step 5.** Use the same program as in the previous steps to examine the I/O addresses in use on your lab computer and complete the following table. These are important I/O addresses to remember! If a device has more than one range of addresses, enter all ranges in the I/O Address Range column. Some of the ports listed may not exist on your computer.

| Device | I/O Address Range |
|---|---|
| COM1 |  |
| COM2 |  |
| COM3 |  |
| COM4 |  |
| LPT1 |  |
| Keyboard |  |
| Primary IDE Channel |  |
| Secondary IDE Channel |  |

lab

ⓗint

*There is yet another way to view resources. Many BIOS setup programs enable you to view and to do limited configuration of these settings. If you are feeling brave, you may explore the BIOS setup program on your computer. The user manual will help you with this.*

**Step 6.** Your investigation of resource usage on Alice's computer shows no conflict, but she gives you yet another task. Until now this computer had not been on the LAN at Alice's. She found an old ISA bus network card that she would like you to install. Sure enough, you discover that the only IRQs it can be configured to use (via jumpers on the card) are 3 or 5. A PnP BIOS will permit you to disable the IRQ, or the port using the IRQ, for use by PnP. Then the IRQ will be available for the network interface card.

In the classroom, read the user manual for your computer to see how to access the BIOS setup program. Go into the setup program, use the instructions in the user manual, or browse the setup program menus to see where you would make such a change. Don't make any actual changes, but record below the version of BIOS you are using (for example, AMI BIOS 1999) and the steps that you would take to reserve IRQ 3 or 5 for the network interface card.

_____

_____

_____

_____

lab
**Warning**

*"Explore" means look, not change. Inappropriate changes to the BIOS setup can make your computer unusable because these settings are used to recognize system components. Be very careful to first write down (or print out) the existing settings and do not make any changes to BIOS at this point.*

## LAB EXERCISE 1.04

**I Hour**

# Connecting Monitors, Printers, and Other Devices to Your Computer

A new client, Bill's House of Flowers, needs a new computer in their store. You have picked up the computer, monitor, keyboard, mouse, printer, external modem, and scanner, along with all the necessary cables. Your job is to deliver the system to Bill's and to connect all peripherals.

## Learning Objectives

In this lab, you connect a monitor, mouse, keyboard, printer, external modem, and scanner to a computer. Before you begin, you build a reference library of connector technology for yourself. By the end of the lab, you'll be able to:

- Build a reference library of charts, glossaries, and web sites
- Identify physical connector hardware in the classroom using a connector reference chart

■ Research the connection technologies of USB and FireWire/IEEE 1394

■ Connect a variety of external peripheral devices to a personal computer

## Lab Materials and Setup

To complete this lab you need:

■ A computer running Windows 95, or a newer version of Windows

■ A parallel port on the computer you are using

■ A connection to the Internet (because you will be doing some research over the Internet)

■ An operating printer with a parallel cable

■ A USB port on the computer and a USB cable (optional)

■ A FireWire port on the computer and a FireWire cable (optional)

In many industries, technicians and mechanics invest a great deal of money accumulating all the right tools for their work. Computer technicians also need the right tools. The physical ones (screwdrivers, multi-meters, and so on) are usually provided by the employer. But the less tangible tools—the right references—often are not provided. In fact, it can be difficult to find all the information that you need on peripheral ports, cabling, and connectors in one place.

In this lab you will build such a reference to use on the job. This reference can include some handy charts to keep with you. But, because computer technology changes so quickly, it is also very valuable to have a list of web sites where you can find current information. Altogether, you should have a personal reference library that includes hard copy (books and printouts), as well as an online library of web sites.

In this lab, as you build a reference library including one or more charts, a glossary, and a list of good web sites, you will also research information on some of the newer connection technologies.

Your final task is to connect peripheral devices to a computer.

## Getting Down to Business

The following steps explain how to build a connector reference.

**Step 1.** To begin building a connector reference, go to a web site and download both a chart of the connectors you may encounter as a technician, and a glossary. You may use the site recommended for this lab, one recommended by your instructor, or one that you find on your own. The recommended site is ckp.made-it.com, home of Connectivity Knowledge Platform (CKP). The home page contains an index of links to references on connectors, cables, and connectivity devices. From the index, select the link titled Connector reference chart. Print the chart and save it in your *A+ Certification Study Guide* or in a three-ring notebook. This chart contains more than you need for the exam, but will be very handy on the job.

**Step 2.** Identify the connectors that are physically available to you in the classroom and check them off on the reference chart you made in Step 1.

**Step 3.** At the same web page, or another of your choosing, find a glossary of terms and print them out (if a printer is available and connected). Save this glossary in your notebook to be used as a reference along with the chart.

lab
&#9416;int    *Two online web sites with good glossary searches are www.webopedia.com and www.whatis.com.*

**Step 4.** Use the web site you used in the previous steps, and that of a cable manufacturer, such as Belkin Company (www.belkin.com), to research the questions below on FireWire/IEEE 1394 and USB. Note: At this time the CKP site has excellent information on USB, but no information on FireWire. You will find FireWire information at the Belkin site.

### FireWire/IEEE 1394

1. What speeds are shown for FireWire?

_____

_____

2. How does FireWire compare with USB?

   _____

   _____

3. How many devices are supported on a FireWire bus?

   _____

   _____

4. Describe the number and type of connectors used for FireWire.

   _____

   _____

## USB

1. What are the three device types defined in the USB standard?

   _____

   _____

2. What are the two speeds supported by USB?

   _____

   _____

3. Define a USB host.

   _____

   _____

4. How many USB hosts may exist on a USB network?

   _____

   _____

5. Define a USB hub.

   _____

   _____

6. Define a function.

 

7. Create a list of Internet sites that you can use as your online reference library. Include the sites used for this lab, as well as others that you have encountered.

 

**Step 5.**   Next, research two older technologies that are associated with connectors: RJ11 and RJ45. For RJ11 there is a nice page describing the very, very basic RJ11 implementation at (how well can you type?) www.shout.net/~wildixon/telecom/rj/rj.html. This page is worth the trouble to reach because it describes and has links to information on the many different versions of Registered Jacks (RJ).

**lab**

**Warning**   *Internet sites come and go, so be sure to update your lists and test your bookmarks on a regular basis (perhaps once a month).*

**Step 6.**   Now you will practice physically connecting peripherals to your computers. Power down your computer. If the printer is already connected to your computer with a parallel cable, power down the printer and disconnect the cable from the computer. Examine the cable and identify the connection type—it is most likely to be parallel at the computer end. At the printer end of a parallel cable it will probably be Centronics, a standard in use for many years that uses a 36-pin Amphenol connector. This connector, originally made by the Amphenol Company has a locking clip at each end to firmly hold the connector to the printer.

Many newer printers use USB cables to connect to the computer. Some will have a permanently connected cable at the printer end with a USB plug at the computer end. Others will only have a USB socket at the printer end and you will have to provide a separate USB cable to connect the two units. Examine the USB cable and note that there are different plug types on each end: USB type A and USB type B.

Now connect the printer to the correct connector on the computer.

**Step 7.** Disconnect the monitor and examine the connector. This will be a 15-pin connector. Notice that the connector on the computer is female.

**Step 8.** Perform the same procedure with all the cables and devices you have available for this lab.

**Step 9.** Reconnect all the devices before proceeding. If this is the computer you are using for your Internet access, ensure that it can boot up and that it is fully functional at the completion of the lab.

**lab**
**Hint**

*As a rule, physical devices must be connected to a computer when the computer is powered off. However, PnP changes the rules for us, especially when connecting a new USB device to a PnP computer with a PnP operating system. In this case, the computer must be powered up, with the operating system running, before you connect the USB device. Therefore, if you have a USB device, wait until you have connected all non-PnP devices, then power up the computer, bring up the operating system and connect the USB device. As with all devices, it is important to read the manual or instructions that come with a USB device. Some will have you install software before plugging in a USB device; others will prompt you for the software after it's plugged in.*

# LAB ANALYSIS TEST

1. You're installing a hard drive into a computer. The IDE ribbon cable is in place and connected to the motherboard, but the free end will not plug into the hard drive. What could the problem be?

_____

_____

2. You have solved the problem with the cable, but you notice that the ribbon cable actually has two connectors that fit the hard drive—one on the end of the cable, and one in the middle of the cable. What rule do you use to decide which connector to use for installing a single hard drive in a computer?

_____

_____

3. You're at a client's site installing an ISA network card provided by the client. There is no documentation for it. You went to the manufacturer's web site on the Internet and found information on installing this card, including the following cryptic instruction: "Give your network card 16 bytes of I/O address starting at 36Ch." Calculate the address range. The computer also has a parallel port configured as LPT1 and using I/O range 0378-037F. Will there be a conflict if you install this card? What steps should you take next?

_____

_____

4. Another client has asked you to install an ISA sound card in a Windows 95 computer. How will you discover the resources required by the ISA sound card and how you will determine what resources are in use?

_____

_____

5. You have been asked to bring a new mouse to Bill's House of Flowers to replace their current mouse. What information do you need from Bill in order to take the appropriate type of mouse?

_____

_____

# KEY TERM QUIZ

Use the following vocabulary terms to complete the sentences below. Not all of the terms will be used.

IRQ
memory
pin grid array (PGA)
power supply
processor
random access memory (RAM)
system board
system modules
nonmaskable interrupts (NMIs)
modem

1. Internal and external components, such as hard drives, printers, video cards, and so on, are connected (directly or indirectly) to the _____.

2. Most computer components are designed to perform only one or a limited number of functions, and they do so only when it is specifically requested of them. The device responsible for organizing the actions of these components is the _____, also referred to as the central processing unit.

3. Older processor models, such as the Intel 80286, 80386, and 80486, have _____ form. The earliest Pentium models used this, and the newest Pentium IIs and IIIs have returned to this form. This form is square, with several rows of pins on the bottom. These pins are used to attach it to a motherboard, referred to as a ZIF (zero insertion force) connector, or, more commonly, as a socket.

4. The _____, typically located at the back of the computer's interior, has several very important functions. It is responsible for converting the alternating current (AC) voltage from wall outlets into the direct current (DC) voltage that the computer requires.

5. _____ are used by memory to indicate a possibly fatal condition, and the processor is stopped mid-task.

# Lab Wrap-Up

You have accomplished a lot! You have studied, explained, experimented, researched, and practiced both the physical and theoretical aspects of the first four objectives for the A+ exam. We also hope you have gained skills that will be useful on the job. With your readings and lab experience you have identified hardware, removed and reinstalled field-replaceable unit, worked with hex notation, discovered the resource usage of a computer, and considered the variety of connection types that you are likely to encounter on the job. Now it is time to move to Chapter 2.

# LAB SOLUTIONS FOR CHAPTER 1

## Lab Solution 1.01

In Figure 1-1, you were to identify the components of a typical motherboard.
Following is the key:

| Component | Identifier # |
| --- | --- |
| 3.3-V power input connector | 7 |
| PCI expansion card connectors | 13 |
| DIMM memory sockets | 1 |
| Power supply | 4 |
| System board jumpers | 11 |
| Primary IDE/EIDE channel connector | 9 |
| Secondary IDE/EIDE channel connector | 2 |
| ISA expansion card connectors | 12 |
| Microprocessor | 3 |
| Floppy disk drive interface connector | 8 |
| Control panel connector | 10 |
| Power input connector | 5 |
| Battery socket | 6 |

The backside of the computer is the central connection point for the peripherals
that are added. Figure 1-2 reveals these connectors.

| TABLE 1-5 | Component | Identifier # |
| --- | --- | --- |
| | Serial port (9-pin male) | 5 |
| Components visible from the back of the PC | Slot covers | 9 |
| | Power supply cooling fan | 1 |
| | USB (Universal Serial Bus) port | 4 |
| | Cooling fan | 6 |

**TABLE 1-5**

Components
visible from the
back of the PC
(continued)

| Component | Identifier # |
|---|---|
| Power supply | 2 |
| Monitor port (15-pin female) | 8 |
| Keyboard and PS/2 mouse connectors | 3 |
| Parallel port | 7 |

Servicing the computer motherboard, adding internal components, or adding expansion cards calls for accurate identification of parts and connections. Figure 1-3 features the following items:

| Component | Identifier # |
|---|---|
| Power supply connectors | 6 |
| Cooling fan | 1 |
| PCI expansion slot | 4 |
| IDE flat data ribbon cable | 7 |
| CPU (processor; central processing unit) | 2 |
| 168-Pin DIMM memory | 5 |
| Processor socket | 3 |

Most users are familiar with the different things found on the face of the computer cabinet. Figure 1-4 shows the following components:

| Component | Identifier # |
|---|---|
| Floppy disk drive bays (3.5-inch size) | 3 |
| CD-ROM drive | 1 |
| Floppy disk drive | 4 |
| Additional CD-ROM or tape drive bay (5.25-inch size) | 2 |

Making proper connections on the inside of the computer can make or break the technician, let alone the computer. Figure 1-5 points out these components:

| Component | Identifier # |
|---|---|
| Additional CD-ROM or tape drive bays (5.25-inch size) | 9 |
| Power cable | 5 |
| CMOS battery | 1 |
| Master/slave jumpers | 2 |
| CD-ROM drive | 6 |
| Additional connector for another IDE/EIDE device | 8 |
| Sound card connector | 3 |
| IDE/EIDE cable | 4 |
| Power supply connectors | 7 |

Close examination of the motherboard will reveal smaller features you need to work with.

| Component | Identifier # |
|---|---|
| Jumper configuration settings | 3 (It is printed on the motherboard) |
| Configuration jumpers | 1 |
| Floppy disk drive cable | 2 |

## Lab Solution 1.02

The procedures will vary, depending on the actual equipment supplied for classroom. Fairly detailed steps were provided with the lab instructions because of the nature of the lab. The information below is purely supplemental to that in the lab instructions.

**Step 1.**   The setup information recorded here is critical. If these settings get erased from CMOS memory during the lab, the computer may fail to recognize the hard drive and be unable to successfully boot up. In that case, you will need to rerun setup and manually enter this information.

**Step 2.** For safety's sake, we are referring you to the ESD information that will be more formally explored later in the course.

**Step 3.** Your notes should include a rough sketch of the system with the cover off, but without any components removed.

**Step 4.** It is sometimes daunting to actually remove all the components of a PC, especially when you are not sure you can get them all back together and actually have it work. Keep the faith—you can do it!

**Step 5.** If there are extra parts, or if the cover does not fit as it did previously, review your notes and carefully examine all the components that you reinstalled.

**Step 6.** If the computer does not power up at all, recheck the power cord connection. Ask for the instructor's guidance. If you decide to open up the computer again, please refer to all the precautions described earlier in this lab.

**Step 7.** If you are allowed to perform these steps on a laptop, be sure to remove only those components identified by the instructor.

## Lab Solution 1.03

**Step 1.** A kilobyte is a notation used in binary systems. It represents 1024 bytes. The value 64KB is 64 times 1024 bytes, or 65,636. However, even knowledgeable people talk about the value as if the K equaled 1000.

**Step 2.** Remember to include the first byte when you calculate the range of addresses. The solutions are:

1. 02F8-02FF = 8 bytes
2. 0330-0331 = 2 bytes

**3.** 0376-0376 = 1 byte

**4.** 03F2-03F5 = 4 bytes

**5.** 03F8-03FF = 8 bytes

**Step 3.** The IRQ 0 usage does not show in WINMSD, but it does show in Windows 2000 Device Manager. You can confirm the usage of this IRQ in Windows 2000 by using Device Manager to view the properties of the System Timer.

The answers will vary somewhat based on the configuration of the lab computers. The table below shows common IRQ usage.

| IRQ # | Device |
|-------|--------|
| 0 | System timer |
| 1 | Keyboard |
| 2 | Cascade, redirect to IRQ 9 |
| 3 | Serial ports (COM2 and COM4) |
| 4 | Serial ports (COM1 and COM3) |
| 5 | Parallel port (LPT2) |
| 6 | Floppy disk drive controller |
| 7 | Parallel port (LPT1) |
| 8 | Real-time clock |
| 9 | Redirected from IRQ2 |
| 10 | Available |
| 11 | Available |
| 12 | PS/2 mouse |
| 13 | Math coprocessor |
| 14 | Hard disk controller |
| 15 | Secondary hard disk controller |

**Step 4.** Answers will vary. On an older computer that does not support enhanced capability parallel ports (ECP) or have the newer DMA controller, you may only see one DMA channel in use—channel 2, which is used by the floppy disk controller

(important to remember). On a newer computer that has these capabilities, and has them turned on in BIOS, you could get results similar to those in the following table.

| DMA Channel | Device |
|---|---|
| 2 | Standard floppy disk controller |
| 3 | ECP Printer Port (LPT1) |
| 4 | Direct memory access controller |

**Step 5.** I/O address ranges of the selected devices listed in the table will vary. Following is one possible set of results.

| Device | I/O Address Range |
|---|---|
| COM1 | 03F8-03FF |
| COM2 | 02F8-02FF |
| COM3 | 03E8-03EF |
| COM4 | 02E8-02EF |
| LPT1 | 0378-037F |
| Keyboard | 0060-0060<br>0064-0064 |
| Primary IDE Channel | 01F0-01F7<br>03F6-03F6 |
| Secondary IDE Channel | 0170-0177<br>0376-0376 |

**Step 6.** Answers will vary, depending on the BIOS setup program you are using.

## Lab Solution 1.04

**Step 1.** Information that can serve as a quick reference is worth printing out and keeping in your tool kit. Detailed information on standards and specifications are best if they are relatively handy—for example, in books in your work area or at home—where you can get to them when you are studying and researching. Another great source, of course, is the Internet, which is why you build a list of Internet sites to use as references. The Internet sites will also be more dynamic and up-to-date than your paper references.

**Step 2.**   The results of this comparison of the connectors in the chart and those in the classroom will vary. The instructor will help you if you cannot match up one in the classroom with one on the chart.

**Step 3.**   You may find more than one glossary that you want to save. In the mid-1980s, we attempted to build our own glossary of computing terms, but found it to be an unending job. Now, we are content to use the excellent glossaries that we find in books such as the *A+ Certification Study Guide* and at online sources. Another good online glossary can be found at www.technologyforce.com.

**Step 4.**   At the Belkin site, the page for FireWire products has very little technical information about FireWire, but there is a link on that page titled All About FireWire, which provides more detailed information on FireWire.

### Answers to the FireWire/IEEE 1394 questions:

1. FireWire has speeds up to 400 MBps (50 Megabytes per second).
2. FireWire has a bandwidth nearly 30 times that of USB.
3. Up to 63 hot-swappable devices are supported on a FireWire bus.
4. There are two connector types. The 6-pin is used to connect storage devices, scanners, printers, and hubs to a computer, while the 4-pin is used to connect audio/video devices, such as digital camcorders and cameras.

### Answers to the USB questions:

1. The three device types are hosts, hubs, and functions.
2. The two speeds supported by USB are 12 MBps and 480 MBps.
3. A USB host is an initiating device, such as a PC.
4. Only one USB host may exist on a USB network.
5. A USB hub is a multiport repeater for the serial USB network.

6. A function is a dumb device on a USB network, such as a keyboard, mouse, or printer.

7. Answers will vary. A minimum list might include all the sites used in this lab. Following is such a list—some sites were not previously suggested, but represent sites the students may have discovered on their own.

   www.webopedia.com
   ckp.made-it.com
   www.whatis.com
   www.pcmech.com
   www.belkin.com
   3com.com
   www.google.com
   www.informationweek.com
   techweb.com/enclyclopedia
   www.microsoft.com/technet
   ieee.com
   www.technologyforce.com

**Step 5.** The activity is complete within itself.

**Step 6.** Your experience will vary based on the hardware you have available.

**Step 7.** Your experience will vary based on the hardware you have available.

**Step 8.** Your experience will vary based on the hardware you have available.

**Step 9.** Be sure all the equipment you need to continue is in working order!

# ANSWERS TO LAB ANALYSIS TEST

1. If the IDE cable cannot be plugged into the hard drive, perhaps the cable is oriented the wrong way. The data/control connector on a hard drive subsystem and the connector on the cable are often (but not always) keyed so that they fit only in one orientation. Try reversing the orientation of the connector on the hard drive.

2. The simple rule when you are installing just one IDE hard drive is to attach it to the end of the ribbon cable. However, this is no longer necessary with newer implementations of IDE/EIDE, which will properly detect the master drive on either position on the cable. In Chapter 2, you encounter the special configuration procedures for installing more than one hard drive.

3. There will be a conflict between this network interface card and LPT1. The 16-byte range of addresses begins at 36Ch and ends at 37C, which overlaps the range of addresses used by LPT1. Suggestions: Research further to see if there is a way to configure the card to use another range. It is remotely possible that there is a table printed on the adapter itself. Don't waste too much more time on this research, because network interface cards are very inexpensive. After you have made a good faith effort to configure this card for the client, advise the client to purchase a new card—preferably a PCI card. In the remote possibility that the computer only has an ISA bus, the customer could purchase a new ISA card, which would have complete installation documentation with it, and be less likely to conflict with the known LPT1 address range.

4. It can be very difficult to configure an ISA sound card. They are often very inflexible about the resources that they will use, and they are a notorious source of conflicts. IRQ 5 is a de facto standard among these old cards, even when the documentation indicates one will use either 5 or another IRQ. To determine the resources that are required by the ISA sound card and how to configure the card, you would read the documentation for the card. Because this is older technology, and probably a card that the client has had floating around for a while, it may have separated from its documentation. In this case, you will use the Internet to search for this information—beginning at the web site of the manufacturer (or the site of the company that bought them out, as is often the case). After you discover the resources needed by the card, use Device Manager in Windows 95 to discover what resources are in use. If this is a new career for you, you have just had an indication of how interesting life will be from now on!

5. Before taking a mouse out to Bill's shop, ask him if the old mouse was a serial mouse or a PS/2 mouse. You may need to ask him to look at and to describe the connector on the old mouse. If the old mouse was a PS/2 mouse, you can safely take a new PS/2 mouse; however, if the old mouse was a serial mouse, it is still possible that the computer has a PS/2 port on it. Therefore, describe a PS/2 port to the client and ask him to examine the back of the computer to see if there is one. Real world—if there is any doubt, take both types of mice to the client. You could also have available an adapter that will convert from 9-pin to PS2 configuration.

## ANSWERS TO KEY TERM QUIZ

1. System board

2. Processor

3. Pin grid array (PGA)

4. Power supply

5. Nonmaskable interrupts (NMIs)

EXERCISES • QUESTIONS • ANSWERS

# 2

# Installation, Configuration, and System Optimization

**Y**ou are gaining more experience and confidence as an information services technician. Today you are preparing to upgrade several desktop and laptop computers. Your tasks will include configuring and installing three IDE devices in a desktop computer; installing and configuring USB devices; installing a SCSI card and internal SCSI tape drive in a desktop computer; and upgrading components in a laptop computer.

The following labs are designed to prepare you for upgrading, extending, and optimizing system performance.

**LAB EXERCISE 2.01**

# Upgrading a Desktop Computer

1 Hour

Wanda's Wedding Wonderland has hired you to upgrade one of their office computers in anticipation of installing new graphics software. The computer will need a second IDE drive and a new CD-ROM drive. You have asked how Wanda wants to use the drives and have learned that she wants to leave her operating system and program files on the first drive, and reserve the second drive for the data generated by her programs, especially the graphics application. You verified that the BIOS in Wanda's computer includes support for hard drives larger than 528MB using LBA (logical block addressing) or a similar technology. Most BIOSs in Pentium-based systems do support large hard drives. Only on 486-based systems or the very earliest Pentiums should you expect to encounter lack of support for large hard drives. Considering her planned use of the two hard drives, you have decided to place them on separate IDE/EIDE channels—each as a master. This will effectively load-balance the predicted drive usage by having I/O for the OS and program drive on its own channel, and the I/O for the data on the second channel. (The A+ exam objectives do not indicate that you need to understand the usage patterns before placing IDE/EIDE devices, but you will want to know this when you are on the job.)

She wants the CD-ROM drive to replace a failed drive. She uses the CD-ROM drive mainly to install software from CDs. She knows that the new graphics software, which she will use to design wedding cakes, has a library of images on CD, which she will copy to her new hard drive. Again, considering the planned usage of the drives, you will install the CD-ROM drive as a slave on the secondary IDE/EIDE channel. Remember that you can have only two devices per channel!

## Learning Objectives

In this lab, you upgrade a computer. You will be adding a second IDE hard drive and an IDE CD-ROM drive. By the end of this lab, you'll be able to:

■ Plan for the effective use of IDE devices

■ Install multiple IDE devices in a desktop computer

## Lab Materials and Setup

The materials you need for this lab are:

■ One desktop computer system unit with motherboard, power supply, and floppy drive. Ensure that the computer has both a primary and secondary IDE/EIDE connector on the motherboard. This system should be open, with the power supply, memory, and floppy drive in place. Hard drives and CD-ROM drive should be removed before the lab.

■ Two IDE/EIDE hard drives—one identified as the existing hard drive with the operating system installed; the second will be the data drive.

■ One IDE/EIDE CD-ROM drive.

■ Installation guide(s) for the hard drives and CD-ROM drive, if available.

■ Two IDE/EIDE cables, each with two 40-pin drive connectors and one 40-pin connector for the IDE/EIDE connector on the motherboard.

■ A large, open workspace with an anti-static mat (if possible).

■ A Phillips screwdriver or appropriate nut driver.

■ One or more containers in which to place and organize screws and other small parts.

■ A notepad on which to take notes and make sketches of the computer and components.

■ The user manual for the computer.

*If this is the same computer that you used in the Chapter 1 labs, and if you saved your drawings and notes, you may reuse those drawings and notes in this lab.*

## Getting Down to Business

You're now getting into the actual hands-on process of removing and installing components. The steps below will guide you through your task.

cross
**Reference**

*If you are unsure of the safe procedures to follow, read ahead in the* **A+ Certification Study Guide,** *beginning with the section titled "Personal Safety Procedures" in Chapter 4 stopping at Exercise 4-2.*

**Step 1.** Prepare for the task at hand. Observe safe electrostatic discharge (ESD) procedures. If necessary remove the case cover by following the manufacturer's instructions in the user manual for the computer or by following your instructor's directions. Be very careful not to disturb cables inside the system unit as you remove the cover. Place any screws or other removed attachment hardware in a container so that they don't disappear. Stop now and draw a rough sketch, identifying the components and their locations. Also make any notes that will aid you when reassembling the computer.

**Step 2.** Prepare the two IDE/EIDE hard drives for installation. Since each drive will be a master on a separate IDE/EIDE channel, be sure to configure both drives as masters by setting the jumpers per the instructions for each drive (usually on a sticker on the drive). Write down the type and capacity information for the second drive, in the event that you might need it later for the BIOS configuration. Install and secure the two drives in drive bays inside the system unit. Install the IDE/EIDE cables to the primary and secondary IDE/EIDE channels on the motherboard. (Remember that the stripe on one side of the ribbon cable must go to pin 1 on both the motherboard and the drive!) Connect the drive containing the operating system to the cable connected to the primary channel, and connect the second drive to the cable connected to the secondary channel.

**lab**

**Warning**   *Be sure that the screws you use to install the hard drives are the correct ones. Screws commonly used in computers come in at least two sizes. Although the smaller ones will fit into the mounting holes in the drives and seem to be secure, they can come loose and the disk could cause damage. Also, make sure to use the correct length of screw. Some hard drives have internal components very close to the edge. Using a screw that is too long might cause a problem if it contacts an internal component.*

**Step 3.**   Prepare and install the CD-ROM drive. Set the jumper on the drive for the appropriate setting for installing the drive as a slave. Physically install the drive in a drive bay. Connect the drive to the remaining connector on the IDE/EIDE cable on the secondary channel.

**Step 4.**   Ensure that all internal and external cables are connected to the computer. Replace the cover of the system unit, securing it with the necessary screws or fasteners.

**Step 5.**   Power up the computer. Start up the CMOS setup program. If the primary master drive was the one previously installed in this computer, it should not need further configuration in Setup. For the second drive, the default "auto" detection is preferable. If this does not work, then enter the new drive's type and capacity in the BIOS settings. Again, this information is usually found on the label on the drive. Exit from Setup, saving your changes, and allow the computer to reboot.

**Step 6.**   Once the operating system loads, confirm that the drives are recognized. If the second hard drive was not previously partitioned and formatted, it will not be recognized in Windows Explorer, but you may use another tool, such as Disk Manager, Disk Administrator, Device Manager, or WINMSD (depending on the operating system) to confirm the presence of the drive. Do not attempt to partition or format the second drive at this time, because it is beyond the scope of this chapter. You will learn more about partitioning and formatting hard drives in Chapters 8 and 9.

**LAB EXERCISE 2.02**

# Installing a SCSI Controller and Device

1 Hour

Plochmann's Flower Wholesale has requested that you install a SCSI tape backup system in a file server. There is no SCSI controller in the server, so you need to install both a SCSI controller and the SCSI tape backup system.

## Learning Objectives

While IDE/EIDE is the common interface for drives and tape backup systems in desktop computers and entry level servers, on the job you will, from time to time, encounter the need to install and configure SCSI devices, such as tape backup systems and older scanners. If you work with medium to high-end servers, SCSI is the drive interface of choice because it is faster than IDE/EIDE and supports more devices. After you've completed this lab, you will be able to:

- Identify the proper procedures for installing SCSI controllers and devices
- Identify the proper procedures for configuring SCSI controllers and devices
- Resolve SCSI device address and termination conflicts
- Identify internal versus external SCSI devices
- Identify the type of SCSI used

## Lab Materials and Setup

The materials you need for this lab are:

- One desktop computer system unit with motherboard, power supply, hard drive(s) (installed), CD-ROM drive, and floppy drive. Ensure that the computer has an available expansion slot that fits the SCSI controller provided for the lab. This system should be open, with all components in place, with the exception of the SCSI controller. Verify that an unused power connector is available from the power supply, if an internal SCSI device is to be installed.
- Windows 95 or later version of Windows installed on the computer.

- One SCSI controller card with appropriate internal interface cable.

- One internal or external SCSI tape drive.

- An open drive bay (if installing an internal tape drive).

- Installation guides and drivers for the SCSI controller and SCSI device, if available.

- A large, open workspace with an anti-static mat (if possible).

- A Phillips screwdriver or appropriate nut driver.

- One or more containers in which to place and organize screws and other small parts.

- A notepad on which to take notes and make sketches of the computer and components.

- The user manual for the computer.

cross
**Reference**    *Before you begin this lab, read a good reference on SCSI, which may be an Internet source, such as articles at www.pcmech.com or the entire section titled "Certification Objective 2.02" in the* **A+ Certification Study Guide***.*

## Getting Down to Business

The following steps will guide you through the process of installing a SCSI tape backup system. Because the actual details of an installation will differ slightly depending on whether you are installing an internal or an external drive, we have left these details out of the following steps. Use the installation guide(s) for the SCSI controller and SCSI device for those details.

lab
**Hint**    *If this is the same computer that you used in the Chapter 1 labs, and if you saved your drawings and notes, you may reuse those drawings and notes in this lab.*

**Step 1.**    Prepare for the task at hand. Observe safe ESD procedures. If necessary, remove the case cover by following the manufacturer's instructions in the user manual for the computer, or by following your instructor's directions. Be very careful not to disturb cables inside the system unit as you remove the cover. Place any screws or other attachment hardware in a container so that they don't disappear. Stop now and draw a rough sketch, identifying the components and their location, and make any notes that will aid you when you reassemble the computer.

**Step 2.**   Locate the internal and external connectors on the SCSI controller card. If you are installing an internal tape drive, prepare for installation of the SCSI controller card by connecting the interface cable to the internal SCSI device connector on the card. In the space provided below, identify the type of SCSI card you are installing, and give the characteristics of the SCSI-type that enabled you to identify it.

_____

_____

**Step 3.**   Configure the SCSI bus controller by performing the following steps based on the instructions in the manual for the controller: 1) Ensure that it is properly terminated. 2) Set the logical unit number (LUN) for the controller. The LUN identifies the SCSI controller and distinguishes it from other SCSI controllers in the same system. 3) Configure the controller with its device ID, which should be 7 for the controller. Device ID is similar to LUN, only it identifies multiple devices on the same controller. 4) Determine what resources (IRQ, I/O, etc.) must be assigned and perform configuration on the card if necessary. 5) Install the controller into the computer.

**Step 4.**   If you do not actually have a SCSI tape drive, skip to Step 5. If you do have one, first do any necessary configuration, such as termination for the last device in the chain, and the device ID in the chain, per the manual. Install the tape drive into an empty drive bay and connect the SCSI interface cable if it's an internal drive, or simply connect the SCSI interface cable to both the drive and the controller card if it's an external drive. Also connect a power connector from the computer's power supply to the internal drive (an external drive contains it own power supply).

**Step 5.**   Ensure that all internal and external cables are connected to the computer. Close up the system unit, securing it with the necessary screws or fasteners.

**Step 6.**   Power up the computer. Take any necessary steps to install a driver for the SCSI controller and set the SCSI ID.

**Step 7.**   Install a driver for the tape drive, and confirm that the drive is recognized.

**cross Oeference**

_Be sure to carefully study Table 2-1 in the A+ Certification Study Guide before taking the A+ Core Hardware exam._

**LAB EXERCISE 2.03**

# Installing and Configuring Peripheral Devices

**30 Minutes**

Technicians at Nerd Matrix work with both external clients and internal clients. The external clients are the main focus of the business but, like all other companies, Nerd Matrix has their own infrastructure to support. You have been called to the operations department to install two new peripheral devices on a desktop computer—a mouse and video camera.

## Learning Objectives

Although peripherals come in all shapes, sizes, and technologies, you can apply a standard set of procedures to the installation and configuration of peripherals. After you complete this lab you will be able to:

- Identify the proper procedures for installing peripheral devices
- Identify the proper procedures for configuring peripheral devices
- Identify specific steps to take when installing USB devices
- Identify specific steps to take when configuring USB devices

## Lab Materials and Setup

For this lab exercise, you'll need:

- One fully PnP desktop computer with motherboard, power supply, keyboard, hard drive(s), CD-ROM drive, and floppy drive. Ensure that the computer has two USB connectors. This system should be completely assembled, closed, and ready to be powered up.

- Windows 95 with USB support (Windows 95b or 95c) or later version of Windows installed on the computer.

- One USB mouse.

- One additional USB device (optional—the lab steps use a camera).
- The user manual for the USB device(s).
- The user manual for the computer.

lab
**Warning**    *Windows NT does not provide USB support.*

## Getting Down to Business

In this exercise, you'll install a mouse and video camera on a desktop computer. In doing so, you will see that you install these USB devices while the computer is running, because USB is both Plug and Play (detected automatically) and hot swappable, meaning that a USB device can be added or removed while the computer is running.

**Step 1.**    As with all new peripherals (or any hardware for that matter), read all documentation that came with the USB devices. Then remove the device from its packaging. Remove any packing material from within the device and any items taped or otherwise attached to it. Perform any assembly or other steps that are described in the documentation.

**Step 2.**    Power up the computer and log on, if necessary. After the desktop appears, plug the USB mouse into one of the USB ports. The mouse should be automatically recognized, without the need for additional software, unless the mouse driver is not available with your operating system. Record your observations below, as well as any action you were required to take after installing the mouse:

_____

_____

lab
**Warning**    *Make sure the system is running before plugging in a USB device for the first time. If the system is not running when a USB device is plugged in for the first time, it cannot recognize that the device has been connected, and you will spend considerable time trying to figure out why an easy-to-install PnP device doesn't work. Also note that with Windows 2000 or later, the user who is logged on during the initial connection of a USB device must be a member of the local administrators group, because only an administrator can install a driver. After the initial connection and installation of the driver, a non-administrator may reconnect the device without problem.*

**Step 3.**   Unplug the USB mouse and describe what appears on your monitor as a result of this action:

_____

_____

**Step 4.**   Plug the USB mouse back into the computer and record your observations below:

_____

_____

**Step 5.**   Plug in your second USB device, taking any necessary steps, and record your observations below:

_____

_____

**cross Reference**

*For more information on upgrading computers by installing and configuring peripheral devices, read the section titled "Installing and Configuring Peripheral Devices" in the A+ Certification Study Guide.*

**LAB EXERCISE 2.04**

**I Hour**

# Using Disk Utilities to Upgrade System Performance

The shop foreman at LabelPerks, a major producer of custom labels and stickers, has complained to you that some of the computers on the production floor seem slower than other, similarly configured computers. Experience has taught you that system performance can often be improved by regular defragmentation of the data on the hard drives, as well as by testing and resolving problems such as lost clusters, cross-linked clusters, and bad sectors.

Microsoft has included drive defragmentation software in all Windows versions beginning with Windows 95, with the exception of Windows NT. For Windows NT, you will need to use a third party program, such as Diskeeper from Executive Software.

*For instructions on defragmenting a hard drive with the Microsoft utility, see Exercise 2-5 of the A+ Certification Study Guide. For information about Diskeeper, check out www.diskeeper.com.*

Microsoft has provided two programs, CHKDSK and ScanDisk, in order to solve the problems of lost clusters, cross-linked clusters (sometimes referred to as cross-linked files), and bad sectors. Windows NT, and Windows 2000, and Windows XP  use CHKDSK, while Windows 95/98 uses ScanDisk.

On a FAT file system volume, lost clusters occur when the FAT table indicates that one or more clusters contain data, but there are no directory entries that point to these clusters. CHKDSK and ScanDisk resolve lost clusters by creating directory entries that point to the clusters. You will see these entries as filenames in the root of the drive, all with the CHK extension.

What causes lost clusters? The most common cause of lost clusters is the abnormal ending of a program or operating system. This can be a "crash" in which the software behaves very poorly and takes the computer down, a rude shutdown by the user (hitting the big red switch rather than using the Shutdown command), software "freezing" or "hanging up," or other similar events. What they all have in common is the abrupt interruption of an application or the operating system. This leaves files open on the hard drive. On a FAT volume, this can mean that the space was allocated through the FAT table, but a directory entry was either not created or not updated.

Cross-linked files are nearly (but not quite) the opposite problem—two or more directory entries point to the same clusters resulting in conjoined files. CHKDSK and ScanDisk will give the disputed space to one of the two files, but this is not usually a complete resolution. It may leave one of the files with missing parts and the other file with extraneous parts. The files that result from the repair of lost clusters and cross-linked files by CHKDSK and ScanDisk are usually, but not always, useless. The "found" lost clusters are often the temporary files created by your applications, not the actual data files. Once you determine that no data is missing, you can delete the files. The best solution is to delete the resulting files (*.CHK) and restore the files from a backup that predates the damage.

Allocation problems, such as lost clusters and cross-linked clusters, are common with the FAT file systems, but rare with NTFS because it has built-in recovery capabilities.

In addition to detecting the logical problems of lost clusters and cross-linked files, all of these utilities are also capable of detecting bad surfaces—identified as bad sectors. In this case, the utility cannot actually fix the damage, but will mark the cluster that contains the bad space as "bad" in the allocation table of the file system so that no new data will be written to this space.

**lab**
**Warning**

*Be sure to verify that no data is missing before deleting the \*.CHK files. We have gone for years without finding actual data in lost clusters. However, a consultant we know had a system failure, after which he could not find a very important Microsoft Access database. He ran CHKDSK /F, which converted many lost clusters to files. Then he noticed that one of the \*. CHK files was the size of the missing database. He rescued the database by renaming the file. When the renamed file was loaded into Access, it was, indeed, the missing data. He was a hero, and his contract with that Fortune 500 company was renewed!*

## Learning Objectives

To enhance the performance of hard drive systems, service technicians must know how to work with disk utilities. Once you've completed this lab, you will be able to:

- Use CHKDSK to detect and correct file allocation problems
- Use ScanDisk to detect and correct file allocation problems

**cross**
**Reference**

*Try Exercise 2-5 in the **A+ Certification Study Guide** in which you defragment a hard drive.*

## Lab Materials and Setup

The materials you'll need for this lab are:

- A computer running Windows 95 or greater.
- If you are running a Windows operating system other than Windows 95 or 98, you will need to be logged on with local administrator privileges to run these utilities.

## Getting Down to Business

In this lab you will use the CHKDSK and/or ScanDisk commands to test your hard drive for logical problems such as lost clusters or cross-linked files, and physical problems, such as bad sectors. A bit of advice: Always turn off any screen saver that may be running before using ScanDisk because it can interfere with the test.

**Step 1.** Open a command prompt and enter the command CHKDSK. The results you receive will vary depending on the operating system you are running:

■ **Windows 95/98** will immediately display a message stating that CHKDSK has not checked the drive for errors, and that you must use ScanDisk to detect and fix errors on the drive. It will also display statistics of disk capacity, usage, allocation unit size, and the total bytes of memory (REAL mode memory only!). So if you are running Windows 95/98, you must run ScanDisk. See the ScanDisk GUI program in the following illustration.

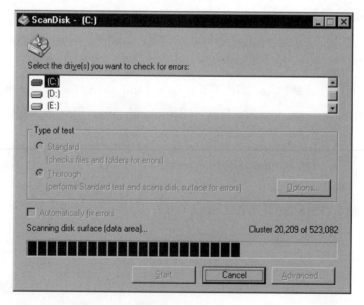

■ **Windows 2000** will take several minutes to examine the current drive. On a FAT volume, CHKDSK will examine the contents of the FAT table, root directory, and subdirectories, performing an audit to ensure that all clusters indicated as being in use in the FAT table are referenced (either directly or indirectly) from the directories.

On an NTFS volume, CHKDSK has three stages. In stage 1 it verifies files, in stage 2 it verifies the NTFS indexes, and in stage 3 it verifies the security descriptors. Following these three stages, CHKDSK continues with a verification of the USN Journal, which is the Change Journal on a Windows 2000 NTFS volume (further defined in Chapter 8). When this last step is complete, it displays the results of the tests plus disk statistics. See the output from CHKDSK in the following illustration. Notice that, although the tests were run, CHKDSK did not fix any errors because we did not run CHKDSK with the /F option. We did not do this because we wanted to see the results of the analysis. If you run CHKDSK with the /F option on a volume that is in use (as C: was in this example), it will display a message that it cannot lock the current drive and cannot run because the volume is in use by another process. It then asks if you would like to schedule the volume to be checked the next time the system restarts and gives you the good old "(Y/N)" option. If you enter "Y" it will run CHKDSK /F the next time the computer boots. This will occur after you select that installation of Windows 2000 from the boot menu. At that time, if you are watching carefully, you will see a black character mode display in the middle of the screen with a graphical band displaying the Windows 2000 logo above and a smaller, plain blue/gray band below. You will have 5 seconds to choose not to have the CHKDSK program run. If you do nothing, CHKDSK runs.

```
Command Prompt                                       _ □ ✕

WARNING!  F parameter not specified.
Running CHKDSK in read-only mode.

CHKDSK is verifying files (stage 1 of 3)...
File verification completed.
CHKDSK is verifying indexes (stage 2 of 3)...
Index verification completed.
CHKDSK is verifying security descriptors (stage 3 of
3)...
Security descriptor verification completed.
CHKDSK is verifying Usn Journal...
Usn Journal verification completed.
Correcting errors in the Volume Bitmap.
Windows found problems with the file system.
Run CHKDSK with the /F (fix) option to correct these.

   8393930 KB total disk space.
   6180964 KB in 47025 files.
     17860 KB in 2794 indexes.
         0 KB in bad sectors.
    142710 KB in use by the system.
     44032 KB occupied by the log file.
   2052396 KB available on disk.

      4096 bytes in each allocation unit.
   2098482 total allocation units on disk.
    513099 allocation units available on disk.

C:\>
```

■ **Windows NT** behaves similarly to Windows 2000, displaying less status information while it runs, and without the tests for the enhancements to the NTFS files system. If you use the /F switch, NT also displays a similar message to the one previously described and prompts you to choose to run CHKDSK at the next reboot. At that time, it runs CHKDSK (actually, the AUTOCHK program) during the initialization stage of the operating system startup, displaying CHKDSK progress information in the blue character mode screen. It will reboot the computer at the conclusion of the CHKDSK operation.

lab
**Hint**

*If you choose to have CHKDSK run the next time the computer boots, you will need to watch carefully in order to see it run. Once CHKDSK completes, the operating system completes its startup procedure or (in the case of NT) reboots the computer. If you look away at the wrong time you will miss it all.*

**Step 2.** Enter your observations on the previous step, including which operating system you used and the results of running CHKDSK. If you are running Windows 95/98, indicate the results of running ScanDisk in both Standard and Thorough modes:

_____

_____

**Step 3.** Now run the program through the GUI. From My Computer or Windows Explorer, right click on the drive, select Properties | Tools | Error-Checking, and click Check Now. On Windows 95 and Windows 98 it runs ScanDisk, while Windows NT 4.0, Windows 2000, and Windows XP run CHKDSK.

cross
**Reference**

*Do not be overly concerned with the FAT or NTFS file systems now. The discussion here is only for the purpose of defining ways to optimize system performance. We will examine the particulars of the various file systems in Chapter 8. Are you too curious to wait? Check out the section labeled "Certification Objective 8.04" in the A+ Certification Study Guide.*

**Step 4.** There is much more to the CHKDSK story. In this step you will research and learn more about CHKDSK. Use your Web browser to connect to the Microsoft Technet site at www.microsoft.com/technet. In the Search box enter "Q187941" (without the quotation marks) and click the GO button. Read the article titled "An Explanation of CHKDSK and the New /C and /I Switches." This article contains an excellent explanation of how CHKDSK works. Answer the following questions:

a) Name two utility DLLs used by CHKDSK.

_____

_____

b) When is the optional fourth pass of CHKDSK performed?

_____

_____

c) Give one reason for running CHKDSK in read-only mode, and then give a reason for not running it in read-only mode.

_____

_____

## LAB EXERCISE 2.05

**I Hour**

# Upgrading a Portable Computer

Once again, this is an inside job. The sales manager of Nerd Matrix needs to have his portable computer upgraded. His present hard drive is running low on disk space, and he wants it replaced with a new, larger one. The BIOS also needs to be upgraded because of a problem it has with recognizing USB devices.

## Learning Objectives

After you complete this lab you will be able to:

- Identify the proper procedures for replacing a hard drive in a portable computer
- Identify the proper procedures for upgrading the BIOS in a portable computer

## Lab Materials and Setup

It is often true that portable computers become obsolete before they need components upgraded. However, there are exceptions, especially when a computer is heavily used, as in the case of the sales manager. Nerd Matrix recommends these portables to many of their clients and has a contract with the supplier for components. The hard drives are considered field replaceable units (FRUs), and the manufacturer includes instructions on upgrading, or "flashing," the BIOS. When the new hard drive came in, other technicians, using special hardware, brought it up to Nerd Matrix specifications by placing the standard Sales Department image on the drive in advance of your installing it.

The materials you need for this lab are:

■ One portable computer, completely assembled, closed, but powered off

■ Windows 95 or later version of Windows installed on the computer

■ A large, open workspace with an anti-static mat (if possible)

■ A Phillips screwdriver or appropriate nut driver

■ One or more containers in which to place and organize screws and other small parts

■ A notepad on which to take notes and make sketches of the computer and components

■ A hard drive that fits the computer

■ The user manual for the computer

If you do not have a spare hard drive, simply remove and reinstall the same one.

lab

**Warning**

*Do not do any step of this lab for which you do not have clear documentation and instructions for the exact model of portable on which you are working. Flashing a BIOS is a very delicate matter that should be done only when absolutely necessary, and only using careful instructions from the manufacturer. A technical trainer we know had two laptop computers that he used in classes. He successfully installed beta 3 of Windows 2000 on both of these machines, but could not install the released version of the product. The manufacturer provided him with a flash upgrade, which he ran on both machines. The flash upgrade had a bug in it and caused both machines to be absolutely unbootable. Had he run the program on just one machine at a time, he would have had at least one machine that would boot (without the released version of Windows 2000). The next week, the manufacturer sent him a patched flash program and he was back in business.*

## Getting Down to Business

In the following steps you will prepare the portable computer by removing the current hard drive, then you will install a replacement hard drive and test it to be sure it is recognized and boots up. Finally, you will determine what steps would be necessary to upgrade the BIOS. You will perform a BIOS upgrade only if appropriate.

lab

**Hint**

*Flash BIOS is common in both desktop and laptop computers. A few years back, flash BIOS was not common, and the BIOS could be upgraded only by replacing the ROM BIOS chip. You might run into such a situation on an older machine, in which case you must contact the manufacturer of the BIOS to get a newer version, if one is available.*

**Step 1.**    Prepare for the task at hand. Be sure the computer is powered down and observe safe ESD procedures. Use the manufacturer's instructions to determine how to remove the hard drive in the portable. In some portables you do not have to use any tools—simply unlatch the hard drive compartment. In others you must open the computer case. Consult the user manual for your computer for the procedure, and remove the hard drive. Describe how you did it below:

_____

_____

**Step 2.**   Consult the user manual for your computer and install the new hard drive into the drive bay. Once it is installed, take any necessary steps to have the hard drive recognized, then test it by booting up the computer. Finally, describe below how you installed the hard drive, and any changes you had to make to BIOS setup:

_____

_____

**Step 3.**   Consult the user manual for your computer and determine what steps must be taken to upgrade the BIOS in the computer. Do not actually upgrade the BIOS, unless your instructor tells you to do so. Write down what steps must be taken to upgrade the BIOS on the portable computer.

_____

_____

**cross**
**Reference**

*For information on upgrading system performance on portables by replacing batteries, adding memory, and installing PC cards, read the section titled "Portable Computer" in Chapter 2 of the* **A+ Certification Study Guide**.

# LAB ANALYSIS TEST

1. A customer, the Aerobatics Alliance, has asked you to install a second hard drive into a system that presently has a single hard drive and a CD-ROM drive. What information do you need before you do the actual install?

   _____

   _____

2. After one of your customers purchased a SCSI tape backup system for his departmental file server, he realized that the server does not have a SCSI controller on the motherboard. He is now convinced that the tape drive cannot be installed in that server. What can you do to help the customer?

   _____

   _____

3. Harry, in the shipping department of a mail order company, has complained to you that he connected his USB video camera to his Windows 2000 computer, but the Found New Hardware wizard did not know what type of device it was. When he attempted to install the driver that came with the camera, a message appeared stating that the program was incompatible with that version of Windows. Clicking the Details button on that message directed him to visit the Microsoft Web site. He connected to the site and clicked on the Compatibility link, which took him to the Hardware Compatibility page. A search on the brand and model of the camera failed to find the product. What advice do you have for Harry?

   _____

   _____

4. You have upgraded memory on several different models of Toshiba laptops. Now you are getting ready to upgrade the memory on laptops from Compaq and you have some extra memory modules from the Toshiba computers. Will you be able to use the same memory modules in the Compaq laptops?

   _____

   _____

5. Your computer suffered a crash this afternoon. After booting it up again, what procedure should you follow?

   _____

   _____

# KEY TERM QUIZ

Use the following vocabulary terms to complete the sentences below. Not all of the terms will be used.

> CHKDSK
>
> hot swappable
>
> BIOS
>
> hard disk controller
>
> master/slave configuration
>
> IEEE
>
> CMOS
>
> primary/secondary configuration
>
> ScanDisk
>
> terminate

1. When you have two IDE/EIDE drives installed on a single channel, they have a relationship that is described as a _____.

2. When connecting a new SCSI device to a chain, if you do not properly _____ it, you can make every device on the chain unusable.

3. USB devices are both PnP and _____.

4. The Windows 2000 and Windows NT program for resolving problems with disk allocation and bad sectors is _____.

5. If a computer is unable to work with a new device, you may need to upgrade the _____.

# LAB WRAP-UP

Another hard day in the lab! You installed IDE/EIDE devices, giving some thought to how they will be used. After that you installed a SCSI controller and device, remembering to terminate the SCSI chain and assign the proper ID to the device. You connected at least one USB device and observed PnP in action (we hope). Then you worked with a utility to resolve disk problems, such as lost clusters, cross-linked files, and bad sectors. Finally, you swapped a new hard drive in a portable computer and determined the steps for upgrading the BIOS on that particular model computer. It is time to go home and kick back!

# LAB SOLUTIONS FOR CHAPTER 2

In this section, you'll find solutions to the lab exercises, Lab Analysis Test, and Key Term Quiz.

## Lab Solution 2.01

**Step 1.** The instructions on Step 1 are complete.

**Step 2.** It is always easier to configure the jumper settings for master/slave on drives before securing them in the computer. Once you have configured each hard drive to be a master (per instructions on the drive or in the installation manual for the drive), secure both drives in appropriate bays, using only the screws that properly fit the hard drives. Hard drives (unless they are removable) are not accessed from outside the computer, so they can be installed in bays without external access. Once the drives are secured inside, connect the hard drive from which you want to boot the operating system to the end of the cable you have connected to the primary IDE/EIDE channel. Connect the hard drive you intend to use for data to the end of the cable you have connected to the secondary IDE/EIDE channel on the motherboard. Connect the power connectors to each hard drive.

**Step 3.** There are several different methods of installing drives into computers. Some have a drive bay that directly fits the hard drive. You simply slide the drive in and insert four screws through appropriate slots in the computer frame and into appropriate threaded holes in the drive. Other computers use a drive bay that is wider than the drive and that has slots to hold rails that are attached to the drive. This system is designed for quick and easy installation and removal of drives, but it requires that rails be attached to the drive and then the drive slid into the computer. See Figure 2-1 for a close-up of a 4-inch wide SCSI drive with attached adapter plates and rails, and Figure 2-3 for a photo of that same SCSI drive resting on a 5.75-inch wide CD-ROM drive with screw holes in the sides. Also look at Figure 2-2 to see a photo of a computer with a rail-mounted hard drive and CD-ROM drive and an empty slot showing the rail guides.

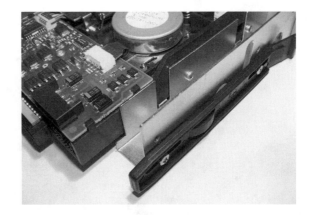

**FIGURE 2-1**

SCSI Drive with
Adapter Plates
and Rails

Remove the cover from an unused half-height drive bay. Slide the CD-ROM drive into the bay from the front. Be sure to line up the slots on the side of the bay with the holes in the drive, and ensure that the front of the drive is even with the other drives. Secure the drive with screws. Connect this drive to the remaining connector of the IDE/EIDE cable that is connected to the secondary channel on the motherboard. If the drive will be used for multimedia applications, connect the audio cable from the motherboard or sound card to the CD-ROM drive. Connect the power connector to the drive.

**FIGURE 2-2**

Computer with
Rail Mounted
Hard Drive,
CD-ROM Drive,
and an Open
Rail-Mount Bay

SCSI Drive with
Rail Mount and
CD-ROM Drive

**Step 4.** The actual actions you take for this step will depend on the computer itself, and how it is configured. If you are unsure of how to close up the system unit, check the documentation for the computer and the devices that are installed. Be sure to reconnect the keyboard, mouse, and monitor if they were disconnected for the lab. Don't forget to also connect the power cords to the CPU and monitor!

**Step 5.** The instructions in the lab are complete, although the exact actions will depend on the BIOS setup program.

**Step 6.** You can confirm that the computer recognizes the drives by going into Windows Explorer. You may be surprised to see the CD-ROM drive recognized, but not the second hard drive. If the second hard drive is brand new and has never been partitioned or formatted, it will not appear in Explorer. You can still confirm its existence in NT with Disk Administrator, and in Windows 2000 (or greater) by using Disk Manager. In Windows 95/98 you run the FDISK program from a command prompt to view the drive and partition it. Working with these utilities is beyond the scope of this chapter, but will be explored further in Chapters 8 and 9.

# Lab Solution 2.02

**Step 1.**   The instructions for Step 1 are complete.

**Step 2.**   When preparing a SCSI controller card for connection to an internal SCSI device, connect the internal interface cable to the card before installing it into the computer, because it can be difficult to this do once the card is installed. You will see in Figure 2-4 a picture of a SCSI card with an internal cable attached. Once the cable is connected, select an open expansion slot on the motherboard. Remove the slot cover for this connector from the back of the computer. You should not have to configure the controller for its SCSI ID because it should, by default, be configured to use SCSI ID 7, the highest priority ID. But check the documentation for the controller and verify that it is configured correctly.

Answers to the question concerning the type of card will vary. The card used in our test lab, shown in Figure 2-4, is an Ultra SCSI-3 (Fast-20) with an 8-bit bus width and a maximum throughput of 20 MBps. It can be identified by the 50-pin high-density external connector that is only 1¼ inches wide. The internal cable resembles IDE hard drive ribbon cabling. Basically, if you have a 50-pin cable, the SCSI bus is 8-bit. The 16-bit SCSI bus uses 68-pin cables, and the 32-bit SCSI uses 110-bit cables. External connectors on older SCSI controllers look like Centronics parallel printer connectors, but are slightly wider, while the newer SCSI bus controllers use high-density connectors.

**Step 3.**   Install the SCSI controller card by pushing it firmly into the selected expansion slot. Apply pressure as needed until the edge connector is completely and firmly seated. Remember to wiggle the card only back and forth lengthwise if you need to get it inserted, not at 90 degrees to the slot. Secure the SCSI card in place with a screw (the one you removed with the slot cover).

**Step 4.**   If you do have a SCSI tape drive, this step will vary based on whether the drive is internal or external. An external drive connects by SCSI cable to the external connector on the controller card at the back of the computer. It also requires termination. If you install an internal drive, you first remove the front punch-out panel from an empty drive bay, slide the drive into the bay from the front, secure the drive in the bay, then connect the drive to the internal interface cable and connect the power cable.

FIGURE 2-4

FIGURE 2-4

SCSI Card with
Cable Attached

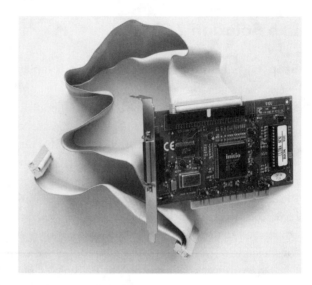

**Step 5.** Close up the system unit, being careful not to dislodge cables.

**Step 6.** If the system fails to boot up after power is turned on, or if there are error messages associated with the SCSI controller (other than a missing driver), power down the computer and troubleshoot your configuration. SCSI problems center around improper termination of the SCSI bus and incorrect addressing of devices on the bus. If the system boots up and successfully loads the operating system, you should see a message that a new device is detected (except if you're using NT, which is not PnP). If the driver is already available on the computer, you may not have to do anything else. Otherwise you may have to provide device driver software when prompted. You may need to use Device Manager in Windows 95/98, Windows 2000, or Windows XP to troubleshoot problems with the controller. In Windows NT, you may have to run the SCSI Adapters program from Control Panel to add the driver.

**Step 7.** A device driver for the tape drive must be installed. This is done through a Control Panel program—Add/Remove Hardware in Windows 2000 and Windows XP, Add New Hardware in Windows 95/98, and Tape Devices in NT. Once the driver is installed, if you have a tape for the drive, test the installation by using your backup program. If you plan to use the backup program that comes with Windows, run the backup program (NTBACKUP for NT and Windows 2000, MSBACKUP for Windows 95) to see if it recognizes the drive. If it does not recognize the drive, it may only work with a third-party backup program.

## Lab Solution 2.03

**Step 1.** Reading the documentation is an important step because, with some devices, you may actually be required to install software before connecting the device. This is true of some of the cameras we have tested.

**Step 2.** Answers will vary. When we installed a Microsoft Optical Wheel Mouse on a computer running Windows 2000, the Found New Hardware message box was displayed with the following message: USB Human Interface Device. No additional steps were required.

**Step 3.** Answers will vary, but in general, this is a non-event, with no message displaying. If there is no other mouse on the computer, you will lose the mouse cursor.

**Step 4.** Observations will vary, but this is, once again, a non-event. In Windows 2000, the message described in Step 2 occurs only the first time the mouse is installed. If this is your only mouse, you will regain the mouse cursor.

**Step 5.** Observations will vary. If the device is detected, but there is no driver, the Found New Hardware wizard appears, and you may go through several screens to install the driver. If there is no driver available for the device, go to www.microsoft.com/windows, click on the link for your version of Windows and search for a driver for your device. In some versions this will be found under a link titled "Compatibility." If you fail to find the driver or information about the device at this site, look on the manufacturer's web site. When you locate the driver, download it and follow the instructions to install it.

## Lab Solution 2.04

**Step 1.** Open a command prompt and enter the command CHKDSK. The results you receive will vary depending on the operating system you are running:

- Windows 95/98 will behave as described in the lab.
- Windows 2000 will behave as described in the lab.
- Windows NT will behave as described in the lab.

**Step 2** The observations will vary, but here are some possible observations: Windows 95/98 ScanDisk is a GUI program. In ScanDisk you have a choice of tests to run. A Standard check will check only for logical problems, such as lost clusters and cross-linked files, and runs fairly quickly. A Thorough test will perform a Standard test, and also scan the disk surface for errors. It will fix the errors as described in the beginning of the lab. It takes much longer to run, but should be run on a regular basis as a means of preventive maintenance to prevent data from inadvertently being placed in areas of the disk that may have become damaged.

On a test computer (400 MHz Pentium III with 256MB RAM) the Standard test took 15 seconds on a 2.1GB drive, while the Thorough test took 5 minutes 10 seconds. That is nearly 21 times longer—and we did not select write check or error correction!

Windows NT and Windows 2000 CHKDSK perform as described in the lab.

**Step 3.** Step 3 is complete and no answer is required.

**Step 4.**

a) Two utility DLLs used by CHKDSK are UNTFS.DLL and UFAT.DLL.

b) The optional fourth pass of CHKDSK performed when the /R switch is used.

c) A good reason for running CHKDSK in read-only mode is to run it during a period of low system usage just to predict how long it will take to run it on that volume. A reason not to run CHKDSK in read-only mode is that if read-only mode encounters errors in the earlier phases, it may falsely report errors—reporting that a disk is corrupted when that is not the actual error detected. This occurs because read-only mode does not lock the volume, and therefore may become confused by alterations made to NTFS on behalf of other processes while it is running. Running CHKDSK with /F or /R (write mode) will lock the volume and avoid these invalid errors.

## Lab Solution 2.05

**Step 1.**    Answers will vary from model to model. On one portable, turning the computer over, locating the hard disk drive latch, unlatching it, and sliding the case containing the hard disk out of the bay accessed the hard drive. See Figure 2-5 for a photo of the hard drive in its case and the empty bay.

**Step 2.**    Answers will vary from model to model. To install a new hard drive in the same computer, you may need to remove the old hard drive from the case. This requires removing two screws—one on each side of the case—and carefully disconnecting the cable within the case. Once the old drive is removed, the new drive can be inserted into the case and the screws refastened. Then, the case is reinserted into the bay until the latch clicks shut.

**Step 3.**    Answers will vary from model to model. In our test computer, the instructions for upgrading the BIOS were in the manual under the heading, "Updating the Flash ROM BIOS." This type of BIOS can be updated with

**FIGURE 2-5**

Portable with
Hard Drive
Removed

software, rather than physically replacing the BIOS chip. The action of updating this type of BIOS is often called "flashing" the BIOS. In order to do this, you must first obtain the flash program with the updates to the BIOS from the manufacturer, then follow the instructions to flash the BIOS. On some systems you may have to set a special set of dip switches inside the computer and reboot before running the flash program. Many do not require a hardware change like that.

# ANSWERS TO LAB ANALYSIS TEST

1. Answers will vary. First, you need to know what type of hard drive and CD-ROM they presently have. A desktop PC is most likely to use IDE/EIDE, but it doesn't hurt to ask. If you determine that the drives are IDE/EIDE, then knowing the make and model of the PC will help you to determine whether you will have any problems with BIOS compatibility for a new, many-gigabyte hard drive. Once you know the make and model, you can often find the information you need at the manufacturer's web site. You may actually need to update the BIOS. Directions for doing this should be at the site.

    Then, because each IDE/EIDE channel can have a maximum of two devices, you will have to confirm that there are two IDE channels available—this information too should be on the web site or in the owner's manual for the computer.

    Finally, ask the customer how he plans to use the second hard drive and the CD-ROM drive. See the information in Lab 1.01. Basically, you want to give the drive with the most traffic its own channel. Some CD-ROM drives cannot be alone on a channel, but others can. So if you decide that the CD-ROM drive should be alone on its own channel, you may also have to check this out. The most likely configuration will be to have the present hard drive (containing the operating system) remain as master on the primary channel, install the new hard drive as master on the secondary channel, and install the CD-ROM drive as slave on the secondary channel.

2. You can tell the customer that he can still use his tape drive if they have an available expansion slot, and if he purchases a SCSI card and connector cable that is compatible with the tape drive.

3. I would recommend that Harry contact the manufacturer to see if they have released a new driver for the device. If the device is more than two years old, it is possible that the manufacturer has no plans to create a driver for Windows 2000.

4. Not likely! Most laptop manufacturers use proprietary memory modules.

5. After a system crash, you probably have lost clusters and even cross-linked files on your disk. Therefore, run the CHKDSK or ScanDisk program. After the program runs, check to see if it produced *.CHK files. If it did, attempt to verify that you are not missing any important files on that drive. If data is missing you may want to try to retrieve it from these files or restore the files from a backup. When done with the files, delete all the unneeded files.

## ANSWERS TO KEY TERM QUIZ

1. master/slave configuration

2. terminate

3. hot swappable

4. CHKDSK

5. BIOS

EXERCISES • QUESTIONS • ANSWERS

# 3

# Diagnosing and Troubleshooting Problems

## LAB EXERCISES

T he problem with learning how to solve problems is that they do not spontaneously occur when you would like them to—unlike in a lab situation where you can calmly note the symptoms and apply rational troubleshooting procedures to them. They occur in real life when you have other priorities piling up. When you're dealing with system failures and errors in real life, it takes discipline to block out the ordinary stresses and focus on resolving the problem. This can be particularly difficult to do when you are tired, overworked, facing deadlines, and feeling pressured. But keeping your focus on resolving the problem, and consciously working to put the other stresses out of your mind for the moment can result in successful problem solving.

In order to give you some problems to solve we actually have you break your computer—several times—in the following labs. Now, this does give you an unfair advantage—since you break it in the first place, you know what is broken. So what's the point? Well, you get to see the symptoms displayed by the computer when these failures occur. The clues (or lack of clues) you receive may surprise you.

In the first lab you do some research before the real fun begins. Your research will give you troubleshooting references to add to the technical portfolio that you began building in Lab 1.04 of Chapter 1, when you created a connector reference and a list of useful web sites.

In the remaining labs, you will work your way through your computer, wreaking havoc on major components and peripherals. In each lab you will first disable some components, then observe the symptoms displayed, and then fix the computer. We hope you think of additional things to break—but be sure you can fix them!

**lab**
**Warning**
*Use extreme caution; some of the steps in these labs could result in an unusable computer! Disconnecting cables always carries the risk of bending or breaking a pin. Bus connectors were not intended to have interface cards added and removed several times a day! In fact, the manufacturer's specifications for most connectors state that they are certified only for a limited number of times that connectors can be attached and removed. Remember that being cautious with delicate circuitry is part of the job!*

**LAB EXERCISE 3.01**

# Building a Reference
# for Diagnostics and Troubleshooting

**I Hour**

It is Monday morning at Nerd Matrix, and you are preparing for the week ahead. Already on the board is a job ticket from the Practical Bank, where the loan manager reports that when he attempts to boot up his computer, it beeps several times and fails to load the operating system. It sounds like there are audio error signals to be interpreted, but you do not have a reference to interpret those signals for the BIOS in his machine.

Another job ticket calls for you to flash (upgrade) the BIOS in several computers at J&B Financial, in preparation for upgrading them to Windows XP. You know that J&B has several types of computer systems, and you need to be prepared with the correct programs to upgrade their BIOSs. Therefore, before you leave to go to these customer sites, you decide to do some research on the Web to be prepared for these and similar situations. This research will expand your list of web sites by adding diagnostics and troubleshooting information for various BIOSs.

In this lab you will explore the web sites of several BIOS manufacturers looking for helpful troubleshooting information. The references you are searching for are BIOS error codes and sources of replacement BIOS chips, as well as BIOS upgrade programs—a much simpler solution than replacing BIOS chips.

Ever since the first IBM PC, our personal computers have tried to tell us what ails them. This is not done with sophisticated artificial intelligence; rather it is done with simple diagnostic routines programmed into BIOS. This series of tests is collectively called the Power On Self-Test (POST). They include tests of the motherboard circuitry, processor, memory, keyboard, drives, ports, and whatever other diagnostics have been programmed into the BIOS. At the end of the POST, the system may produce an audio code (a beep or series of beeps) that indicates that the POST tests completed successfully, or it may produce an audio or video error code. In general, the audio error signals are produced for failures that might prevent the error code from being displayed on the screen.

These error codes are usually specific to the BIOS in the computer. In order to interpret them you should have a reference of the codes for the BIOSs with which you work. It may require some detective work. For instance, if you visit the site of

American Megatrends, publisher of the AMI BIOS, and hope to find a list of their codes, you will be disappointed. Instead they direct you to the individual computer manufacturers who use the AMI BIOS. Similarly, you begin your search of Phoenix and Award BIOS issues at the Phoenix site (they acquired Award), but from there you use links to go to other sites where you will find the information you seek. The major computer manufacturers, Compaq and HP, have their own proprietary BIOSs or versions supplied and modified for them by one of the major names, such as AMI, Award, or Phoenix.

## Learning Objectives

Once you complete this lab, you will be able to:

■ Update your list of web sites with sites for troubleshooting

■ Find references for BIOS error codes

■ Use a tool to gather BIOS information

## Lab Materials and Setup

The materials you'll need for this lab are:

■ A computer running Windows 95 or greater

■ Online access to the Internet

■ Acrobat Reader (free download at www.adobe.com/products/acrobat/readstep.html)

■ A printer connected to the network or directly to your computer (optional)

## Getting Down to Business

In the following steps you explore web sites to gather information about BIOS upgrades. After exploring the sites suggested in these steps, you may think of other sites to try. At the end of the lab, add all the useful sites to your list of web sites.

**Step 1.**   Use your web browser to connect to www.phoenix.com. From the home page, select the link labeled "BIOS Upgrades." Read the information on this page. Where can you find the BIOS upgrades for Award and Phoenix BIOSs?

_____

_____

**Step 2.**   From the BIOS Upgrade page, click on the link labeled "Phoenix BIOS User's Manual." Use Acrobat Reader to read this manual. Record the URL for this manual and describe the chapters that you believe will be most helpful to you for troubleshooting and solving BIOS problems.

_____

_____

**Step 3.**   Use your web browser to connect to www.hp.com. Locate the "Search" box on the home page and enter "BIOS upgrade" (including the quotes). Then click  the arrow to the right of the search text box to start the search. When the results appear, observe the number of results and answer the following questions:

 1. If you supported HP computers that needed BIOS upgrades, would this site be useful to you? Why?

_____

_____

 2. How would you modify your search of the site?

_____

_____

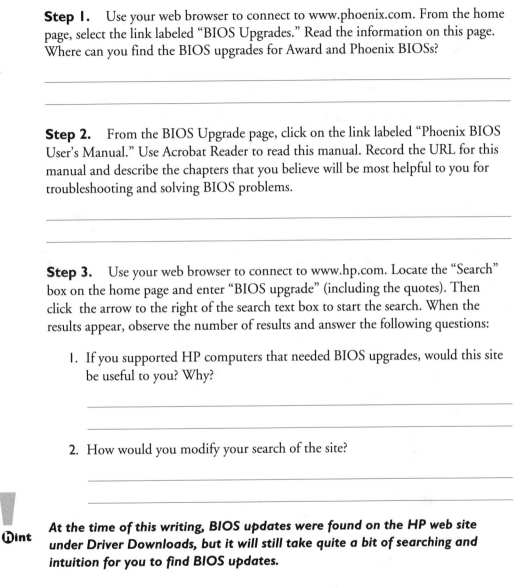

lab
ⓗint   *At the time of this writing, BIOS updates were found on the HP web site under Driver Downloads, but it will still take quite a bit of searching and intuition for you to find BIOS updates.*

**Step 4.**   In this step you will connect to the site of computer manufacturer Gateway and look for BIOS updates for portable computers. Use your web browser to connect to www.gateway.com. Navigate through the site, looking for BIOS update files available for download. List three BIOS updates shown on this site.

_____

_____

**Step 5.**   Add the new web sites that you found useful to your list of Web sites that you began in Chapter 1.

_____

_____

lab

**⚠️arning**   _Do not allow your list of web sites to become outdated. Take time on a regular basis to review the sites for recent articles and to search for other new sites to add to your list. If a site isn't updated in several months, it may leave you with incomplete or obsolete information for problem solving._

**Step 6.**   Locate a general reference for BIOS error codes. Connect to the PC Guide site at www.pcguide.com. Click on the link titled "Search the PC Guide." Read the paragraph above the "Search for" box, then search on "bios and beep" (without the quotation marks). Record at least three BIOS articles that you find in your search. Remain at this site for the next step.

_____

_____

**Step 7.**   At the PC Guide site research the possible causes of continuous beeping on a PC with an AMI BIOS, and record the results you discover below.

_____

_____

**Step 8.**   When a computer boots up and/or when you run the BIOS setup program, you can gather information about the version of BIOS. However, you would like to have a program that you can run from an operating computer to gather information about the BIOS in that computer. At one of the sites you explored above, you discovered that one exists and decide to download and test it before going to the customer site. Use your web browser to connect to the site for Award BIOS upgrades that you recorded above. At this site, notice the BIOS Agent icon. Click on the agent and follow the instructions to download it, being sure to select the option to save the file to disk. Select a location on your local hard drive in which to save it (the Windows Desktop is easy to remember). The file BA.EXE is copied to the location you specify. After the program is downloaded, double-click on BA.EXE. The BIOS Agent screen appears. Click on the button labeled "Get BIOS Info" to run an analysis as shown in Figure 3-1.

Record the results below from running BIOS Agent on your machine:

BIOS ID: _____

BIOS Date: _____

BIOS Signon: _____

BIOS Type: _____

Super I/O: _____

Chipset: _____

OEM Signon: _____

**Step 9.** After you have recorded the results that appear on the screen, print a report or save the results to disk. After printing or saving the report, compare it to

**FIGURE 3-1**

Get BIOS
Info Screen

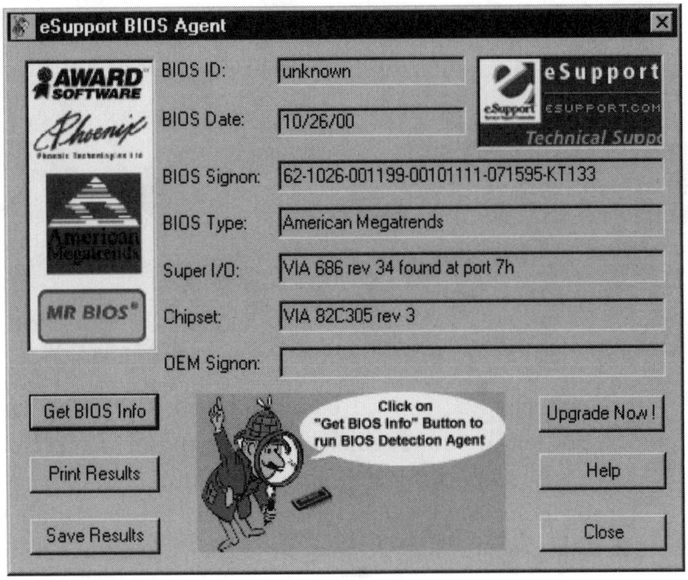

the results on the screen. Do all the fields from the screen appear on the report and are they in the correct order? Record your observations below:

_____

_____

**Step 10.** To find out what the field descriptions in the BIOS mean, click the Help button and fill in the information below:

BIOS ID: _____

BIOS Date: _____

BIOS Signon: _____

BIOS Type: _____

Super I/O: _____

Chipset: _____

OEM Signon: _____

Now you are armed with more knowledge about system BIOS, you know web sites where you can research specific BIOS information, and you have a utility that you can use to glean information about system BIOS without having to reboot a computer. You are ready to help your customers with problems associated with system BIOS.

**LAB EXERCISE 3.02**

**30 Minutes**

# Identifying Symptoms and Problems Associated with Memory

In this lab and the ones that follow in this chapter, you will see that the most important tool in troubleshooting is your own common sense, applied with a careful assessment of the symptoms. This is followed in importance by technical knowledge. In these labs you actually cause the problems that you have to solve, so you are not required to perform logical troubleshooting steps.

*cross* *Reference*

*Before proceeding with this lab read the section titled "Basic Troubleshooting Procedures" in the* **A+ Certification Study Guide** *and complete Exercise 3-2 at the end of that section.*

In these labs, as you observe the symptoms of the problems that you cause to happen, imagine yourself in a situation in which you are confronted with these symptoms without knowing what caused the problem. Take time to apply these troubleshooting procedures which expand slightly on those in Exercise 3-2 of the *A+ Certification Study Guide.*

1. Observe and note the error messages, investigate the computer history, and think of questions you would ask the customer in order to learn what specific actions he or she took prior to the time of the failure. You may need to ask the question "What has changed?" multiple times in order to get to what really happened.

2. Consider how you would reproduce the problem.

3. Observe the symptoms and determine if the problem is hardware or software related.

4. Most problems do not require high tech solutions. Therefore, apply the "simple" rule. Ask yourself, "What is the simplest thing that could cause this problem?" Then check that the system or problem component has power and is properly connected—simple things that can be overlooked. An experienced technician develops an internal checklist of the "simple" things that can cause problems.

5. Make sure the correct device driver (if applicable) is loaded and that there are no resource conflicts.

6. If possible and practical, isolate the failed component and test it on another computer. Or test an identical component from another computer in the failed computer.

7. Proceed with checking all components, working your way further into the computer.

8. Test the most central components of the computer, such as the BIOS, motherboard, memory, and processor. Do this by carefully observing the POST for the amount of memory detected and any error codes or messages displayed.

lab
**Hint**

*These steps are not carved in granite. For instance, when you see a symptom that points to BIOS, skip the intervening steps and focus on the BIOS to solve the problem.*

While writing this chapter, we encountered a failure on one of our desktop computers. It would not recognize the hard drive. The error messages indicated that no hard drive was present. This was extremely dismaying, because this particular machine had financial records that had not been backed up to the server in 5 days (many lessons to be learned here). Staying calm and noticing that not only was the hard drive not recognized, but the floppy drive was not recognized either, made us decide that the problem may have been in the motherboard. This moved us to step 6 above—we removed the hard drive from this computer and installed it as the primary master in one of our test lab computers. Sure enough, the operating system on the hard drive started up normally. The new computer had many components that were different from those in the desktop but, because the hard drive had a plug and play operating system, it detected the new hardware, and we soon had all the correct drivers installed, and were back in business. First order: back up the financial records and pledge to do this daily!

To sum things up: Don't panic. Gather information, use your best powers of observation, apply the "simple rule," isolate the problem, and always use common sense.

## Learning Objectives

Once you complete this lab, you will be able to:

- Recognize symptoms of memory problems
- Apply troubleshooting techniques to problem solving

## Lab Materials and Setup

The materials you'll need for this lab are:

- One working desktop computer running Windows 95 or greater, with multiple DIMMS or SIMMS installed
- A large, open workspace with an antistatic mat (if possible)
- A Phillips or Torx screwdriver or appropriate nut driver
- One or more containers in which to place and organize screws and other small parts

■ A notepad on which to take notes and make sketches of the computer and components

■ The user manual for the computer

## Getting Down to Business

Now you will simulate computer problems, observe the symptoms, and solve the problems. Perform the steps below, recording your observations or responses in the space provided.

**Step 1.** Power down the computer. Unplug the power cable and open the case. Remove a single RAM module NOT in the first slot, but in the last occupied slot. Close the case, reconnect the power cord, and power up the computer. Record your observations below:

_____

_____

**Step 2.** Power down the computer. Unplug the power cable and open the case. Reinstall the RAM module. Close the case, reconnect the power cord, and power up the computer. Verify that the memory is recognized and that the computer boots up successfully. If it does not boot up correctly, troubleshoot and resolve the problem.

**Step 3.** Power down the computer. Unplug the power cable and open the case. Remove the RAM module from the first slot. Close the case, reconnect the power cord, and power up the computer. Record your observations below:

_____

_____

**Step 4.** Power down the computer. Unplug the power cable and open the case. Reinstall the RAM module. Close the case, reconnect the power cord, and power up the computer. Verify that the memory is recognized and that the computer boots up successfully. If it does not boot up correctly, identify and resolve the problem.

Not all memory problems produce overt symptoms. We have to remain alert to problems of insufficient memory, such as when a user reports that he cannot run an application that he previously could run. They may or may not receive a message indicating that the application will not run due to insufficient memory.

**LAB EXERCISE 3.03**

# Identifying Symptoms and Problems Associated with BIOS and CMOS

**I Hour**

An accounts payable clerk from Great Eats Organic Food Wholesaler has noticed an error message that briefly appears on the BIOS screen during boot up. While he does not notice any problem when working with the computer, you stop by his office to check it out in case it is something that could cause problems later. While you are there you are asked to look at a computer in the warehouse that is not keeping time accurately. They have to correct the time on it every day, which is causing problems, because they run an inventory application that schedules tasks based on the system time and date.

## Learning Objectives

Once you complete this lab, you will be able to:

- Troubleshoot problems with incorrectly configured BIOS settings
- Replace a failed CMOS battery

## Lab Materials and Setup

The materials you'll need for this lab are:

- A computer running Windows 95 or greater with only one floppy drive
- A large, open workspace with an antistatic mat (if possible)
- A Phillips or Torx screwdriver or appropriate nut driver
- One or more containers in which to place and organize screws and other small parts
- A notepad on which to take notes and make sketches of the computer and components
- The user manual for the computer (more than just a "nice-to-have")

# Getting Down to Business

In the following steps you will create an incorrect BIOS setting and look to see what (if any) problems this causes. Then you will do some research on the topic of CMOS battery and go through the steps necessary to change the battery on your computer.

**Step 1.**   You are going to "tell" your computer that it has a device that does not actually exist in the computer. In this case, you will tell it that it has a second floppy drive. Power up your computer and start the BIOS setup program. Take the necessary steps to configure the BIOS for a second (Drive B:) floppy drive. Exit and change your settings. Reboot the computer, watching carefully for the symptoms. Record your observations below:

_____

_____

**Step 2.**   Reboot the computer, run the BIOS setup program, and remove the setting for the second floppy drive. While you are in the setup program, write down all the settings as a precaution before you perform Step 4. Reboot the computer again, and ensure that the error message does not appear.

**Step 3.**   Before proceeding to the next step, connect to the PC Mechanic's site at www.pcmech.com and search on "battery." Among the articles in the resulting list, select the article titled "CMOS Backup Battery." Read this article before proceeding, paying close attention to the battery replacement procedure while performing the following steps.

lab
**Warning**

*Some computers do not have an on-board battery. So if your lab computer is one of these, you will not be able to use it to do steps 4 & 5 in this lab.*

**Step 4.**   In this step you will simulate a failure of the battery supporting the CMOS. Power down the computer. Unplug the power cable and open the case. Locate the battery. If it is a removable battery and the computer manual discusses how to remove it, remove the battery. If the manual's instructions are incomplete, use those in the article you found in Step 3. Close the case, reconnect the power cord, and power up the computer. Record your observations below:

_____

_____

**Step 5.** Power down the computer. Unplug the power cable and open the case. Reinstall the CMOS battery. Close the case, reconnect the power cord, and power up the computer. Ensure that the computer boots up properly and has the correct time and setup information. Troubleshoot any problems that occur.

**lab**
**Hint**   *If you have not visited the PC Mechanic web site before, spend some time exploring the other articles at this site.*

## LAB EXERCISE 3.04

# Identifying Symptoms and Problems Associated with Peripherals

**I Hour**

Ace Shipping and Freight has called you to their administrative office to check out a few problems. They moved their office over the weekend and now, when they attempt to start up one of the computers, it beeps several times and the monitor remains blank, even though it is powered on. Also, another computer is no longer able to print to its local printer.

## Learning Objectives

Once you complete this lab, you will be able to:

- Troubleshoot common problems with peripherals
- Define ECP parallel port mode
- Define bi-directional

## Lab Materials and Setup

The materials you'll need for this lab are:

- A computer running a PnP operating system: Windows 9x, Windows 2000, or Windows XP
- A PnP printer
- An IEEE 1284 bi-directional parallel printer cable

## Getting Down to Business

In the following steps you will simulate a monitor connection problem, then go through the procedures you would do to troubleshoot and resolve a problem with the parallel port mode on a PC.

**Step 1.**   Power down the computer. Then unplug the video cable that connects the monitor to the computer's video adapter. Power up the computer and record your observations below:

_____

_____

**Step 2.**   Power down the computer and reconnect the monitor. Power up the computer and confirm that the computer can boot up normally.

**Step 3.**   Before proceeding to the next step, take a few minutes to learn about the IEEE 1284 standard and the parallel port modes known as EPP (Enhanced Parallel Port) and ECP (Enhanced Capabilities Port). Connect to the web site of Warp Nine Engineering at www.fapo.com. Under the "1284 Info" heading click on the link titled "IEEE 1284 Info." On the next page scroll down to the list of articles and select the link titled "Introduction to the IEEE 1284 Parallel Port Standard." Which mode do new generation printers and scanners most often use, EPP or ECP?

_____

_____

lab

ⓘint   *While you do not have to have ECP or EPP mode to support bi-directional communications between a peripheral and the PC, your BIOS setup Standard mode may not be bi-directional. We have seen BIOS setup with 4 choices: Standard, Bi-directional, ECP, and EPP. However, some BIOS have a Standard mode that includes bi-directional support. The only way to be sure is if it is stated in the BIOS setup or in the documentation for your computer.*

**Step 4.**   Your research has shown you that the newer ECP and EPP modes are both bi-directional and faster than standard bi-directional mode. Use Device Manager to see if ECP mode is enabled on your computer. On a Windows 2000 computer a parallel port with ECP enabled can be seen in Device Manager, as shown in Figure 3-2.

**Step 5.** Now you will go "under the hood" to see where you configure the parallel port mode. Reboot the computer and enter the BIOS setup program. Verify that the parallel port is configured for ECP/EPP mode. If it is not set for one of these enhanced modes, change to that mode now, then save the settings and exit from the setup program. Power the computer down, and connect the printer to the computer using an IEEE 1284 parallel cable. Then power up the printer and the PC. Your operating system should display a message that it has discovered a new device. Proceed to install the device driver. (If the operating system does not have a driver for your printer, you may have to go to the manufacturer's Web site and download one.) After the device is installed, open Device Manager and open the Ports object. You should see a symbol for a working ECP port. Make sure the printer has paper and verify that the printer works by printing a document from Notepad.

**Step 6.** Reboot the computer and enter the BIOS setup program again. In the BIOS setup program, change the setting for the parallel port to disable ECP or EPP. (For some versions of BIOS you select "Normal" as the Parallel Port Mode.) Save your settings and exit from the BIOS program, and then boot up into the operating system. After you log on you should see a systems Settings Change message stating

FIGURE 3-2

Device Manager
(Windows 2000)

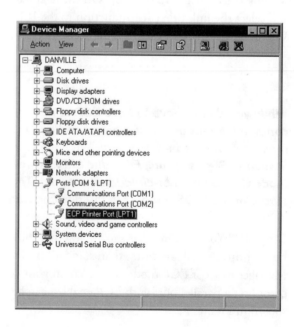

that the operating system has finished installing new devices and, if you are running Windows 95/98, you must restart your computer before the new settings take effect.

**Step 7.** Open Device Manager and look under the Ports object. Is there a symbol for an ECP Printer Port? Test the printer by opening Notepad and printing a document. Record your observations below:

_____

_____

**Step 8.** Reboot the computer and start the BIOS Setup program. In the BIOS setup program, change the setting for the parallel port to enable ECP or ECP+EPP mode. Save your settings and exit from the BIOS, booting up into the operating system. Once again, test the printer by printing a document from Notepad.

In this lab you simulated a troubleshooting experience in which the computers had been moved. The disconnected monitor could very easily happen after a move, because it is very common for people to fail to make the correct connections when they move a computer. The second problem could have occurred if someone had made a change to the BIOS setup. Because of the recent move, you should first check the connections before pursuing the BIOS solution.

**LAB EXERCISE 3.05**

**1 Hour**

# Identifying Symptoms and Problems Associated with Drives

The Fine Catering Company has called to report problems with the floppy drive on one of their computers. They cannot read a disk in drive A. Before going to their office to troubleshoot the problem, you experiment with the drives in one of the lab computers.

## Learning Objectives

Once you complete this lab, you will be able to:

- Identify symptoms and problems associated with drives

## Lab Materials and Setup

The materials you'll need for this lab are:

- A working computer running Windows 95 or greater with a single floppy drive and a single IDE/EIDE drive
- A large, open workspace with an antistatic mat (if possible)
- A Phillips or Torx screwdriver or appropriate nut driver
- One or more containers in which to place and organize screws and other small parts
- A notepad on which to take notes and make sketches of the computer and components
- The user manual for the computer

## Getting Down to Business

The following steps have you simulate possible floppy drive problems in order to prepare you to troubleshoot these problems.

**Step 1.** Shut down your computer. Insert a formatted but non-bootable floppy disk in drive A, then turn the computer on and observe any error messages that appear on the screen. Record your observations below:

_____

_____

**Step 2.** Remove the floppy disk from drive A and shut down the computer. Unplug the power cable, open the case, locate the data cable to the floppy drive, and remove it. Reconnect it in a reversed position (i.e. with the colored wire on the ribbon cable NOT connected to pin 1), close the case, reconnect the power cord, and power up the computer. Record your observations below:

_____

_____

**Step 3.** Shut down the computer. Unplug the power cable and open the case. Locate the data cable to the floppy drive, and disconnect it. Close the case, reconnect the power cord, and power up the computer. If it successfully completes the boot up, insert a diskette into the floppy drive and try to access it in Windows Explorer. Record your observations below:

_____

_____

**Step 4.** Shut down the computer. Unplug the power cable and open the case. Reconnect the floppy drive data cable, being sure to orient it properly. Now disconnect the hard drive data cable. Close the case, reconnect the power cord, and power up the computer. Record your observations below:

_____

_____

**Step 5.** Shut down the computer. Unplug the power cable and open the case. Reconnect the IDE/EIDE cable to the hard drive, connecting the hard drive to the middle connector on the cable. Close the case, reconnect the power cord, and power up the computer. Record your observations below:

_____

_____

**Step 6.** If your computer is not fully functional, take the necessary steps to correct all problems and ensure that it can successfully boot up.

In this lab you simulated disk failures in order to observe the symptoms and practice correcting the problems.

*Chapter 3 of the* **A+ Certification Study Guide** *lists additional symptoms and problems.*

# LAB ANALYSIS TEST

1. Brown and Jones, a structural engineering firm, has hired you to do BIOS upgrades or replacements on 300 computers before they are upgraded to Windows XP. Of these computers, about 100 are Compaq desktop models, 50 are Toshiba laptops, and the balance are desktop systems from various vendors. How will you prepare for this upgrade?

   _____

   _____

2. The manager of the mail order department at a retail outlet has called to report that his computer will not run a new order-fulfillment application. It is reporting insufficient memory. Maintenance records show that this computer was among those that recently received an upgrade from 64MB to 128MB of RAM in preparation for this new application. How do you proceed?

   _____

   _____

3. During routine maintenance of the inventory control computer from the Cream Puff Bakery, you notice that the floppy drive is not functioning at all. You are puzzled as to why no one had reported this as a problem, especially since the computer is rebooted every day. What could explain the fact that no one reported problems with the computer?

   _____

   _____

4. While preparing to deliver and install a client's new HP printer, you read the manual for the printer and discover that it is designed to take advantage of the ECP parallel port mode. How can you determine if ECP mode is enabled on the parallel port of the computer? If it is not enabled, how can you enable it, provided that the computer can support ECP mode?

   _____

   _____

5. Martin from the Nerd Matrix dispatch center stopped you in the hallway first thing this morning to tell you that, when he started his computer this morning, he could hear it power up then heard some beeps, but the monitor remained blank. You have agreed to help Martin. How will you proceed?

   _____

   _____

# KEY TERM QUIZ

Use the following vocabulary terms to complete the sentences below. Not all of the terms will be used.

DIMM

flash

expand

POST

ECP

EPP

beep codes

CMOS

bank

unit

1. During bootup, audio error signals may occur when the _____, a series of diagnostics tests, is run.

2. If a computer does not maintain the setup information after it is powered down, change the battery that supports the _____ RAM.

3. _____ is a special fast parallel port mode used by some newer printers and scanners.

4. When a system's BIOS code is out of date, you may have to replace the chip or simply modify the BIOS software. When a BIOS can be modified, we say that we can _____ the BIOS.

5. When installing SIMM memory, you must install a complete _____, which may be a single slot, but is often two slots.

# LAB WRAP-UP

Good work! You now have expanded your portfolio of Internet technical resources that you started in Chapter 1 to include sites with information for troubleshooting BIOS problems. You had hands-on experience identifying symptoms of problems associated with various system components including CMOS, BIOS, memory, disk, and peripherals, such as monitors and printers. You are now ready to move on to the next chapter on power protection and safety procedures.

# LAB SOLUTIONS FOR CHAPTER 3

## Lab Solution 3.01

**Step 1.** The BIOS replacements and upgrades for Award BIOSs can be found at the web site of Unicore Software at www.unicore.com, while the replacements and upgrades for Phoenix BIOSs are located at the site of Micro Firmware at www.firmware.com.

**Step 2.** The URL for the Phoenix BIOS manual is http://www.phoenix.com/pcuser/ PDF-Files/userman.pdf. The chapters that would be most helpful are Chapter 1, "The Setup Guide;" Chapter 2, "Boot Utilities;" and Chapter 3, "Phoenix Phlash" (cute!).

**Step 3.** 1) Yes, if you supported HP computers that needed a BIOS upgrade, this site would be useful because it provides the BIOS upgrade software for all the HP computers. 2) If you supported HP computers and suspected that one of them required a BIOS upgrade, you would search on the model name rather than on the string "BIOS upgrade." This would return information about that model. You can then search for references within that topic. For instance, if you search on "Pavilion," then select the recommended link to Support for your HP Pavilion PC you will find a list of Pavilions by model number. By selecting Product Support, and then the "Update Software & Drivers" link next to the model in question, you can find the specific information needed.

**Step 4.** Answers will vary because the drivers offered on this site will change over time. At the time of this writing, there were BIOS updates with the following descriptions: BIOS update version P09 for the BIOS prefix EA8A510A, BIOS update version P07 for the E-3400, and Solo 9550 Flash BIOS version 29.00 for Windows 98/Windows ME.

**Step 5.** Answers may vary if you found other web sites on your own. The following web sites should be included in your list, along with others you have discovered:

www.phoenix.com

www.unicore.com

www.firmware.com

www.gateway.com

**Step 6.** Answers will vary, as the PC Guide is updated. References at this time include: "Troubleshooting BIOS Beep Codes—Other Brand" "Troubleshooting BIOS Beep Codes—Award BIOS;" "Troubleshooting BIOS Beep Codes—Phoenix BIOS;" and "Troubleshooting BIOS Beep Codes – AMI BIOS."

**Step 7.** According to the article titled "Troubleshooting BIOS Beep Codes—AMI BIOS," continuous beeping is a symptom of a memory or video problem.

**Step 8.** When you click on the Download Agent from the home page it takes you to the BIOS Agent page where it explains what the program is and how you can use it. Clicking the download link will bring up the File Download dialog. You should choose "Save this program to disk" and then choose a location on the local hard drive to save the program. After the file is downloaded, open Windows Explorer or a command prompt and execute the program BA.EXE. It opens a window that gives you several options. Click on the Get BIOS Info button. Results will vary. The following information resulted from running the BIOS Agent program on a computer with BIOS by SystemSoft, a manufacturer not supported by this version of the BIOS Agent. However, it still returned some helpful information on the BIOS date and chipset.

| | |
|---|---|
| BIOS ID: | Unknown |
| BIOS Date: | 05/15/99 |
| BIOS Signon: | unknown |
| BIOS Type: | unknown |
| Super I/O: | SMC 869 rev 0 found at port 3F0h |
| Chipset: | Intel 440BX/ZX rev 3 |
| OEM Signon: | (blank) |

**Step 9.** If you choose to save the results, it will use the default location and filename of c:\bios.txt unless you override this by typing in a new location and filename. Once saved, the file can be read with any text editor, such as Notepad.

The information in the report does not align very well with what is displayed on the screen. First of all, the version number of the BIOS Wizard appears, which may be useful information. At this writing, the BIOS Wizard Version is 1.5. However, only 4 items, or fields, appeared on the report, as opposed to the seven that were displayed on the screen. In addition, the items that do appear are not in the same order as on the screen. Some that do not appear were unknown or blank on the screen, but two unknown items did appear. You would probably be wise to manually record the results yourself.

**Step 10.**   The BIOS Agent Quick Help screen is shown in Figure 3-3 with the definitions of each field.

## Lab Solution 3.02

**Step 1.**   Observations will vary based on the type of RAM and the design of the computer. Our test computer had 128MB of SIMMs arranged in 2 banks, each with

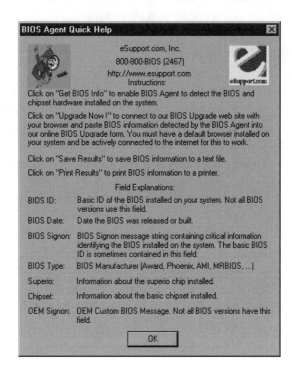

**FIGURE 3-3**

The BIOS
Agent Quick
Help screen

two 32MB SIMM modules. When we removed only one SIMM module and rebooted, the computer refused to recognize the entire bank that had the missing module. It recognized only 64MB of the 96MB installed in the computer. Otherwise, the system booted normally and the operating system ran. The missing memory would not be discovered unless someone had difficulty running an application that required more memory. If you do this lab on a computer with only one bank of SIMMs you will not be able to boot up the computer.

**Step 2.**    No additional information is needed for this step. If the computer did not start up correctly, then you should power it down again and follow correct troubleshooting procedures in which you make sure the RAM is correctly installed and that all other connections are properly made, including the power cord.

**Step 3.**    Observations will vary, depending on the type of RAM, BIOS version, and system design. One of our test computers had 256MB of DIMMs in two slots; each DIMM had 128MB of RAM. After removing the DIMM from the first slot we reconnected and powered up the computer. No error messages were noted, and the operating system (Windows 2000) successfully started up. We ran the System Information tool from the System Tools menu. It showed just 128MB of RAM installed.

**Step 4.**    No additional information is needed for this step. If the computer did not start up correctly, then you should power it down again and follow correct troubleshooting procedures in which you make sure the RAM is correctly installed and that all other connections are properly made, including the power cord. The most likely problem is that the RAM is not correctly seated in the slot.

We actually did something we do NOT recommend you try. On a test computer with two 128MB DIMMs we only partially inserted the DIMM in the slot, so the clip on one side was not engaged. As a result, the computer would not even begin the boot up process. No messages displayed on the screen, and there were no beeps and no error codes. We could hear only the fans on the power supply and processor, but we had a blank display. We powered down and reseated the module in the slot, after which the computer booted up normally.

## Lab Solution 3.03

**Step 1.** Answers will vary, depending on the BIOS version of the computer. On a test machine, after adding a second floppy drive to the BIOS setup, we rebooted and briefly saw a message stating "B: Drive error. Press F1 to resume. Press F2 to run Setup." The system continued the bootup process (without the requested press of F1), and the operating system successfully booted.

**Step 2.** There is no additional information required for this step.

**Step 3.** No response is required for this step.

**Step 4.** Answers will vary, depending on the BIOS version and system design. On a test machine, the system booted up without displaying an error and actually had the correct date and time, as well as the correct setup information! On older machines, you will probably see a request to set the time, and may have difficulty successfully booting up.

Observations will also vary based on the computer itself. The extremes go from losing BIOS settings and not booting up at all, to no apparent symptoms. Losing track of time is common.

**Step 5.** No response is required for this step.

## Lab Solution 3.04

**Step 1.** Answers will vary. The computer we tested had one long beep, 3 short beeps, and a blank monitor.

**Step 2.** No additional instructions are needed for this step, and there are no observations required.

**Step 3.** New generation printers and scanners most often use ECP. EPP is used by CD drives, tape drives, hard drives, and other non-printer devices.

**Step 4.** No observations or answers are required for this step.

**Step 5.** If you are working on a computer that is several years old, you may not have this option and will not be able to complete this lab.

**Step 6.** No observations or answers are required for this step.

**Step 7.** On the test computer, there was no longer a symbol for an ECP Printer Port, and the print job failed with a message: "There was an error found when printing the document 'Untitled – Notepad' to LPT1. Do you want to retry or cancel the job?"

**Step 8.** No answers or observations are required. You should now be able to print again.

## Lab Solution 3.05

**Step 1.** After powering up the computer with a non-system disk in drive A, we received a message "Non-System disk or disk error. Replace and strike any key when ready."

**Step 2.** Exact results will vary based on the BIOS. After reversing the ribbon cable connector on the floppy drive and restarting, we did not observe an error during boot up. However, once the operating system loaded (Windows 2000), we inserted a diskette in the drive and attempted to read drive A: in Windows Explorer, and received a message box titled "Insert disk" with the following message, "Please insert a disk into drive A:."

**Step 3.** Exact results will vary based on the BIOS. On a test computer, during the power up after disconnecting the floppy drive data cable, the system beeped twice and displayed an error message that the floppy drive was unavailable. It then went on to detect the hard drive and beeped once. Then it booted from the hard drive and the operating system came up. However, once the operating system loaded (Windows 2000), and we attempted to open drive A in Windows Explorer, we received a message box titled "Insert disk" with the following message, "Please insert a disk into drive A:" as shown here.

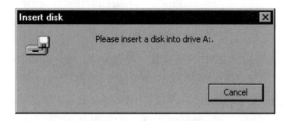

**Step 4.**   Results will vary slightly, depending on the BIOS. On a test machine we heard a single beep at the end of the POST, then after the system failed to locate a Boot Record from the Floppy and CDROM, this message displayed as shown here.

```
Searching for Boot Record from CDROM . . Not Found
Searching for Boot Record from Floppy . . Not Found
Searching for Boot Record from SCSI . . Not Found

Drive Not Ready
Insert BOOT diskette in A:
Press any key when ready
```

When we pressed a key, the system again attempted to locate a Boot Record and displayed the Boot Failure message again.

**Step 5.**   On most computers manufactured in recent years, this will not be a problem. In other words, the primary master hard drive can be positioned in either position on the cable and still be recognized. However, on the job you might encounter an old computer that requires the master hard drive be connected to the end plug on a cable.

**Step 6.**   No observations or answers are required for this step.

# ANSWERS TO LAB ANALYSIS TEST

1. Answers will vary. They should include researching the appropriate BIOS upgrade programs for the known models. This would include locating BIOS information on the Compaq and Toshiba sites. For systems in which the BIOS is unknown, we would use a tool, such as the BIOS Agent used in Lab 3.01 to determine the BIOS version. Although we can gather some information by going into the BIOS setup program on these computers, a utility is less intrusive.

2. Answers will vary. One approach would be for you to instruct him to reboot the computer and observe the total amount of memory reported during the system bootup. If it shows only 64MB of RAM it is possible that the memory was not installed or not installed correctly, or there is a problem with the memory. In this case you will have to pay a visit to the computer, and you should take along a memory module for the computer.

3. Answers may vary, based on the vintage of the computer. If a floppy drive fails, many computers can still successfully boot up, as long as the drive is not needed during the bootup. Therefore, if no one using the computer actually attempted to use the floppy drive, the problem would have gone unnoticed.

4. Answers will vary. If the operating system is Windows 95, Windows 98, Windows 2000, or Windows XP, you can look at the ports in Device Manager and see if it lists an ECP Parallel Port. On any computer, you can reboot and run the BIOS setup program. This will tell you if it supports ECP at all. If you discover, through one of these methods, that ECP mode is not enabled, you can enable it through BIOS setup if the BIOS supports it.

5. Answers will vary. You should quickly check the video connection to the monitor to see if the problem could be something as simple as a loose or disconnected monitor cable. If the connection seemed loose, or if the cable were actually disconnected, you would correct that, then power up the computer. If that did not solve the problem you would observe the symptoms for yourself. If there were more than the single beep that most systems use to indicate a successful POST, you would check a reference of audio beeps for the BIOS to find out what the BIOS was trying to tell you.

# ANSWERS TO KEY TERM QUIZ

1. POST
2. CMOS
3. ECP
4. flash
5. bank

# 4

# Power Protection and Safety Procedures

Y ou have spent time in the previous chapters learning how to install, configure, and upgrade computers. You also practiced responding to problems with PCs and honing your diagnostic abilities and troubleshooting skills. Now you will practice the proactive procedures required of computer technicians. This includes learning power protection and safety procedures and practicing preventive maintenance procedures.

The first of the following labs gives you experience with preventive maintenance tasks. Then you will explore the symptoms and solutions for power problems, followed by researching personal safety hazards and procedures. Finally, you will define environmentally friendly disposal procedures for computer components and byproducts.

## LAB EXERCISE 4.01

I Hour

# Identifying Preventive Maintenance Products and Procedures

Fay's Fabulous Fabrics specializes in fabric and supplies for quilters in a five-county area. However, because fabric being stored, shown, and cut generates a great deal of dust and fiber debris, it is a very inhospitable environment for the five computers used in the retail area and the back office. You visit Fay's once every three months to do preventive maintenance, which includes removing all the dust from the computers before it can cause serious problems.

## Learning Objectives

In this lab, you will do preventive maintenance on a computer system and monitor. By the end of this lab, you'll be able to:

- Work with various preventive maintenance products
- Select the correct procedures for preventive maintenance

## Lab Materials and Setup

The materials you need for this lab are:

- One desktop computer system unit and a monitor
- A bottle of isopropyl alcohol
- Distilled water
- An environmentally-safe compressed air product (such as Canned Air)
- A small vacuum—ideally one designed for computer maintenance (antistatic)
- Two or three lint-free cloths
- Cotton swabs
- Glass cleaner
- A diskette cleaning kit (optional)
- A large, open workspace with an antistatic mat (if possible)
- A Phillips or Torx screwdriver or appropriate nut driver
- One or more containers in which to place and organize screws and other small parts
- A notepad on which to take notes and make sketches of the computer and components
- The user manual for the computer

**cross**
**Reference**

*Read the entire section titled "Preventive Maintenance Products and Procedures" in the **A+ Certification Study Guide.***

## Getting Down to Business

In this lab you are going to dismantle and completely clean a PC system. This is something that needs to be done periodically to every PC system, but in actual practice it seldom is. When you commence working in the field, you will often find yourself dealing with very dirty PCs. It is worth the effort to clean them before working on them!

**Step 1.** Power off the computer, remove the power cord, and observe safe ESD procedures. Remove the case cover by following the manufacturer's instructions in the user manual for the computer, or by following your instructor's directions. Be very careful not to disturb cables inside the system unit as you remove the cover.

Place any screws or other removed attachment hardware in a container so that they don't disappear. If you have not already documented this computer, stop now and draw a rough sketch, identifying the components and their location. Make any notes that will aid you when you reassemble the computer.

**lab Hint**

*We're sure you have noticed that we consistently ask you to make a sketch of each computer you open, identifying the components and their relative locations to aid you in reassembling the computer. It will not be long before you will be so familiar with each component and the various versions and types of each component, that you will feel this step is unnecessary. We feel, however, that it is still necessary, even for experienced technicians, because there are so many components, and so many types of motherboards and cabinet layouts that even experienced technicians become confused. We recommend you always do it!*

**Step 2.**   Gently remove all plug-in expansion cards and examine the contacts on the connectors. If any appear soiled or dusty, use compressed air to blow the dust off the connectors, being careful to direct the dust away from the computer. If that does not do the trick, use isopropyl alcohol on a cotton swab to clean the contacts. Alternatively, use a white pencil or pen eraser to remove the dirt. Record any observations below:

_____

_____

**lab Warning**

*Do not be over zealous in cleaning delicate components. Rough or careless handling can leave the computer unusable.*

**Step 3.**   Examine all cables and replace any that are frayed or cracked. If you found damage, record the action you took below.

_____

_____

**Step 4.**   Use the compressed air to blow dust out of hard-to-reach areas inside the computer case.

**lab Warning**

*Be very careful to not blow dust and dirt into the floppy or CD drives. This could render them useless.*

**Step 5.** Hold the keyboard over a wastebasket and turn it upside down, gently shaking all loose debris into the basket. Then use the vacuum to remove all dust residue from the keyboard and inside and around the computer system. Be sure to vacuum all vents and fans. Use a damp cloth to clean the keyboard and the computer case if necessary.

*For details on cleaning a keyboard, see the sidebar titled "From the Classroom" in Chapter 4 in the **A+ Certification Study Guide**.*

**Step 6.** Clean the mouse by following the instructions in Exercise 3-1 in Chapter Three of the *A+ Certification Study Guide.*

**Step 7.** Using the glass cleaner and a lint-free cloth, clean the monitor screen per Exercise 4-1 in Chapter Four of the *A+ Certification Study Guide.*

**Step 8.** Referring to the notes you made as to where each board was located in the motherboard slots, reinstall any plug-in expansion cards that were removed, and ensure that the boards are securely seated in the connectors. Carefully reconnect all internal cables. Close up the system unit, securing it with the necessary screws or fasteners. Reconnect all external cables.

**Step 9.** If you have a diskette cleaning kit, follow the instructions in the kit to clean the floppy disk drive.

*Be very careful not to allow any liquids to run or drip into the computer.*

**Step 10.** Power up the computer and confirm that it is fully functional.

In this lab you performed preventive maintenance procedures using some very basic products and tools. In addition to the steps taken here, you might also use a mild soap to clean smudges off the outside of the computer case, the monitor case, and any other attached peripheral device cases.

Preventive maintenance can include being innovative. In arid climates, there is often so much dust in the air that you may have to take extra steps to maintain the health of your computer. You may need to add extra filtration to the air in the room, or even go so far as to add filters to the outside of the case to keep dust from being sucked into the case by the fan(s).

## LAB EXERCISE 4.02

# Researching Symptoms and Solutions for Power Problems

**I Hour**

Nerd Matrix has customers ranging from very small one-person offices to large multi-national companies. The large customers usually take care of their own power problems, but you often have to advise the small-to-medium customers on symptoms of power problems, and how to protect against damage from fluctuating and failing power sources. In this lab you will research power problems, their symptoms and consequences, and the devices needed to protect against power problems.

## Learning Objectives

After you've completed this lab, you will be able to:

- Recognize the signs of power problems
- Define various power problems
- Identify devices for protecting computers from power problems

## Lab Materials and Setup

The materials you need for this lab are:

- One desktop computer with Windows 95 or later installed
- Internet access

*Before completing this and the following labs, read the section titled "Certification Objective 4.02" in the A+ Certification Study Guide. For this lab, pay special attention to the "Scenario & Solution" in this section.*

## Getting Down to Business

It is unfortunate that in real life today the electrical power we draw from the power grid is not as stable as it was just a few years ago. This is due to many factors, ranging from politics to cost to incredibly increased demand upon limited resources. The problem is exacerbated by the sensitivity of our (relatively) delicate electronic computers. It is important, both now and increasingly in the future, that we take whatever steps we can to ensure that the equipment we work on is provided with the cleanest power possible.

This lab will guide you through some of the terminology, concepts, and resources available to you to make sure that the power your computers receive is appropriate for them.

**Step 1.**   Go to the web site of Sutton Designs (or another web site where you can see a glossary of electrical power terms) at www.suttondesigns.com. At the Sutton site, click the Glossary link and search on each of the following terms, supplying definitions for them in the space provided:

blackout _____

brownout _____

EMI _____

joule _____

line conditioner _____

RFI _____

sag _____

surge _____

surge suppressor _____

UPS _____

**Step 2.**   Use your Internet browser to connect to the web site of the PC Guide at www.pcguide.com. Click the Search The PC Guide link. In the search box enter "suppressor" and select two or three documents to read in order to research power protection. This site may have new, related, articles when you search it, but at the time of this writing one article was particularly useful: "Protection against Power Problems."

a. You are shopping for a surge suppressor and are comparing two surge suppressors that seem nearly identical, except that one, rated to protect to 600 joules is more expensive than one rated at 400 joules. Explain which you would choose, and why you would choose that one. Include a definition of joules.

_____

_____

b. You notice a tag on the surge protector certifying that it has met a certain set of standards. What is the name of the organization that is responsible for product safety testing and standards? What is the standard that covers surge suppressors?

_____

_____

c. The definition for UPS at the Sutton site was rather limited. Find a more complete definition in the PC Guide articles.

_____

_____

d. The word spike was not defined at the Sutton site. Search the PC Guide site for this word.

_____

_____

**lab**
**Warning**
*Never plug a surge protector into a UPS. Likewise, never plug a laser printer into a protected outlet on a UPS either, because the power surge required during the start-up phase while a laser printer is heating up can severely affect the UPS. Some newer UPS units include non-protected outlets that can power a laser printer or similar device.*

**Step 3.**   Several of the terms defined above are power problems. Using the *A+ Certification Study Guide* and Internet sources, such as the PC Guide, provide a description of the symptoms you would expect to observe for each of the following problems, and how you would go about solving the problems:

blackout _____

_____

brownout _____

_____

EMI _____

_____

surge _____

_____

spike _____

_____

noise _____

_____

In this lab you researched power problems, their symptoms, and the devices that protect from such problems.

## LAB EXERCISE 4.03

**30 Minutes**

# Identifying Personal Safety Hazards and Procedures

Now you will move from protecting the hardware to protecting yourself from hazards. These hazards include lasers, high-voltage equipment, power supplies, and cathode ray tubes.

## Learning Objectives

After you've completed this lab you will be able to:

- Identify potential hazards
- Identify steps to take to avoid hazards

## Lab Materials and Setup

- One desktop computer with Windows 95 or later installed
- Internet access

## Getting Down to Business

Often people are more careful about the equipment they work on than they are about themselves and their own health. In actual fact, although most present-day computer equipment uses voltages that are too low to cause personal injury (outside of power supplies and power line cords, that is), there are many other hazards that are more insidious which you should be aware of. This lab will help you discover what some of those hazards are, and how to protect yourself against them.

**Step 1.** Using the *A+ Certification Study Guide* and web sites, such as Webopedia, PC Mechanic, and PC Guide, research the hazards of lasers and answer the following questions:

a. What common computer components use lasers?

_____

b. What are the consequences of mishandling lasers?

_____

c. How can you protect yourself from being injured by lasers?

_____

**Step 2.** Using the *A+ Certification Study Guide* and/or web sites, such as Webopedia, PC Mechanic, and PC Guide, research the hazards of high-voltage equipment and answer the following questions:

a. What are two common high-voltage computer components?

b. What can be the consequences of mishandling high-voltage components?

c. How can you protect yourself from being injured by a high-voltage component?

**LAB EXERCISE 4.04**

# Identifying Environmentally Friendly Disposal Procedures

**20 Minutes**

So far, you have worked to protect computers from power problems and to protect yourself from high-voltage computer equipment. Now let's look at protecting the environment and ourselves from the hazardous materials in our computer equipment, as well as working to keep items that can be recycled out of our landfills.

Nerd Matrix has adopted a policy of educating their clients to be conscious of how they dispose of used computer supplies and equipment. All the technicians are instructed to remind clients to dispose of their hazardous materials safely, and to recycle any component for which you can find a recycling source. To do this, you can start with each municipality and learn what it offers in recycling and hazardous waste disposal services. You can also find out what the federal government standards are for disposing of a particular component, and finally, you can contact the manufacturer. Some, like Hewlett-Packard, will accept your old equipment—disposing of it or recycling portions, as appropriate.

## Learning Objectives

Once you've completed this lab, you will be able to:

- Safely dispose of computer equipment and other related hazardous waste
- Research proper disposal procedures for a component.

## Lab Materials and Setup

The materials you'll need for this lab are:

- A computer running Windows 95 or greater
- Internet access

## Getting Down to Business

In this lab you will research how to dispose of batteries, monitors, system boards, chemical solvents, and cans in your community. Then you will research the special document, called a Material Safety Data Sheet (MSDS) for several common computer products.

**Step 1.** Using your Internet browser, locate the web page of your hometown, or the nearest large city. You will find search engines very valuable for this— try the Google site at www.google.com. Once you find the web page for one of these municipalities, research what provisions they have for disposing of each of the following, and describe these provisions in the space provided:

a. Batteries – _____

_____

b. Toner kits and cartridges –_____

_____

c. Chemical solvents and cans –_____

_____

d. Computers, other consumer electronics, and rechargeable products – _____

_____

**Step 2.** Remember all that documentation you found packed with the last laser printer you unpacked? One item was a Material Safety Data Sheet (MSDS) that described the proper disposal procedures. If you no longer have the data sheet, you can use your Internet browser to connect to the Cornell University Material Safety Data Sheets web page at http://msds.pdc.cornell.edu/msdssrch.asp. Search on LaserJet and look at the data sheet for the HP LaserJet 4V toner cartridge, C3900A. Is the toner hazardous? How should toner be disposed of? Does the cartridge consist of hazardous metals? How should the cartridge be disposed of?

<br>

lab
**ⓦarning**

*Regardless of the toxicity (or lack of it) of laser toner it is still a very fine powder, and must be handled with respect. You must always take precautions when handling such super-fine powders.*

**Step 3.** Another option you can pursue if you are unsure of how to dispose of a component is to contact the manufacturer for more information, as you do in this step. Use your Internet browser to connect to the web page of Hewlett-Packard at www.hp.com. From the home page, click the Products and Services link. On the Products and Services page scroll down to the list of services labeled Business Services and click the Return and Recycle link. Use the information on this page and linked pages to answer the following questions:

a. Is there a charge for the hardware recycling service?

b. What does HP do with returned inkjet supplies?

c. What steps has HP taken that increased their ability to recycle their LaserJet printer cartridges?

# LAB ANALYSIS TEST

1. You have been called to the plant manager's office of a corn packing plant where they pack sweet white-corn kernels into cans. They just completed their busiest time of year, and are giving the offices and plant a thorough cleaning. The manager's desktop computer has a keyboard with keys that "stick." How will you proceed?

   _____

   _____

2. You are cleaning out a system unit for a customer. You have vacuumed out the inside of the computer, but you can see dust in crevices that you cannot reach with the vacuum. What can you do to remove this dust from the computer?

   _____

   _____

3. A new client is a glassworks company that makes fine art glass items, employing 40 glass artisans and an office, shipping, and store staff of 17. Their workshop, offices, and mail order facility are all located in a rural setting. Since moving to this location one year ago, they have discovered that brownouts and brief blackouts are frequent, and they have lost several computers to surge damage in spite of using surge protectors on all their computer equipment. Their equipment includes a single file and print server, a dedicated firewall, and ten desktop computers. What solution will you pursue for this customer?

   _____

   _____

4. Yet another Nerd Matrix client is a large (20-bay) diesel truck repair center. One of their mechanics, Bruno, is the de facto computer support person at their site. He is also your contact there, and it is important for you to maintain a good relationship with him. His experience with diesel engines has taught him that if he can get something apart, he can fix it. You stop by one day to find him dismantling the laser printer, and trying to open the laser assembly. What information does Bruno need?

   _____

   _____

5. While on a service call to a customer site you notice several laser print cartridges and a chemical solvent can in a waste basket. Why is this a concern? What will you tell this customer?

   _____

   _____

# KEY TERM QUIZ

Use the following vocabulary terms to complete the sentences below. Not all of the terms will be used.

UPS

resistors

blackout

suppressor

EMI

brownout

monitor

MSDS

lasers

batteries

**1.** Flickering lights can be a symptom of a/an _____.

**2.** Because _____ and chemical solvents contain hazardous material, they must be disposed of properly. Check with your local municipality to determine the proper disposal method.

**3.** Included with the documentation that came with your new LaserJet printer, you found a special data sheet called a/an _____ with information about disposal of components.

**4.** CD-ROM drives and certain printers have _____, which can be harmful if directed in your eyes. These devices are designed so the operation of this component is disabled if the casing is opened or broken.

**5.** Never open a/an _____ or power supply because there is a danger of electrical shock—even when the power cable is disconnected from the wall outlet.

# LAB WRAP-UP

In these labs you researched some of the proactive activities you will need to perform as a computer technician. You explored the use of preventive maintenance products and learned practices to keep your computer equipment from being overwhelmed by dust and debris. Then you determined proper power protection and safety procedures—both for the equipment and for yourself.

# LAB SOLUTIONS FOR CHAPTER 4

## Lab Solution 4.01

**Step 1.** Step one is complete and does not require any answers or observations.

**Step 2.** Observations will vary based on what you find in the computer.

**Step 3.** Observations will vary based on what you find in the computer.

**Step 4.** No observations or answers are required. Be sure to use the compressed air very carefully.

**Step 5.** No observations or answers are required.

**Step 6.** No observations or answers are required.

**Step 7.** No observations or answers are required.

**Step 8.** No observations or answers are required.

**Step 9.** No observations or answers are required.

**Step 10.** No observations or answers are required.

## Lab Solution 4.02

**Step 1.** Answers will vary, but should substantially match the following:

- **blackout** a total loss of power.
- **brownout** a condition of lower than normal AC voltage.
- **EMI** Electro-Magnetic Interference is unwanted electrical "noise" on a power line that may "leak" from the power line, in which case it constitutes a magnetic field that may affect electronic equipment and damage data.

- **joule**   a measure of the amount of energy delivered by one Watt of power in one second, or 1 million Watts of power in one microsecond.

- **line conditioner**   a true Line Conditioner is a device that provides automatic voltage correction and conditioning, and produces a clean, filtered, sine wave output.

- **RFI**   Radio Frequency Interference comprises noise signals that travel over a significant distance. These signals can be received by power cords and wiring and converted to EMI.

- **sag**   a brownout lasting from a few milliseconds to a few hundred milliseconds. Computer equipment malfunctions can occur when sag lasts longer than 10 to 20 milliseconds.

- **surge**   a momentary transient overvoltage on an AC power circuit, data circuit, or telephone circuit that has the potential of damaging connected electronic equipment. "Momentary" may be from a few billionths of a second (nanoseconds) to a few thousandths of a second (milliseconds). Transient voltage increases that do not exceed the safe operating voltage of a circuit are not usually defined as surges. On an AC power circuit, a surge is defined as voltage greater than a few hundreds of volts. On a data circuit, a surge is defined as a few tens of volts.

- **surge suppressor**   a device used to protect equipment from transient overvoltages on AC power, data, or telephone circuits. A surge suppressor may absorb the surge, as in the case of the shunt-type of surge suppressor, or it may block the surge from flowing, as in the case of the series-type of suppressor. These two methods may also be combined within one device.

- **UPS**   Uninterruptible Power Supply. A device that contains a battery that is being constantly kept at full charge and that can supply power for a limited time if the external power fails.

**Step 2.**   Answers will vary, but should substantially agree with the following:

a. Given the choice between a surge protector that protects to 400 joules and one that protects to 600 joules, choose the latter. A joule is a measurement of energy. While 400 joules is good protection—better than the basic protection of a unit that can absorb 200 joules, 600 joules offers much higher protection.

b. Underwriters Laboratories is the organization responsible for product safety testing. The standard for surge suppressors is UL 1449, Transient Voltage Surge Suppressors.

c. A UPS provides backup battery power. A good UPS also provides filtering and conditioning of the power. There are two types of UPSs – standby UPS and online UPS. With standby UPS, the primary power to the devices connected to the UPS output comes from the AC power source, and the backup battery power kicks in only when there is a failure of the AC power source. This is the opposite of an online UPS, in which the primary source of output from the UPS comes from the battery, and the AC power source becomes the power source to the UPS output only when the battery fails.

d. A spike is a power surge of very short duration—perhaps a few thousandths of a second—in which the voltage quickly increases from 110 to, perhaps, over 1,000 volts.

**Step 3.**    Answers will vary, but should cover the following key points:

■ A **blackout** is pretty obvious, since there is a total lack of power. However, the scope of the blackout can vary. It may be isolated to a single circuit, or it may include a neighborhood or even an entire city. Nothing requiring AC power (unless it is on backup power) will be operating within the geographic scope of the blackout. The disruption of power can cause data to be lost, and the resumption of power can result in a surge or spike of current.

The backup battery power of a UPS is the best protection from blackouts because, although it may provide power for only a few minutes, it allows time for the computer to be shut down safely. (Note that you should also have your monitor plugged into a protected outlet on a UPS. If it isn't, and the power fails, you can't see the screen to shut your computer down!) If you do not have a UPS, be sure to turn off and/or disconnect computers and peripherals from the power source before electrical service is restored. Doing this will prevent damage from the surges and spikes that may occur as power is restored. Also, it is always wise to keep a flashlight near your computer systems so you can see what you are doing in the dark!

■ During a **brownout**, lights will go dim—often for less than a second. Like a blackout, a brownout can be followed by a power surge or spike. A surge protector, or UPS that provides surge protection, is the best protection from brownouts.

- **EMI** (electromagnetic interference) can be the cause of dips and surges in power. The dips have the same symptoms as brownouts, and you may see lights dim because of EMI. The surges can damage the equipment. You deal with EMI by avoiding exposing wiring to high-voltage equipment that can cause EMI, and by protecting your computers from surges by using surge protectors. Also, be sure that cables, including network cabling, are not kinked, bound together, or coiled, all of which can cause EMI interference.

- The usual symptoms of a **surge** are the damages that occur as a result of a surge. Therefore, focus your efforts on preventing a surge by using a surge protector.

- A **spike** is more likely to do damagethan a surge, even when a surge protector is in use. This is because a spike may happen too fast and be too strong for a surge protector to be successful in mitigating the effect of the surge.

- **Noise** is the presence of EMI on a line. Therefore, the result of noise can be surges, spikes, and/or brownouts. These symptoms are discussed above. The best solution for noise is a noise filter, which removes EMI. The noise filter can be a separate component, or it can be integrated with another device, such as a surge suppressor or UPS.

## Lab Solution 4.03

**Step 1.**   Answers will vary, but should include the following:

a. Two common components that use lasers are CD-ROMs and laser printers.

b. The consequences of mishandling lasers can include eye damage. These devices use lasers that normally cannot burn the skin, but can do damage to the eye if the beam is focused on the eye.

c. You can protect yourself from being injured by lasers by operating and maintaining them in the manner that the manufacturer describes in the user manual. Normal operation of CD-ROMs and laser printers does not allow the laser to be aimed at your eyes. In fact, these devices are designed to disable the laser as soon as the case is removed or opened. Avoid tampering, or otherwise trying to defeat this safety mechanism of the device.

**Step 2.**    Answers will vary, but should include the following:

a. Common high-voltage computer components include the power supplies (computer and printer) and the cathode ray tubes (CRTs) of the monitor.

b. The consequences of mishandling high-voltage components can be electrical shock that can lead to serious injury or death.

c. You can protect yourself from a life-threatening electrical shock by *never* opening up a CRT monitor, power supply or other high-voltage component. And remember to always remove your ESD strap when working around them. You must also unplug the devices from the power outlet. But don't get too confident because these devices can store electrical charges long after they are unplugged, and must be treated with the same respect you give them when they are plugged in.

## Lab Solution 4.04

**Step 1.**    Answers will vary considerably. The following was the result of searching the Minneapolis, Minnesota, web site:

a. **Batteries**    Household batteries are disposed of through recycling collection. They must be in a clear plastic bag. Auto batteries must be returned to a store that sells auto batteries.

b. **Toner kits and cartridges**    No mention of this on the Minneapolis site. HP and other manufacturers have return/recycling programs.

c. **Chemical solvents and cans**    Take to a drop-off center in a tightly sealed and labeled container, no larger than 5 gallons. Do not mix hazardous wastes together.

d. **Computers, other consumer electronics, and rechargeable products**    Take to a drop-off center.

**Step 2.**    No, neither the HP LaserJet toner nor the cartridge is considered hazardous. However, be aware that the toner in laser cartridges and copiers is made up of extremely fine particles, and you should always be careful not to breathe any such particulate matter into your lungs if you are exposed to it. The cartridge is made up of metal and plastic parts, and the toner should be treated as a plastic for the purposes of disposal.

**Step 3.** Answers may vary, because the terms of the return program may have changed. At the time of this writing the following was true:

a. There is a charge to return hardware to HP. They have an on-line service that charges from $13 to $34 per item, and they also mention customer price quotes.

b. The returned cartridges are processed, and materials are separated for purification into raw materials. Recycled HP inkjet cartridge material ends up in automobile parts, trays for microchip fabrication, copper wire, steel plates, and the precious metals are used in electronics and electrical equipment.

c. HP has taken several actions to increase their ability to recycle their LaserJet printer cartridges. They have reduced the average use of plastic resins by 44 percent since 1992, reduced the average number of parts by 22 percent, and they now mark plastic parts weighing more than 25 grams with internationally recognized ISO symbols so that they can be properly recycled. HP toner cartridges also come with a UPS label for returning the used cartridges, on a no-charge basis.

# ANSWERS TO LAB ANALYSIS TEST

1. The most likely reason for keys that "stick" is debris in the keyboard. Therefore, carefully clean the keyboard, by following the instructions in steps one and two of Lab 4.01. Also, take an extra keyboard to the customer site because this is a very inexpensive component, and if a cleaning does not fix the problem, the manager should not be inconvenienced by having to wait for a new keyboard.

**lab**
**Hint** *One "folk tale" about keyboard cleaning suggests that you put the keyboard in a warm shower! We don't recommend techniques like this.*

2. To remove dust from the hard-to-reach places in the computer, use compressed air, being very careful to not blow air into the drives or onto other components in the computer.

3. This customer needs protection from blackouts, brownouts, surges, and probably EMI. Pursue UPS products that contain integrated suppressor and noise filters as well as the UPS function. All their systems will need to be protected, so you should also consider larger UPS products that can handle multiple computers.

4. Bruno needs to know that he should never tamper with the laser device because he might defeat the safety feature that keeps the laser from operating when the case is opened. While you are at it, you should also talk to him about the danger of tampering with power supplies and CRT monitors. None of these is safe to service, unless you are specifically trained to do so.

5. There are two concerns: the hazard posed by the chemical solvent and the wastefulness of throwing out laser cartridges that have components that can be recycled. You should probably gently remind the customer that it is preferable to recycle laser cartridges (it's free!) and appropriately dispose of chemicals.

## ANSWERS TO KEY TERM QUIZ

1. brownout

2. batteries

3. MSDS

4. lasers

5. monitor

EXERCISES • QUESTIONS • ANSWERS

# 5

# Motherboard, Processors, and Memory

## LAB EXERCISES

**E**arlier chapters in this lab manual helped you to become familiar with the roles of the central components in personal computers. In the labs in this chapter you will revisit those components—motherboard, processor, memory, CMOS, and BIOS setup— in order to further understand their characteristics and capabilities. This knowledge is important in your career as a technician because it will enable you to make intelligent choices when configuring new systems and upgrading existing systems.

In working with processors, memory, and motherboards, you must understand their capabilities, and you must also understand their form factor. This is a term that is often used in the physical description of processors, memory, motherboards, and other components. The word "form" refers to the shape of something, while the word "factor" refers to the elements that make up an object. These words used together refer to computer components—the minimum definition of which includes the physical dimensions of a component, and can also relate to where sub-components are located.

In this chapter we will look at the important characteristics of processors, memory, and motherboards, including the form factors in which they are available. In processors we will look at the various socket and socket form factors, while in memory we will discuss SIMMs, DIMMs, and other form factors. Then we will define the main motherboard form factors: AT, Baby AT, and ATX.

You have probably noticed that we have asked you to use the Internet to research certain things. This is because the Internet has become the most powerful source of information available. However, as in learning anything, it takes time and practice to develop skill in the use of the Internet as a source of specific information. As a technician you will often be faced with unfamiliar hardware, and you will often need to find drivers for specific equipment. The more familiar you are with using the Internet to find the information you need at the moment, the easier your life will become. Therefore, these labs require you to do extensive Internet research.

Note that some web sites present information in a logical and easy-to-use format, while others seem to delight in making things obscure and difficult. The authors of this book found that they could not find answers to a couple of the questions you will be asked—specific details on processors. Maybe you can succeed where we couldn't! Good luck!

**LAB EXERCISE 5.01**

# Identifying CPU Chips

**1.5 Hours**

Hardware technicians are often called upon to determine the computer configuration that will best meet the needs of an end user. To this end, technicians at Nerd Matrix are required to demonstrate a detailed knowledge of the capabilities and specifications of processors made by various manufacturers. You also must keep up to date on the latest processors available. Therefore you have been directed to do specific research on the Internet to create tables of characteristics for the families of CPU chips made by the principal chip manufacturers.

## Learning Objectives

In this lab, you will research the capabilities of the non-Intel processors, building tables for each manufacturer similar to Table 5-1, Intel Pentium Processors, in the *A+ Certification Study Guide.* You will also look for the existence of new Intel processors. By the end of this lab, you'll be able to distinguish between the popular CPU chips based on their:

■ Physical form

■ Socket type

■ Voltage

■ Speeds

■ Cache capability

## Lab Materials and Setup

The materials you need for this lab are:

■ A desktop computer with Windows 95 or later version installed on the computer

■ Online access to the Internet

To best prepare for this lab, read the entire section "Certification Objective 5.01" in the A+ Certification Study Guide and complete Exercise 5-1.

## Getting Down to Business

**Step 1.** There is some confusion between socket and slot connections for motherboards. It can be said that both are forms of sockets, in that each is a type of connector into which a microprocessor is plugged. When talking about sockets that accommodate processors, we use the term socket when the processor has a pin grid array (PGA) form factor, and we use the term slot for a Slot 1 processor form factor. Table 5-1 was built from information provided in the *A+ Certification Study Guide*, and arranged roughly in chronological order. Notice that there was a change at the Pentium II to Slot 1, which was also used for the first Pentium III, then Intel offered another form factor for the Pentium III–socket 370. The AMD and Cyrix processors of the same generation stayed with the Socket 7 form factor.

| TABLE 5-1 | Past processors you may encounter in legacy equipment |
| --- | --- |

| Processor/Speed | # of pins | Socket # |
| --- | --- | --- |
| Pentium 60 and 66 | 273 | Socket 4 |
| Pentium 75-200 | 296 | Socket 7 |
| Pentium Pro | 387 | Socket 8 |
| AMD K5 | 296 | Socket 7 |
| Cyrix MI | 296 | Socket 7 |
| Pentium II | 242 | Single-edge contact (SEC) Slot 1 |
| AMD K6 | 296 | Socket 7 |
| Cyrix MII | 296 | Socket 7 |

Remember that when you look at a motherboard that requires a PGA processor, when the processor has been removed, you will see a grid of holes in which a PGA processor of the correct form factor can be installed. This is a socket. An example of a socket 8 connector on a motherboard is shown in Figure 5-1. Notice how clearly it is labeled.

When you look at a motherboard that requires a processor using a Slot 1 form factor (with the processor removed), you will see what looks like an expansion bus connector, as seen in Figure 5-2. This is a slot.

Examine the hardware available to you in your classroom lab, or that you have gathered on your own. Identify whether the processor form factor is a socket or a slot. Record your observations below:

_____

_____

**Step 2.**    Using the information on AMD processors in the *A+ Certification Guide*, as well as additional information to be found at the AMD Web site (www.amd.com),

**FIGURE 5-1**

Socket 8
connector

**FIGURE 5-2**

Slot I connector

complete the following table. An extra column is provided for a new processor model, if you discover one at their site.

| AMD Processors | AMD K5 | AMD K6 | AMD Duron | AMD Athlon | Any new processor |
|---|---|---|---|---|---|
| Form factor | | | | | |
| Socket/Slot | | | | | |
| Voltage | | | | | |
| Speeds | | | | | |
| L1 cache (KB) | | | | | |
| L2 cache (KB) | | | | | |
| Notes | | | | | |

**Step 3.** Chip manufacturer Cyrix created a line of low-cost microprocessors intended for personal computers and information appliances that competed with AMD, and Intel. They were acquired by VIA Technologies, a Taiwan supplier of chipsets and processors, which now offers the VIA Cyrix MII processor, as well as the VIA C3 processor. Using the information on Cyrix processors in the *A+ Certification Study Guide*, as well as additional information to be found at the VIA web site at

www.viatech.com, complete the table below. Extra columns are provided for any new processor models you discover.

| VIA/Cyrix Processors | Cyrix MI | Cyrix MII | VIA C3 | 1st New Processor | 2nd New Processor |
|---|---|---|---|---|---|
| Form Factor | | | | | |
| Socket/Slot | | | | | |
| Voltage | | | | | |
| Speeds | | | | | |
| L1 cache (KB) | | | | | |
| L2 cache (KB) | | | | | |
| Notes | | | | | |

**lab Warning**

*Knowledge of VIA processor products created since its purchase of Cyrix are not on the A+ exam as of this writing, but may be included in the future. Remember, in order to perform well on the job you also need to keep current on new technologies.*

**Step 4.** The *A+ Certification Study Guide* provides a table of Intel Pentium Processors. However, technology does not stand still, and you need to keep your knowledge up-to-date. Use your Internet browser to go to the Intel web site at www.intel.com to look for any new processors released since the Pentium III, and complete the table below. (Hint: we found three.)

| Processor Name | | | | |
|---|---|---|---|---|
| Form Factor | | | | |
| Socket/Slot | | | | |
| Voltage | | | | |
| Speeds | | | | |
| L1 cache (KB) | | | | |
| L2 cache (KB) | | | | |
| Notes | | | | |

In this lab, you reviewed the different form factors found in processors, and researched the capabilities of processors manufactured by Intel, AMD, and VIA (Cyrix). Keeping up to date on this information is important to you on the job because a hardware technician must understand the technology encountered in personal computers.

**lab**
**Ⓗint**

*Don't forget to enter copies of the tables you created in this Lab into your lab notebook! Remember that this is hard-earned information that will be very useful to you in the future. It must go into your personal database so that you don't have to try to find it again.*

## LAB EXERCISE 5.02

# Identifying RAM Characteristics

**I Hour**

Memory is another important consideration when you must determine a computer configuration that will best meet the needs of an end user. The amount required is often defined in the requirements for software. However, determining the type, speed, and form factor of the memory to be installed is dependent on the motherboard you use.

At Nerd Matrix, technicians are required to keep up to date on the latest memory technologies so these exercises will help you maintain that standard.

**lab**
**Ⓗint**

*This is one of the interesting aspects of being a computer technician. Not only do you have to understand existing and past technology in order to service "legacy" (old and older) computers but, at the same time, you have to keep up with the never-ending proliferation of new technologies.*

## Learning Objectives

In this lab you will use the Internet to research characteristics of various types of RAM. After you've completed this lab, you will be able to:

- Understand categories of RAM
- Describe the physical characteristics of RAM
- Locate RAM within a personal computer

## Lab Materials and Setup

The materials you need for this lab are:

- A desktop computer with Windows 95 or later version installed
- Online access to the Internet
- Acrobat Reader
- A printer connected to the network or directly to your computer (optional)

*To best prepare for this lab, read the entire section "Certification Objective 5.02"* in the **A+ Certification Study Guide** *and complete Exercise 5-2.*

## Getting Down to Business

**Step 1.** Go to the web site of Kingston Technology (www.kingston.com), a manufacturer of RAM chips. From the home page go to the link for the Ultimate Memory Guide. You will need Adobe Acrobat Reader installed to read the guide. Optionally, print it out, but be warned that it is a large document—about 120 pages. Read the section "A Closer Look" then answer the questions below:

*If you do not have Adobe Acrobat Reader, download a free copy from www.adobe.com/products/acrobat/readstep.html.*

a. When attempting to locate the RAM in a PC, look for sockets located near the _____.

b. True or False? A memory bank is a group of sockets or modules that make up two logical units. _____

c. Before purchasing and installing new memory modules for a computer, you need to know the memory configuration rules for that computer. Where would you look for these rules? _____

**Step 2.** Read the section "How Memory Works" and answer the questions below:

a. What part of a computer's chipset controls information flow between the processor and memory? _____

b. What scheme enables memory to run at speeds that do not match the system clock of a PC? _____

c. What type of memory is closest to the processor? _____

**Step 3.** Read the section "How Much Memory is on a Module" and answer the following questions:

a. Complete the following sentence: Memory module capacity is measured in _____, while memory chip capacity is measured in _____.

b. What term describes the transaction between the CPU and memory? _____

c. True or False? RIMM modules can send only 16 bits at a time to a CPU. _____

**Step 4.** Read the section "Different Kinds of Memory" and answer the following questions:

a. True or False? SDRAM memory module speed is measured in nanoseconds.

_____

b. Identify the form factor of the following memory module.

_____

_____

c. Identify the form factor of the following memory modules.

d. Identify the form factor of the following memory module.

e. True or false? When installing a 168-pin DIMM you would install the module at a slight angle to the memory socket in the motherboard, then gently click it into a vertical position, while you would install a 72-pin SIMM straight into the memory socket.

**Step 5.**   Point your web browser to the PC Mechanic's site at www.pcmech.com. Click on the link labeled Memory. On the memory page select the article "SDRAM, PC100, PC133 and DDR." Read the article and answer the questions below:

a.  What is PC100?

_____

_____

b.  Define frontside bus.

_____

_____

c.  Define backside bus.

_____

_____

lab
**Hint**   *If you did not have time to read the entire "Ultimate Memory Guide," bookmark it for later reference because it contains really valuable information for a hardware service technician. If you were able to print it out, make sure to insert it into your personal lab journal—you will need it in your career!*

**Step 6.**   As a hardware service technician you must verify that the software recognizes the hardware. There are several ways to determine the amount of physical memory recognized by your operating system. In Explorer you can click Help | About. Another method is to use the System Information program. System Information is available in all versions of Windows since Windows 95 except Windows NT 4.0, in which you may use the WINMSD.EXE program.

Figure 5-3 shows the System Information program in Windows 98, which you can compare to the System Information program in Windows 2000, as shown in Figure 5-4.

Run the appropriate program for your operating system, then write the amount of memory below:

_____

Windows 98
System
Information

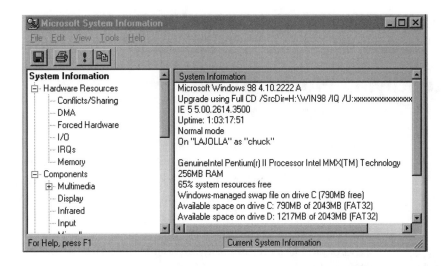

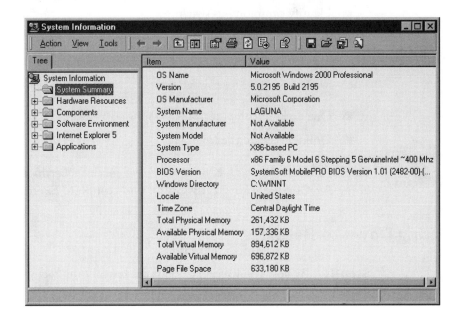

*lab*

**ℌint**

*In Windows 95 and Windows 98 the System Information program organizes information differently than it does in Windows 2000 and Windows XP. For example, on a computer running Windows 98 with 256 MB of RAM, the System Information window displays a line that simply states 256 MB RAM. In Windows 2000 in the System Summary the detail pane Total Physical Memory showed a value of 261,432 KB, which, is (roughly) 256 MB of RAM.*

Windows 2000
System
Information

**LAB EXERCISE 5.03**

# Identifying Motherboards and Their Components

**45 Minutes**

Now that you have accomplished two of the major requirements that your bosses at Nerd Matrix have assigned to you (understanding processors and memory), it's time to work on the elements of a computer which enable those components to function. As a Nerd Matrix technician you will not only have to build and install new computers, but you will often have to visit customers who have computers that have been around for years. Being able to recognize and understand not onlycurrent components, but also those that are out of date and/or proprietary (i.e., those which do not necessarily resemble modern components), will be a critical element in the success of your career.

## Learning Objectives

After you've completed this lab you will be able to:

- Identify various form factors for motherboards
- Identify common bus structures

## Lab Materials and Setup

The materials you need for this lab are:

- One desktop computer with Windows 95 or later version installed computer
- Online access to the Internet

**cross Reference** *To best prepare for this lab, read the entire section "Certification Objective 5.03" in the* **A+ Certification Study Guide** *and complete Exercise 5-3.*

## Getting Down to Business

**Step 1.** By now you have read about the several form factors of motherboards, including AT, Baby AT, and ATX. Standardizing on these few form factors enables manufacturers to build components that interchange with those of other manufacturers. For instance, a motherboard manufacturer who complies with the ATX form factor can accept expansion cards and memory from manufacturers of equipment that connect to the standard connectors (or sockets). You will find ATX motherboards with either slot or socket CPU connectors. See Figure 5-5 and Figure 5-6 for photographs of each.

You will also encounter hybrids of these form factors. However, there are certain characteristics that you can expect with each of these form factors.

Complete the table below. Use references available to you, including books, such as the *A+ Certification Study Guide*, or web sites, such as those of Intel, Webopedia, or the TechWeb Encyclopedia.

| Motherboard | AT | Baby AT | ATX |
|---|---|---|---|
| Dimensions | | | |
| Ports integrated on motherboard | | | |
| Processor location | | | |
| Keyboard connector | | | |
| Power connectors | | | |
| Power | | | |

**Step 2.** Point your Internet browser to www.asus.com. Select the appropriate language and location and click Go in the box next to your country. On the home page for your language, click on the ASUS e-Magazine button and look for an article "ATX Dilemma… the future of "BABY AT." If the article is not available as a link from this page, search for it using the search box on the page. Once you find the article, read it and answer the following questions.

a. What problems have been associated with the Baby AT motherboard form?

_____

_____

b. In what major areas have the ATX boards shown improvement over the Baby AT boards?

_____

**FIGURE 5-5**

ATX
motherboard
with slot 1 CPU
connector

**FIGURE 5-6**

ATX
motherboard
with socket 8
CPU connector

c. What third form is mentioned and described in the article?

_____

_____

**Step 3.**   Based on what you now know about motherboard form factors, identify the form factor in your lab computer. You may do this by opening the computer as you have done in previous labs, or you may discover that you have enough information in the drawings you have made in previous labs to make this determination.

_____

_____

**Step 4.**   Like many technicians, you may have seen many examples of ISA and PCI cards that plug into the most common bus structures. You are not likely to encounter VESA cards except in very old systems. But you may not be as familiar with the newer AGP cards that plug into the AGP bus.

Point your Internet browser to www.techweb.com/encyclopedia. On this page it is important *not* to use the search box at the top of the page because this searches many sites. We want to narrow our search to just the TechWeb Encyclopedia site. Using the box under TechEncyclopedia titled "Define this IT term" type *agp* then click **Define**. The resulting page provides an excellent definition of AGP, as well as a graphic of a motherboard in which you can compare the AGP, PCI, and ISA expansion slots. Scroll down to see a great comparison of the cards that fit into each of these bus types. Notice the EISA bus expansion card. The EISA bus and expansion cards will be found only in older computers—EISA had its heyday back when the 486 reigned as the primo processor!

lab
**Hint**

*When it comes to the motherboard pictured, ISA expansion cards fit only into ISA slots, PCI expansion cards only fit into PCI slots, and AGP video adapters fit only into AGP slots. You may encounter an older computer with EISA slots, which are an exception to this expected rule: an ISA expansion card will fit into an EISA slot. Only the longer connectors of an EISA expansion card can take full advantage of an EISA slot.*

Use the TechEncyclopedia to look at the definitions of all these bus types: PCI, ISA, EISA, Micro-Channel, and VL-bus. AGP and PCI are the main bus types in new computers today, and many new motherboards do not include ISA bus or include it only for downward compatibility with older expansion cards.

**Step 5.** Point your Internet browser to www.webopedia.com and search on "AGP." Read the information presented and answer the following questions:

a. What is the total bandwidth available to an AGP card and how does it compare to a PCI card?

_____

_____

b. How fast are the two faster modes available to an AGP card?

_____

_____

c. What are the three important requirements for a motherboard to use AGP?

_____

_____

_____

## LAB EXERCISE 5.04

# Identifying and Using CMOS

**I Hour**

So far you have satisfied Nerd Matrix's requirements for understanding and being able to recognize the physical and logical components of a computer. Now you must tackle the remaining major element: how the computer knows what it contains and what components it has to control. As a technician at Nerd Matrix, you will need to examine the CMOS characteristics of almost every computer you work on. Being both familiar and comfortable with CMOS commands is perhaps the most important tool you need.

## Learning Objectives

Once you've completed this lab, you will be able to:

- Explain CMOS and define its purpose and how it works
- Understand the elements that CMOS contains and controls
- Change CMOS parameters as necessary

## Lab Materials and Setup

The materials you'll need for this lab are:

- A desktop computer with Windows 95 or later version installed
- Online access to the Internet
- A formatted, non-system diskette
- The user manual for the computer

**cross Reference**

*To best prepare for this lab, read the entire section "Certification Objective 5.04" in the **A+ Certification Study Guide** and complete Exercise 5-4.*

## Getting Down to Business

The following steps will guide you through the processes of examining and changing CMOS settings in a PC. Remember that CMOS contains the parameters that define how the operating system sees the computer that it is residing in. It is important to be very careful when making changes to CMOS, because an inappropriate or incorrect change can cause the computer to cease functioning. A thorough understanding of these steps will ensure that you are a competent and effective computer technician.

**Step 1.** Start up or restart your computer and start the CMOS settings program by using the special key or key combination for your computer. Once in the setup program, browse through the menus. Do you understand all the settings? Write down any settings you do not understand, and in the next step you will research these settings.

**Step 2.**   Point your web browser to www.pcmech.com. Click on the BIOS link. On the BIOS page scroll down and click on the list of articles. Most of these articles define BIOS settings. Browse through the articles to find definitions for the CMOS setup options you listed above and write those definitions below:

_____

_____

**Step 3.**   Most desktop PCs are configured through their system setup program to boot first from the floppy drive, then from the hard drive. Place the formatted non-system diskette in drive A: and reboot the computer. If the computer is configured through its system setup program to boot first from A: you will see an error message. After the error message appears, remove the diskette and reboot, ensuring that the computer now boots from the hard drive.

**Step 4.**   Enter the system setup program (a.k.a. CMOS settings program) and change the bootup sequence so that the hard drive is first. Then reboot the computer with the formatted diskette in drive A. Describe the results below:

_____

_____

**Step 5.**   Restart the computer again, enter the system setup program, and return to the bootup sequence that is preferred for your lab computer. This may be something like A:, C:, or CDROM. If you are in a classroom lab, please ask the instructor what is preferred. Be sure to save the changes and test the results using what you have learned in the previous steps of this lab. The lab is complete when you can confirm that the boot order works as you intend it to work.

# LAB ANALYSIS TEST

1. You have been asked to recommend a computer system for a client who requests a processor with a clock speed over 800 MHz. Which processors will you consider?

2. You are preparing a computer system for a client. They have requested 512 MB of memory. You have examined the motherboard, and know that it has only two memory slots. You have read the user manual for the computer motherboard and found a section "Dual In-line Memory Module (DIMM) Requirements." Following are the requirements:

   - 168-pin 3.3v DIMMs with gold-plated contacts
   - 100 MHz 4-clock unbuffered SDRAM DIMMs
   - Non-ECC (64-bit) memory
   - A minimum of 32 MB (required); a maximum of 512 MB.
   - Module sizes: 16 MB, 32 MB, 64 MB, 128 MB, 256 MB, and 512 MB

   a. Describe your options for choosing RAM for this computer, considering such issues as less expensive tin connectors, slower speeds, and recommended minimums.

   b. Assuming that the processor will be a Pentium III, what are your options for memory module size and number of modules?

3. Maximum Title Company has hired you to define the specifications for 100 new computers they wish to purchase. Mistakes with their last large desktop purchase three years ago left them with computers that could not be upgraded, and that did not have built-in support for USB. What will you be sure to include on the specifications to avoid those problems?

4. Barney's Balloon Factory has a USB printer connected to the USB port of a computer running Windows 2000 Professional. Following the instructions, they connected the printer while Windows was running. However, Windows 2000 Professional is not recognizing the USB port or the printer. What will you check when arriving at their site?

# KEY TERM QUIZ

Use the following vocabulary terms to complete the sentences below. Not all of the terms will be used.

> ATX
>
> backside bus
>
> CMOS
>
> DRAM
>
> L1 cache
>
> L2 cache
>
> memory bus
>
> RAM
>
> SRAM
>
> AT

1. A Pentium III has 32KB of _____.

2. _____, the most common form of RAM, holds data only for a short period of time and must be refreshed periodically.

3. Within a computer the _____ is a data path of parallel wires connecting the memory controller and the memory sockets.

4. The _____ motherboard, released by Intel in 1996 is the most common motherboard form.

5. We can control the configuration for many motherboard components, including I/O ports, bootup sequence, plug-and-play, etc., through a special program based in the system's ROM BIOS. The settings themselves are stored in a small amount of battery-supported RAM, referred to as _____ RAM.

# LAB WRAP-UP

In these labs you performed extensive Internet research into the characteristics of the major components of a PC: processors, memory, motherboards, and busses. You created tables of characteristics for several manufacturers' processors. You studied memory characteristics, you learned to identify various motherboards, and you became more familiar with the contents of CMOS and with how to control it. You are well on the way to becoming a fully qualified A+ certified technician!

# LAB SOLUTIONS FOR CHAPTER 5

## Lab Solution 5.01

**Step 1.** Observations will vary, depending on the hardware available to you.

**Step 2.** You will find information on AMD processors on pages 195 and 196 in the *A+ Certification Study Guide.* For more information, use your web browser to connect to the web site of CPU manufacturer AMD at www.amd.com, then click on the Project Information link. Click on the individual links for the various AMD products in order to gather information for the table below.

| AMD Processors | AMD K5 | AMD K6 | AMD Duron | AMD Athlon | Any new processor |
|---|---|---|---|---|---|
| Form factor | 296-pin PGA | 296-pin PGA | PGA | PGA??? | |
| Socket/Slot | Socket 7 | Socket 7 | Socket A | Slot A | |
| Voltage | 3.62vDC | 3.3vDC | | | |
| Speeds | 75, 90, 100, 116 MHz | 166 – 266 MHz | 700 – 800MHz | 850 MHz –1.2GHz | |
| L1 cache (KB) | 8K | 256K – 1MB | 128K | 128K | |
| L2 cache (KB) | On motherboard | On motherboard | 64K | 256K | |
| Notes | | Competes with Pentium II | Competes with Pentium III *Low-powered derivative of the Athlon* | Competes with Pentium III | |

**Step 3.**

| VIA/Cyrix Processors | Cyrix MI | Cyrix MII | VIA C3 | 1st New Processor | 2nd New Processor |
|---|---|---|---|---|---|
| Form Factor | 296-pin PGA | 296-pin PGA | PGA | | |
| Socket/Slot | | | Socket 370 (PGA370) | | |
| Voltage | 3.3vDC | 3.3vDC | | | |
| Speeds | 100 – 150 MHz | 433 MHz | 800 MHz | | |
| L1 cache (KB) | 16KB | 256KB – 1MB | 128KB | | |
| L2 cache (KB) | N/A | N/A | 64KB Front Side Bus, and 3DNow | | |
| Notes | | | | | |

**Step 4.**    Answers will depend on what new processors have been released by Intel. As of this writing, we found the following:

| New Intel Processors | Pentium 4 | Xeon | Itanium |
|---|---|---|---|
| Form Factor | 423-pin and 478-pin PGA | 330 pin Single Edge Contact Cartridge | |
| Socket/Slot | Socket (Same as above) | SECC Slot | SECC Slot |
| Voltage | 1.7v – 1.75v maximum | 2.8v | |
| Speeds | 1.3 – 2 GHz | 1.4 – 2 GHz | |
| L1 cache (KB) | 12KB instruction, 8KB data | 16KB instruction 16KB data | |
| L2 cache (KB) | 256KB | 256KB – 2.0GB | |
| Notes | Many new features including: Hyper Pipelined Advanced Dynamic Execution 144 new Internet Streaming SIMD extensions (SSE2) | Dual bus architecture | L3 Cache 2 – 4MB |

## Lab Solution 5.02

**Step 1.** Answers will vary, but should substantially agree with the following:

a. CPU (or processor)

b. False. A memory bank is a group of sockets or modules that make up *one* logical unit.

c. Look for memory configuration rules for a specific system in the owner's manual, at the web site for the manufacturer, or use a memory configurator like the one described at the Kingston web site.

**Step 2.** Answers will vary, but should substantially agree with the following:

a. The memory controller controls the flow of information between the CPU and memory.

b. For memory to run at a speed that does not match the system clock of a PC, a multiplication or division factor for synchronization is required.

c. Cache memory is physically close to a CPU. Level 1 cache is the closest since it is physically on the processor.

## Step 3.

a. Memory module capacity is measured in megabytes (MB), while memory chip capacity is measured in megabits (Mb).

b. A transaction between the CPU and memory is a bus cycle.

c. False. While the data path of a RIMM module is only 16 bits, it can transfer four 16-bit packets at a time to a 64-bit CPU.

## Step 4.

a. False. SDRAM memory module speed is measured in MHz.

b. An example of a 144-pin SO DIMM.

c. An example of 72-pin SIMMs.

d. An example of a 168-pin DIMM.

e. False. It is the opposite. When installing a 72-pin SIMM you would install the module at a slight angle to the memory socket in the motherboard, then gently click it into a vertical position, .while you would install a 168-pin DMM straight into the memory socket and retain its position by snapping the clips at either end into place

**Step 5.**

a. PC100 is SDRAM, which meets a certain specification in order to work reliably at 100 MHz.

b. The frontside bus is the data pathway between the processor and the main memory.

c. The backside bus is the data pathway between the processor and the L2 cache.

**Step 6.** Answers will vary based on the amount of RAM installed in your computer.

## Lab Solution 5.03

**Step 1.** Features of the major motherboard form factors (answers):

| Motherboard | AT | Baby AT | ATX |
|---|---|---|---|
| Dimensions | Approx. 12 x 13 inches | 8.5 x 13 inches | 8.5 x 13 inches |
| Ports integrated on motherboard | No | No | Yes |
| Processor location | Near end of expansion slots | Near end of expansion slots | Motherboard is rotated 90 degrees, and processor is located out of the way of the expansion slots. |
| Keyboard connector | DIN-5 | DIN-5 | Mini-DIN-5 |
| Power connectors | P8 and P9 | P8 and P9 | 20-pin |
| Power | ±5vDC and ±12DC | ±5vDC and ±12DC | ±3vDC, ±5vDC, ±12vDC |

**Step 2.**

a. Problems with the Baby AT form include limited compatibility, limited I/O ports, lack of upgradability, and users having to remove all installed cards before upgrading the processor. This last is because an AT motherboard positions the processor socket in front of the expansion slots, so if you install a long expansion board, it must be removed to access the processor.

b. ATX boards show improvements in four major areas: enhanced ease of use, better support for current and future I/O, better support for current and future processor technology, and reduction in total system cost.

c. The Micro ATX form factor is mentioned in the article. It is small, like the Baby AT, but has the benefits of ATX, except that it has fewer PCI slots than ATX.

**Step 3.** Answers will vary. In our test lab we found some old 486-based and Pentium-based computers with the AT or Baby AT form factor, while our newer Pentium II and III computers had either the ATX or Micro ATX form factors.

**Step 4.** No response is required for this step.

**Step 5.**

a. 266Mbps for AGP vs. 133Mbps for PCI

b. 533Mbps and 1.07Gbps

c. Requirements for AGP include:

1. The chipset must support AGP

2. The motherboard must be equipped with an AGP bus slot or have an integrated AGP graphics system.

3. The operating system must be the OSR 2.1 version of Windows 95, Windows 98, or Windows NT4.0, Windows 2000, or Windows XP.

## Lab Solution 5.04

**Step 1.** Answers will vary, based on your knowledge.

**Step 2.** Answers will vary, based on the results of your research.

**Step 3.** No response is required for this step.

**Step 4.** Drive A: should be ignored during the bootup process, and the operating system should boot up normally.

**Step 5.** No response is required for this step.

# ANSWERS TO LAB ANALYSIS TEST

1. AMD Athlon, VIA C3, Intel Pentium III and 4, Intel Xeon, and Intel Itanium.

2. You will use memory that complies with all the specifications.

   a. Tin connectors are not an option because the manual specifies gold connectors. This means that the contacts in the bus are also gold. Mixing gold with tin can cause damage to the connectors because because of the reaction that occurs when two dissimilar metals come in contact with each other.

      You will also be sure that the DIMMs are 100 MHz because this is what is required to work with the motherboard.

      Be sure to exceed the recommended minimums since sometimes the embedded video adapter must also use some of the system RAM. In that case, you do not include the amount of memory used by the video adapter in calculating the RAM that the operating system will actually be able to use.

   b. Your options for module size and number is to install two 256MB modules or a single 512MB module. Since the motherboard can support only a maximum of 512MB, there is no reason to choose the single module solution for the sake of being able to upgrade to more memory. Therefore, choose the combination that meets the requirements at the least cost.

3. You should be sure to require the ATX motherboard form factor, which can be upgraded and which includes USB support.

4. In this situation your first suspicion should be that USB is disabled in the BIOS setup. Therefore, restart the computer and run the system setup program to investigate this.

## ANSWERS TO KEY TERM QUIZ

1. L1 cache

2. DRAM

3. memory bus

4. ATX

5. CMOS

# A+

EXERCISES • QUESTIONS • ANSWERS

# 6

# Printers

# D

o you feel prepared to work with most all computer hardware problems? What about one of the most common peripherals? This chapter focuses on printers: understanding the technology, knowing how to set them up and interface them with your computers, performing routine maintenance, and troubleshooting.

## LAB EXERCISE 6.01

# Researching Basic Printer Concepts, Operations, and Components

**1.5 Hours**

Millie's Marble Marvels has requested that you set up and connect two printers in their business office. A Canon S630 printer must be set up and connected to a computer in their accounting office. An HP LaserJet 5000 printer must be set up and connected to a computer in Customer Service. There is a problem, however. When these printers arrived about a month ago, someone unpacked them and discarded the packing material, including all the documentation and software disks. They also do not have interface cables, which is not unusual. Printer cables are not normally included with a new printer. The computers these printers will be attached to are running Windows 2000.

Before you go on this call you are going to go to the Internet and find manuals (there may be more than one) and drivers for each of these printers. Once you are familiar with the printers, you can physically set up each printer and install the correct driver in the operating system. You will also need to determine the correct interface cables to take with you on the call.

## Learning Objectives

In this lab, you will use the Internet to find the missing documentation. In the process you will learn:

- The basics of inkjet technology
- The basics of laser printing technology
- How to find documentation
- Care of printer cartridges

## Lab Materials and Setup

The materials you need for this lab are:

- A desktop computer with Windows 95 or later version installed
- Online access to the Internet
- An inkjet, bubble jet, or laser printer cartridge in its original package

*To best prepare for this lab, read the entire section "Certification Objective 6.01" in the* **A+ Certification Study Guide** *and complete Exercise 6-1.*

## Getting Down to Business

All major printer manufacturers maintain informative web sites to promote, sell, and support their products. You can learn a lot by visiting these sites—not only what the latest products are, but important technical information, such as changes to the drivers that shipped with a product, and whether there is an upgrade or fix to a problem with a product. In addition, if the documentation has been misplaced, you can often find the entire documentation online. In the following steps you will explore the Canon web site, first looking for information on bubble jet technology. Then you will search for that lost documentation, read it, and print it out so that you have it as a reference before you go to the customer site.

**Step 1.**    Point your web browser to the web site of printer manufacturer Canon at www.canon.com. From the home page select English to get to the English home page. (If you delay, it will eventually switch there automatically.) Then click on the "Canon Technology" link. On the Canon Technology page select "A Look at the Basics." (This animation requires Macromedia Flash Player. If you do not have it you can get it by clicking on the Macromedia download link on the same page.) After reading "A Look at the Basics," select "How Canon Bubble Jet Printers Work." When the tutorial is complete, click the link titled "Return to top of 'Canon Technology'."

**Step 2.**    From the Canon Technology page select "Bubble Jet Technology" and read the information on this page and in related links. At this time those links include: "MicroFine Droplet Technology," "Improved Color Gradation Level," "Portable Bubble Jet Printers," and "Long-Line Bubble Jet Print Head." When you have read all the information at each link, click on the button labeled "Home." At the Canon home page, click on "Products." On the Products page, under Product

Information in the Select Region list box, click on the down arrow and select "America." On the Canon Product Line page click on the link labeled "Corporate Office Products." From here, search for the technical information requested below, and use this information to answer the questions.

a. Find technical information for a Canon S630 printer, including driver downloads and setup information. Did you find information that would be useful to you if you needed to set up this printer and install the driver? Was a Windows 2000 driver available for download? Was a printer manual available for download?

_____

_____

b. From the information you gathered on this printer, determine the cabling required to connect it to the computer and what ink cartridges are required.

_____

_____

**Step 3.** Now do similar research for the HP LaserJet 5000 printer. Point your web browser to the web site of printer manufacturer Hewlett Packard at www.hp.com. From the home page, search the links to find the technical information for the HP LaserJet 5000 printer, including driver downloads and setup information. Use this information to answer these questions.

a. Did you find information that would be useful to you if you needed to set up this printer and install the driver?

_____

_____

b. Was a Windows 2000 driver for this printer available for download?

_____

_____

c. Was a printer manual available for download?

_____

_____

d. Was there any other documentation of interest?

_____

_____

e. What are the options for connecting this printer to the computer at Millie's Marble Marvels? What cabling is required?

_____

_____

f. What toner cartridge does this printer use?

_____

_____

**Step 4.**    It is important to understand how a device works in order to install, support, and troubleshoot it. In this step you will find an Internet resource for learning about laser printing technology. Then you will make up a mnemonic to help you remember the laser printing process. Go to the How Stuff Works site at www.howstuffworks.com and search on "laser printer." The article "How Laser Printers Work" has several sections including The Basic Process, The Controller, The Laser, Toner, Advantages of a Laser, and Lots More Information. Read at least two of these sections and then write the down the six steps in the printing process.

a. _____

b. _____

c. _____

d. _____

e. _____

f. _____

**Step 5.**    Create a mnemonic to help you remember the steps of the laser printing process:

_____

**Step 6.** In general, it is important to make sure that the conditions under which you store and handle printer cartridges do not damage them. Although some manufacturers do not include instructions on the packaging, others do, and it is worthwhile to pay attention to those instructions. The A+ test may have questions about storage and handling of printer media and cartridges.

Examine the package for the printer cartridge you have and look for storage and handling instructions. If you find such instructions, list the main points below.

_____

_____

In this lab you did the necessary research for two printers with missing documentation and you found manuals and drivers at the manufacturers' web sites. This is a scenario you may often really encounter on the job. Even when you have complete documentation, you will want to check out the manufacturer's web site for driver updates and, occasionally, for corrections to the manuals.

You also worked to better understand the laser printing process and the care and handling of print cartridges.

Be sure to add these new web sites to your list of web site resources.

## LAB EXERCISE 6.02

# Setting up a New Printer

**I Hour**

At Millie's Marble Marvels you must prepare the printers for use, including ensuring that all packing material is removed from the inside of each printer, connecting the printers to the computers, and installing appropriate printer drivers.

## Learning Objectives

In this lab you will use the documentation for a lab printer to determine the correct procedures for setting up a new printer. The lab printer does not have to be identical to those mentioned in the previous lab—just a printer for which you have documentation so you can go through the procedures of setting it up as if you have just unpacked it and are installing it for a client. After you've completed this lab, you will be able to:

- Prepare a printer for installation
- Ensure that all necessary items are available
- Install and test a printer

## Lab Materials and Setup

The materials you need for this lab are:

- A desktop computer with Windows 95 or later version installed
- Online access to the Internet
- Acrobat Reader (free download at www.adobe.com/products/acrobat/readstep.html)
- A printer (of any type)
- The printer documentation, including the "getting started" information

**cross Reference**

*To best prepare for this lab, reread the section entitled "Types of Printer Connections and Configurations in Certification Objective 6.01" in the* **A+ Certification Study Guide.**

## Getting Down to Business

When setting up a new printer you first unpack the printer, locate the documentation, and read it, paying special attention to the "getting started" information. Then you proceed with the following steps (in order), guided by the instructions in the documentation:

- Place the printer on an appropriate surface near the computer (see documentation).
- Ensure that all packing material is removed from the printer.
- Connect the correct interface cable to the printer and computer, then connect the printer power cord (see documentation to determine whether the computer should be powered on or off when plugging in the printer data cable).

- Load paper.
- Insert a toner cartridge (laser printer) or print cartridges (Bubble Jet or inkjet printers).
- Power the printer on. (Some printers require power on before ink cartridges can be installed.)
- Run a printer self test printout (if the printer has this capability).
- Install a printer driver.
- Test the printer installation.

In this lab, the actual actions you take will depend on the printer you have chosen to use. If you do not have the documentation for the printer you will use in this lab, please go to the manufacturer's web site and retrieve the documentation as you did in the previous lab. Using that documentation, go through the steps above and record the actions you take in the space provided below:

**Step 1.**   Place the printer on an appropriate surface near the computer (see documentation).

_____

_____

**Step 2.**   Ensure that all packing material is removed from the printer.

_____

_____

**Step 3.**   Connect the correct interface cable to the printer and computer, then connect the printer power cord.

_____

_____

**Step 4.**   Load paper.

_____

_____

**Step 5.** Insert a toner cartridge (laser printer).

_____

_____

**Step 6.** Power the printer on, watching for signs of problems. If problems occur, correct them.

_____

_____

**Step 7.** Insert print cartridges (inkjet printer).

_____

_____

**Step 8.** Run a printer self-test, producing a test printout.

_____

_____

**Step 9.** Install a printer driver.

_____

_____

**Step 10.** Test the printer installation.

_____

_____

In this lab you went through the actual steps for setting up and testing a new printer. You also recorded the details of the steps you took to accomplish this.

*Our printer manual specified an IEEE 1284-compliant parallel cable. If you, like us, have old printer cables around, and are not sure if they are 1284-compliant, you may be able to search the cable manufacturer's web site to find the answer. We had four printer cables in our spare parts room. Only one of these cables was clearly marked as IEEE 1284-compliant. A second cable from the same cable manufacturer (Belkin) was not marked, but a search of the Belkin site (www.belkin.com) for the model number of the connector confirmed that this cable also was IEEE 1284-compliant. A search on the model numbers of two other Belkin cables showed that they were not compliant. You may not have such luck with a different manufacturer, or with homemade cables!*

## LAB EXERCISE 6.03

# Working with Impact Printers

**40 Minutes**

Although you may have thought that impact printers went out of vogue with handheld calculators, they are still very much in use today, and you will encounter them in your career. Their principal use is for printing multi-part carbonless forms where several copies must be printed at once. Impact printers include dot matrix printers and daisy wheel printers. (Actually, daisy wheel printers have pretty much disappeared from the landscape. High-end impact printers, such as chain printers and band printers, were mostly limited to large data centers and have been largely replaced by high-speed laser printers, so you will seldom encounter them.) Although in today's business environment laser, inkjet or bubble jet non-impact printers are what you will mostly be working with, you will still have to deal with impact printers. In fact, just this morning, Nerd Matrix received a call from a customer who needs to replace a failing dot matrix printer they were using to print multi-part forms. Before going on this call you decide to do some research on the terminology that revolves around dot matrix printers.

## Learning Objectives

After you've completed this lab you will be able to:

- Explain how impact printers work
- Explain the strengths and weaknesses of impact printers

## Lab Materials and Setup

To complete this lab you will need the following:

- One desktop computer with Windows 95 or later version installed
- Online access to the Internet

## Getting Down to Business

In this lab you will research terminology and capabilities of dot matrix printers on the Web before shopping for a replacement printer for your client.

**Step 1.**   Use your Internet browser to go to the Webopedia site at www.webopedia.com or the TechWeb Encyclopedia at www.techweb.com/encyclopedia. (Use the Define IT Term box instead of the Search box on the TechWeb site.) Find definitions for the following terms, and write them in the space provided:

a.  dot matrix printer _____

_____

b.  form feed _____

_____

c.  friction feed _____

_____

d.  tractor feed _____

_____

**Step 2:**   Use your Internet browser to connect to www.buyerzone.com. Search on "Impact Printers" and when the results are displayed, click on "Buyers Guide." Read all sections of the Buyers Guide and then answer the following questions.

a.  Can a dot matrix printer print as fast as a laser printer? If so, how?

_____

_____

b. What kinds of forms are dot matrix printers commonly used for?

_____

_____

c. What is the first thing to consider when choosing a dot matrix printer?

_____

_____

d. What criterion indicates purchase of a high-speed printer as opposed to a low-speed printer?

_____

_____

e. What is the second consideration in choosing a printer, and why is it important?

_____

_____

f. Explain the difference between 9-pin and 24-pin printheads. Which one is more acceptable today?

_____

_____

g. Can dot matrix printers handle both tractor-feed and friction-feed paper?

_____

_____

h. What is the main drawback of dot matrix printers?

_____

_____

In this lab you explored the area of impact printers and evaluated the strengths and weaknesses of impact printers. Be sure to add any new web sites that you found useful to your list of web site resources.

**LAB EXERCISE 6.04**

# Practicing Care and Service Techniques

**45 Minutes**

Some technicians do not particularly enjoy doing the routine care and service of peripheral components. But such service, if done consistently and with care, can have great rewards in terms of increased life for the components, a higher quality of output from printers, and much happier (and therefore more loyal) customers and bosses.

## Learning Objectives

After you've completed this lab you will be able to:

- Clean a printer
- Clear a paper jam

## Lab Materials and Setup

The materials you need for this lab will vary, depending on the model of printer you are using. We feel the following list should be adequate for most printers:

- One desktop computer with Windows 95 or later version installe
- Online access to the Internet.
- A soft brush for use inside printers
- Two or three lint-free cloths
- Cotton swabs
- A large, open workspace with an anti-static mat (if possible)
- A Phillips, flat blade, or Torx screwdriver or appropriate nut driver
- One or more containers in which to place and organize screws and other small parts
- The user manual for the printer

## Getting Down to Business

In this lab you will do preventive maintenance on your lab printer. This will include cleaning ink/toner and paper residue from the inside of the printer, as well as performing any maintenance suggested in the printer's documentation.

**lab Warning**

*Be sure to read the printer documentation before proceeding. Do not perform any steps that are contrary to the manufacturer's instructions.*

**Step 1.** Power off the printer and disconnect it from the computer. Remove the power cord, and observe safe ESD procedures. Open the printer, following the manufacturer's instructions. Remove the case cover by following the manufacturer's instructions in the printer user manual or by following your instructor's directions. Be very careful not to disturb cables inside the printer. Although most printers can be opened for routine maintenance without using tools, if you must remove screws or other attachment hardware, place them in a container so that they don't disappear.

**Step 2.** Stop now and examine the inside of the printer, comparing it to the illustrations in the printer documentation. Locate all components.

**Step 3.** Using a soft brush or cloth, remove all ink/toner and paper residue from the inside of the printer. Dispose of the residue without dispersing it into the air.

**lab Warning**

*Never use a vacuum around fine powder particles, such as laser printer toner. These particles are too fine for most vacuum filters, and can be dispersed into the air when vacuumed. Once airborne, they can get into your lungs. Even though they are non-toxic, super fine particles can do lung damage. Some shops will not allow vacuums to be used near laser printers. You also must take care not to blow such particles into the air when using compressed air around printers.*

**Step 4.** Proceed with any additional maintenance described in your printer manual. For instance, on a HP DeskJet 722C, we found a Services tab in the Properties dialog box for this printer. This tab has one section labeled Maintain My Printer, which has buttons for two tasks: *Align the Print Cartridges* and *Clean the Print Cartridges*. The Align Print Cartridges button causes the printer to align the color and black print cartridges in order to fine-tune the placement of black and color inks. (If they are out of alignment your printout may resemble an old 3D comic book, viewed without the special glasses.) This task is recommended every time a print cartridge is replaced or reinstalled, or when troubleshooting instructions recommend doing it. We chose to do this as a maintenance task. The dialog box shown in Figure 6-1 appeared during the first part of the alignment process. When we evaluated the page that printed with the alignment patterns, we found that the best alignment patterns were A7, B7, and C7. We selected them on this dialog box and clicked Continue.

Next, the dialog box shown in Figure 6-2 appeared. We examined the patterns on the printed page and found them to be in alignment, so we clicked on the Done button.

The Clean Print Cartridges task is recommended if the document has blank horizontal lines in it. Clicking the Clean The Print Cartridges button resulted in the dialog box shown in Figure 6-3. We did not perform this task, because there was no indication that this was required or needed.

In this lab you did routine maintenance to your lab printer. At a minimum, you performed the cleaning described in the lab. Then you did any routine maintenance recommended in the printer's documentation.

**FIGURE 6-1**

First dialog box
of Align Print
Cartridges utility

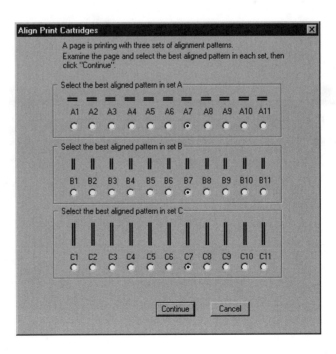

**FIGURE 6-2**

Second dialog box of Align Print Cartridges utility

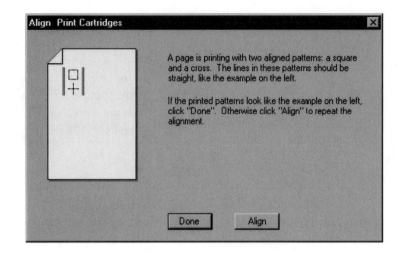

**Align Print Cartridges**

A page is printing with two aligned patterns: a square and a cross. The lines in these patterns should be straight, like the example on the left.

If the printed patterns look like the example on the left, click "Done". Otherwise click "Align" to repeat the alignment.

Done    Align

**FIGURE 6-3**

Clean Print Cartridges dialog box

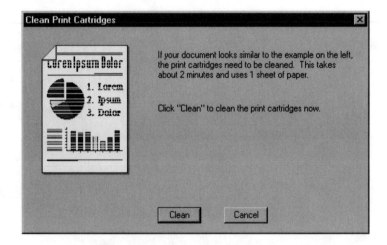

**Clean Print Cartridges**

If your document looks similar to the example on the left, the print cartridges need to be cleaned. This takes about 2 minutes and uses 1 sheet of paper.

Click "Clean" to clean the print cartridges now.

Clean    Cancel

**LAB EXERCISE 6.05**

I Hour

# Troubleshooting Common Printer Problems

When faced with printer problems, you should use troubleshooting procedures similar to those discussed in Chapter 3 with some modification for printers.

1. Observe and note the error messages, investigate the printer history, and think of questions you would ask the customer in order to learn what action he took prior to the time of the failure. Because customers are often not skilled in observing and reporting exactly what is happening in their computer system, you may need to ask the questions several times in order to find out what *really* happened.

2. Consider how you would reproduce the problem.

3. Observe the symptoms and determine whether the problem is hardware- or software-related (driver).

4. Most problems do not require high-tech solutions. Therefore, apply the "simple" rule. Ask yourself, "What is the simplest thing that could cause this problem." Then check that the printer has power, is properly connected, and is "on-line"—the simple things that can be overlooked. An experienced technician develops an internal checklist of the simple things that can cause problems.

5. Make sure the correct device driver is loaded and that there are no resource conflicts (in the case of a printer, this would apply to the computer interface—the port).

6. If possible and practical, connect the printer to another computer. Or test an identical printer on this computer.

7. Proceed with checking all printer components, working your way further into the printer.

8. Test the most central components of the printer by carefully observing the printer's power-up test for any error codes or messages displayed on the printer's display panel, or as an error message on the computer.

## Learning Objectives

Once you've completed this lab, you will be able to troubleshoot common printer problems in the following areas:

- Printer communications
- Paper feed and output
- Paper jams (including effects of humidity, worn feeders, wrong type of paper, etc.)
- Print quality
- Print process

## Lab Materials and Setup

The materials you'll need for this lab are:

- A desktop computer with Windows 95 or later version installed
- Online access to the Internet
- The documentation for the printer

**cross Reference**

*To best prepare for this lab, read the entire section titled "Certification Objective 6.02" in the A+ Certification Study Guide.*

## Getting Down to Business

A high percentage of service and help desk calls are concerned with printing problems. Common printing problems can usually be quickly resolved, and even more obscure ones can be resolved with careful observation and, sometimes, a little intuition. Below are several scenarios in which you will be asked to describe how you would use what you have learned about troubleshooting printers to resolve the problem. In some scenarios, you will need to consult the printer's documentaiton to research the action you would take for the specific lab printer you are using.

lab
**Hint**

*When resolving a printer problem—especially remotely—you may need to see the setting choices in a printer driver, even though you don't have that particular type of printer physically available to your computer. To do this, you can typically install a printer driver within Windows by selecting Manual Install, and then view the printer properties to see the settings. Gee, is that a virtual printer?*

**Scenario 1**    *It never worked!* Rollie, of North-South Realtor purchased a high quality color laser printer for printing personalized color booklets containing the realtors' analysis and valuation of the client's property. North-South does not have a computer support person on staff, and Rollie attempted to install it on his own.

They have called you in to resolve a problem, telling you that they followed the instructions in the documentation for setting up the printer and connecting it to the computer. When the printer is powered up, they can run a self-test using the control panel of the printer. They also seem to have installed the correct driver for the printer. However, the computer doesn't recognize the printer. It is as if the computer were not connected to the printer at all—but they have, indeed, connected a parallel cable. Describe how you would proceed to tackle this problem, and suggest some possible solutions.

<hr>
<hr>

**Scenario 2**    *Double is not always twice as good.* Evelyn of EveryState Insurance Company has called you to solve a printer problem. One of their inkjet printers in the Patient Advocate's office is feeding double pages. This printer has also lately had frequent paper jams. Describe how you would proceed, and suggest some possible solutions.

<hr>

**Scenario 3**    *Poor print quality.* Henry at Helpful HomeHealth Care has reported that one of their printers, an HP DeskJet 722C printer, produces horizontal blank lines. After asking a few questions you discover that this has been a problem only

since they changed the print cartridges. Describe how you would proceed, and suggest some possible solutions.

_____

_____

**Scenario 4** *A blank page is not a good thing.* Manny's Motorcar Repair reports that their venerable HP LaserJet III is producing nothing but blank pages, even when they attempt to do a self-test printout from the control panel of the printer. Describe how you would proceed, and suggest some possible solutions.

_____

_____

lab
**ⓗint**

*Always expect the unexpected. Once when troubleshooting a problem with a LaserJet that yielded only blank pages, we found a staple dangling on the transfer corona wire. Removing the staple (with the printer powered off) solved the problem.*

**Scenario 5** *He was losing his memory!* Harry from the Hazelnut Hut called to say that their HP LaserJet 4 printer was displaying an "out of memory" error while printing a large graphic of a Hazelnut Hut Gift basket. What temporary solution can you give him over the phone, and what should be the long-term solution?

_____

_____

**Scenario 6** *What do we do when the lights come on?* Bioconundrum Technologies had a power outage that affected only their networked laser printers. The rest of the network stayed up, and users were busy sending print jobs to these printers, but found that their jobs didn't print after the printers were back online. What steps might need to be taken after these networked laser printers come back on line?

_____

_____

# LAB ANALYSIS TEST

1. The store manager at Terry's Tot Toys needs a printer in purchasing where they must print out carbon duplicate forms. He was hoping to purchase a laser printer and have it do double duty for other purposes. What is wrong with his strategy?

   _____

   _____

2. Nasturtium Nurseries and Landscaping has a problem with a laser printer that is printing a faint image of the last printout along with the current page. What part of the print process will you troubleshoot?

   _____

   _____

3. You are delivering a new printer to a client. It is still in the box. What do you need to take in addition to the printer?

   _____

   _____

4. What is the most important regular maintenance task for printers? Why?

   _____

   _____

5. You have received calls from two clients with laser printers. Both are having similar problems with the quality of the printouts. At Dion's Doggie Grooming Parlor they have random speckles on the page, but at Fay's Furnace Repair the printouts show speckles repeated in a pattern. Could they have an identical problem? Explain your answer.

   _____

   _____

# KEY TERM QUIZ

Use the following vocabulary terms to complete the sentences below. Not all of the terms will be used.

toner

transfer corona

registration roller

print media

primary corona wire

photosensitive drum

alignment

impact printer

fusing

cleaning blade

1. In the first part of a laser printer cleaning phase a _____ removes excess toner from the drum.

2. A bubble jet or inkjet printer uses ink, but a laser printer uses dry _____.

3. A general term used in printer documentation for the surface on which you print (other than calling it paper, which is too limiting), is _____.

4. Because an inkjet printer uses multiple print heads, it may produce printouts in which the different colors do not line up properly. When this happens, you need to correct the _____ of the heads.

5. If a printout from a laser printer smudges, the _____ phase of the print process is failing due to mechanical failure of the printer, or paper that is too thick or rough textured.

# LAB WRAP-UP

In these labs you researched printer information on different models of printers. Then you went through the steps to set up a new printer, and performed routine maintenance on a lab printer. Finally, you identified trouble-shooting solutions for common printer problems.

# LAB SOLUTIONS FOR CHAPTER 6

## Lab Solution 6.01

**Step 1.** The instructions for Step 1 are complete, and no response is required.

**Step 2.** Answers may vary slightly. You may have gone through the links in a different order, but you should have been successful in finding the information.

a. From the Corporate Office Products page, selecting the "Printers" link displays a page that includes (after scrolling down) a "Color BubbleJet Printers" link. This link brings up a page with many products, including the S630. Clicking on the S630 brings up its product page, which describes the features and specifications of the printer. Clicking on the "Technical Support" link brings up a page with links for downloading drivers and other setup information, as well as problem solving and maintenance—all useful information for setting up the printer and installing the driver. The Windows 2000 driver is available for download, as is the User Guide for this printer.

b. The printer specification for the S630 describes two interfaces: USB and IEEE 1284 ECP parallel port. Therefore, it can be connected to either a USB or parallel port on the computer. The ink cartridges for this printer are described as ink tanks, and are the following Canon models: BCI-3eBK, BCI-3eC, BCI-3eM, and BCI-3eY.

**Step 3.** Answers may vary slightly. You may have gone through the links in a different order, but you should have been successful in finding the information. As this is written, navigation to this information includes the following steps: from the HP home page, click "Support," then under the printing and digital imaging category, click "Printers." On the HP Printers page, click "HP LaserJet Printers," on the next page click "HP LaserJet 5000 Series," and on the following page click "HP LaserJet 5000." The web site may have changed enough so that these were not the exact actions you performed.

a. There is a great deal of useful information under the technical support topic. This includes frequently asked questions and sections on problem solving, setup and install, how to use and maintain, update software and drivers, and manuals.

b.  Windows 2000 drivers for this printer are available for download. The PCL driver uses font technology developed by HP. The PostScript driver uses font technology developed by Adobe. Both of these font technologies are built into the LaserJet 5000. Both drivers should be downloaded and installed so that either font technology can be used. The "Point and Print Bundle" includes drivers for multiple operating systems, and would be a useful download for installing the printer on a network. The drivers can also be downloaded individually.

c.  A User's Guide, a Quick Reference Guide, and a Getting Started Guide are available for download.

d.  Of special interest is a Print Media Guide, which describes paper types, forms, letterhead, labels, envelopes, and transparencies that can be used with HP LaserJet printers. In addition to describing how to select the correct print media, this guide also describes recommended storage conditions for the print media. This is a general reference, and you should refer to the user manual for a particular model of LaserJet printer to make the correct choices.

e.  This printer can be connected to the computer by either serial or parallel (IEEE-1284) interface. Using serial interface for printers went out of vogue about 15 years ago because it is significantly slower than parallel. Therefore, when given a choice between serial and parallel for a printer connection, always choose parallel.

f.  The toner cartridge for this printer is Model C4129J.

**Step 4.**   The order must be the same but, since the laser printing process is a cycle, the list can start at any point and be correct. The *A+ Certification Study Guide* list begins with charging (conditioning), but an article found through the How Stuff Works site begins with cleaning.

a.  Cleaning

b.  Conditioning

c.  Writing

d.  Developing

e.  Transferring

f.  Fusing

**Step 5.** A possible mnemonic for remembering the laser printing process is: <u>C</u>an <u>C</u>arnivorous <u>W</u>hales <u>D</u>ive <u>T</u>oo <u>F</u>ar?

**Step 6.** Answers may vary depending on the manufacturer. When examining an HP laser toner cartridge, the following care and handling instructions are printed on the box:

- Do not expose cartridges to direct sunlight
- Avoid high humidity and store at a temperature between -20°(-4°F) and 40°C (104°F)
- Use cartridges before the expiration date
- Copy quality may deteriorate if you use outdated cartridges
- Do not open the storage bag except when installing the cartridge

## Lab Solution 6.02

Answers will vary, based on the printer used. The following shows the actions taken to set up an HP DeskJet 970Cse printer. This printer comes with a Quick Start poster that guides you through the setup, beginning with unpacking the printer all the way through to installing the printer driver. Also packed with the printer are two User's Guides—one for using the printer with a PC running Windows (several versions), and another for using the printer with a Macintosh.

**Step 1.** Place the printer on an appropriate surface near the computer (see documentation). The Quick Start and setup documentation for the HP DeskJet 970Cse printer does not mention the placement of the printer or environmental requirements. (We have seen such information included with the HP LaserJet printers.) However, under Specifications you can find all the information you require including the dimensions, weight, operating environment, power consumption, and power requirements. If you are preparing to deliver a printer, this information will help you to inform the customer to provide an appropriate space for the printer.

**Step 2.** Ensure that all packing material is removed from the printer. Remember that there may be tape or other material inside the printer too. This information is not included in the documentation, but packing material is clearly marked and easy to remove.

**Step 3.**    Connect the correct interface cable to the printer and computer, and connect the printer power cord. The DeskJet 970Cse has both a parallel and USB interface. We are using the parallel interface, and we are also using an IEEE 1284-compliant parallel interface cable (not included with the printer). We also verify that the computer's parallel port is configured for ECP mode in the BIOS setup. (Recall the printer parallel port information in Chapter 5.) In addition, we connect the printer's power cable (included), and plug it into an outlet.

**Step 4.**    Load paper. This may seem like the easiest part, but you should be sure to verify that you are using paper that complies with the printer's requirements for media. This information can usually be found under Specifications in the documentation. Also, recall that in Lab 6-1, you explored HP's documentation concerning media for their LaserJet printers. We follow the instructions for loading the paper.

**Step 5.**    Insert a toner cartridge (laser printer). We did not do this step, because our printer is an inkjet printer, which must be powered on in order to install the ink cartridges (see Step 7).

**Step 6.**    Power the printer on and watch for signs of problems. If problems occur, correct them. We have no problems at this point. The symptoms of problems will vary by printer, and problem resolution should be done with the help of the printer documentation or information at the manufacturer's web site.

**Step 7.**    Insert print cartridges. The DeskJet 970Cse printer must be powered up before you can install the print cartridges. We follow the Quick Start instructions for installing the cartridges.

**Step 8.**    Run a printer self-test, producing a test printout. On some printers, you will have to initiate this test. On others, such as the DeskJet 970Cse, you do not have to initiate a self-test because the printer automatically prints a calibration page when the cover is closed after installing the new cartridges,.

**Step 9.**    Install a printer driver. The HP DeskJet 970Cse is PnP, as is the computer and operating system (Windows 2000). Another piece in the PnP puzzle for printers is using a PnP interface. USB and IEEE 1284 interfaces (which we use) are both PnP. The last piece required to make this completely automatic is that Windows 2000 has a HP DeskJet 970Cse printer driver. The printer is detected, and Windows loads the driver automatically.

**Step 10.**   Test the printer installation. First go to the printer's Properties dialog box and print a test page. A successful test page printout indicates that the driver and printer are working well. Then test it with an application, such as a word processor, by printing out a document containing a variety of formatting and graphics. It is a good idea to test it with all the installed applications that will use this printer.

## Lab Solution 6.03

### Step 1.

a.  A *dot matrix printer* produces characters or graphics by striking pins against an inked ribbon. The pins are arranged in a matrix. Since these printers work by "impacting" their pins against the ribbon, thus pressing the ink into the paper, they can be used for multi-part, carbonless forms.

 Dot matrix printers feed the paper around a roller or platen—old- fashioned typewriters. Depending on the capabilities of the printer, paper is fed through friction feed or tractor feed or both. Dot matrix printers speed is measured in characters per second (cps). The speed of print for page-feed printers, such as laser printers, inkjet, and bubble jet printers is measured in pages per minute (ppm).

b.  *form feed* is a function of a printer that will advance continuous paper to the top of the next page. With page feed printers, the form feed function will cause the paper to feed or eject the paper. Pressing a button labeled "Form Feed" or FF can usually access the form feed function. Some printers need to be taken "offline" before you can use the form feed function from the front panel. Offline means that the printer is not "listening" to the interface with the computer.

c.  *Friction feed* is a method of feeding paper through a printer by using plastic or rubber rollers to squeeze a sheet of paper and pull it through the printer.

d. *Tractor feed, or pin feed,* is a method of feeding paper through a printer using sprockets on either side of the printer that fit into holes in the side edges of the paper. The sprocket wheel revolves with the platen and pulls the paper through the printer. Tractor feed paper is also called continuous form paper. It comes in either perforated or non-perforated flavors. The perforated edges enable you to tear off the edges with the punched holes and to separate the carbonless sets into single sheets. Continuous form paper also comes in different widths and paper weights. Some business forms, including checks, come on continuous form paper with sprocket holes so that they can be printed on impact printers. The forms may be carbonless forms that require an impact printer.

## Step 2.

a. Yes and no. Although a dot matrix printer generally is not as fast in printing a single page as a laser printer is, it can print on multi-part carbonless paper so it can produce more pages per hour than comparably priced laser printers can.

b. Dot matrix printers are commonly used for printing invoices, purchase orders, shipping forms, labels, and other multi-part forms.

c. The first consideration is the number of pages you expect to print per day. If you expect to print only a few pages per day, an inexpensive, low-volume printer will work just fine.

d. A volume in excess of 50 pages per day indicates that you should select a high-volume dot matrix printer.

e. The second consideration is the number of parts or pages in the forms to be printed. It is important because printers designed to print a large number of parts are often more expensive to buy. There is no need to buy a printer capable of printing more parts than the customer needs, which can save on printhead wear.

f. 9-pin printheads print acceptable, but not high quality, characters on paper. 24-pin printheads can approach typewriter quality printing. However, for the kinds of printing commonly used on multi-part forms, 9-pin printheads perform satisfactorily, are much less expensive to buy, and much faster to use. If you print in draft mode on a 24-pin printer, there is very little difference between them.

g. Yes. Many printers are equipped with both form feed mechanisms. When using friction feed the tractor feed mechanism doesn't interfere with the paper feed.

h. Noise. Dot matrix printers can be quite noisy, and may require a special stand or enclosure to make them acceptable in an office environment.

## Lab Solution 6.04

**Step 1.**　No observations or answers are required. The actual steps you take will depend on the printer and printer documentation. We used an HP DeskJet 722C printer for this lab.

**Steps 2–4.**　No observations or answers are required. The actual steps you take will depend on the printer and printer documentation.

## Lab Solution 6.05
Answers will vary.

**Scenario 1.**　*It never worked!* In this scenario you should probably focus on the interface and cable. Start at the computer and, through BIOS setup, check that the printer port is not completely disabled. If it is not disabled, then a simple thing to do is to try another cable. While newer printers take advantage of the IEEE 1284 standard, not using one shouldn't prevent the computer from seeing the printer at all. Sometimes you simply have a bad cable, so use a new IEEE 1284 cable—no longer than 6 feet.

Beyond the cable, be sure that the printer itself is configured to use the parallel interface. If the printer has more than one interface, it may need to be configured (usually through its own control panel) to use that interface. Also check the computer to see if it has more than one parallel connector. If so, ensure that the printer is connected to the correct parallel port.

**lab**

**⓪int**　*You may even want to play around with cable length. We know of an instance in which an expensive new printer produced only garbled output (usually associated with a bad print driver). After many calls to the printer manufacturer, a shorter cable solved the problem.*

**Scenario 2.** *Double is not always twice as good.* These two problems could have a common cause in the print media itself. Check out the documentation for the printer to find out what the print media requirements are. Then ask the customer questions to determine whether he is using the correct print media *and* if he is storing it properly. Paper of the wrong weight or quality can cause feed and jam problems, as can paper with excess static, which can cause pages to stick together. Static can occur if the paper was improperly stored and allowed to dry out. Also, the opposite problem might exist. If the atmosphere is very humid and the paper has been sitting in a humid environment for a long time, it can become limp from containing too much moisture and can also cause paper jams. A good test of either of these situations is to replace the paper in the printer with fresh paper from an unopened ream.

Also, look inside the printer to see if either of the input areas shows any problems, such as missing or broken parts, or ink/toner and paper debris. Clean the printer and test it. If none of this works, you may need to replace the input friction rollers and/or the internal paper path feed rollers.

**Scenario 3.** *Poor print quality.* This is most likely caused by dirty print heads. The printer driver for this printer comes with a utility that will clean the print heads. This utility is accessed through the Services tab of the printer's Properties dialog box. Figure 6-4 shows the message that is displayed when you run this utility.

**FIGURE 6-4**

The Clean Print Cartridges utility

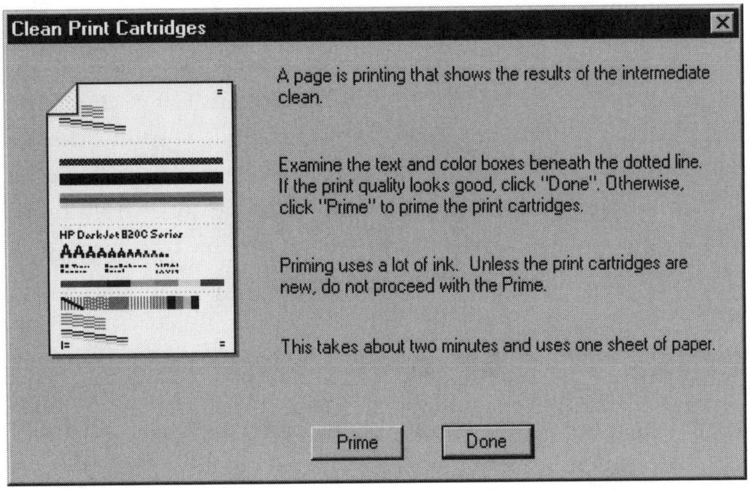

**Scenario 4.** *A blank page is not a good thing.* To troubleshoot this problem, consider the LaserJet print process. The simplest test is to replace the toner cartridge because it contains many of the components central to the print process. If this fixes the problem, you are done and you are a hero. If it does not fix the problem, check out the interior of the printer. A car repair shop is a dusty, dirty environment for computer equipment. If the transfer corona wire is too dirty it will not hold a charge or be able to transfer that charge to the paper. Then the paper will not attract toner, and will remain blank. A good cleaning of the interior, especially of the transfer corona wire may solve the problem. Finally, because it is such an old printer, some major component, such as the fusion assembly or the laser diodes themselves may have failed, so you will need to check out these components. You may want to advise the customer that a replacement of a major component would probably be more costly than purchasing a replacement printer.

**Scenario 5.** *He was losing his memory!* The short-term solution is to suggest that Harry reduce the resolution of the graphic he is printing out. He may actually have to reset the printer to be able to continue, then try reprinting the graphic. The long-term solution should be to add memory to the printer. This is something we never worried about for the old dot matrix printers. However, page printers, especially the laser printers, need to have enough memory to compose an entire page. Often you can add additional memory to the printer so that they can better handle the large, intricate print jobs.

**Scenario 6.** *What do we do when the lights come on?* When the printers lost power, it is likely that there were a number of print jobs queued to those printers from the network server that were unable to print, and became "confused" due to the power outage. To resolve the problem, it may be necessary to have the network administrator delete the print jobs in the queue from the server. Afterwards, the printers should be powered off and then back on again to clear their memory buffers. Users will have to resubmit their print jobs.

# ANSWERS TO LAB ANALYSIS TEST

1. A laser printer cannot print on multi-part carbonless forms. They will need to use an impact printer for this purpose, or print as many copies of each page as they need which takes additional time.

**2.** You would troubleshoot the cleaning phase of the printing process. This problem occurs only on laser printers and indicates that the erase lamps are not functioning properly.

**3.** You will need to take an interface cable. While a power cable is normally included, interface cables are not.

**4.** Cleaning of the printer is the most important maintenance task. This is because a build up of paper and ink or toner debris can affect the quality and the operation of the printer.

**5.** They do not have an identical problem. Random speckles are a symptom of problems caused by debris in the printer. Following the manufacturer's instructions for cleaning the printer should solve the problems. Speckles in a repeated pattern are a symptom of a problem with a drum in a laser printer. If the drum is within the toner cartridge of this printer, try swapping toner cartridges.

# ANSWERS TO KEY TERM QUIZ

**1.** cleaning blade

**2.** toner

**3.** print media

**4.** alignment

**5.** fusing

EXERCISES • QUESTIONS • ANSWERS

# 7

# Basic Networking

**Y**ou are now close to being ready to take your A+ Core Hardware Service Technician Examination. The only area left to explore before you take the exam is Basic Networking.

The following labs are designed to aid you in understanding basic networking concepts, including the common technologies of networks and how to install, configure, and troubleshoot network interface cards (NICs). As you work your way through these labs, you will reinforce the networking concepts you have learned in class so that you can identify network topologies, common network protocols, types of network media, and network access methods. Furthermore, you will examine the differences between full- and half-duplex network communications, and you will troubleshoot common network problems

## LAB EXERCISE 7.01

# Identifying Network Topologies

**I Hour**

Network topology is a basic networking concept that all network professionals must understand. You say you are not planning to be a network professional? Well, since networks connect most computers in business and government, this is also a concept that a hardware service technician must understand. Networks will be part of your working life, whether you specialize in networking or not. In this lab you will research network topologies, then answer related questions.

*cross*
*Reference*

***To best prepare for this lab, you should read the section titled "Topologies" under Certification Objective 7.01 in Chapter 7 of the** A+ **Certification Study Guide.***

## Learning Objectives

Network topologies can be viewed both as physical and as logical topologies. Physical topology defines the hardware connections you make; logical topology defines the flow of data through the network. In this lab you will research and define these topologies. By the end of this lab, you'll be able to:

- Identify common physical network topologies
- Identify common logical network topologies

## Lab Materials and Setup

The materials you need for this lab are:

- A PC with Windows 95 or later version installed
- Internet access and a web browser

## Getting Down to Business

When you are learning about a new topic, it is usually a good idea to use more than one source. This is valuable because you will be exposed to different points of view, and can often gather more information than you can get from just one source. For instance, when researching network topology, you will find that some sources emphasize the distinction between logical and physical topology, while others may not even bother to mention the differences—or, if they do, those differences may not be defined. In this lab you will use information from two different web sites: that of the Wellington Institute of Technology, and the online technical "encyclopedia" Webopedia. At the Wellington Institute site you will use a tutorial to research network topologies. At the Webopedia site, you will research the definitions of the topology terms you encountered on the first site, and expand on what you learned.

lab
**ⓘint**
*The following steps include the use of web sites that may change. If these sites are not available to you, use the Google search engine (www.google.com) to look for other relevant sites.*

**Step 1.** To begin this research, use your web browser to go directly to the Network category at the Webopedia site at www.webopedia.com/networks. Notice the list of links to subcategories and click "Network Topologies." On the Network Topologies page there is a list of links to terms; click the link to "Topology." Notice the general definition, and the list of principal topologies used in local area networks (LANs). Read all the information under Topology and then click the "Network Topology Diagrams" link at the end of the article, where you will find a more complete definition of network topologies.

    a. In your own words, provide a definition of network topology:

_____

_____

**b.** How many major topologies are listed at this site? List them below.

_____

_____

Remain at this site. In the following step you will open a new instance of your web browser so that you can easily and quickly switch between the sites. If you prefer to stay in one instance of the browser, then you will simply have to navigate back and forth between the two sites from within that instance.

**lab**

**Hint** *An "instance" is a single running copy of a program. Some programs can have two or more copies active in memory at the same time. Not all programs can be instanced in this way, but many can, including Internet Explorer. This may not be true of other Internet browsers, or of much earlier versions of Internet Explorer. We are currently using version 5.5, but we have been able to do this for some time. It can be very useful!*

**Step 2.** Open a new instance of your web browser and point it to the web site of the Wellington Institute of Technology at www.cit.ac.nz. From the home page, click the "On Line Computing Course Materials" link, which will bring up a listing of Self Study Guides. Click the "Networks: An Introduction" link, which brings you to a page titled "Networking Fundamentals." On this page, click the "Networking Topology" link on the sidebar, which will bring you to a tutorial on network topology. Click the "Introduction" link, read the information on the page, then answer the following questions:

**a.** Does the definition of network topology on this page agree with the Webopedia definition?

_____

_____

**b.** How many major topologies are listed at this site? List them below.

_____

_____

c. The topologies that are common to both of these sites are the topologies that are considered the most basic network topologies. What topologies are included in the lists at both sites?

_____

_____

d. Of the additional topologies (other than the most basic topologies) listed at these sites, one is really a hybrid of two basic topologies, one is an implementation of a basic topology, and the third is a unique network topology. Please identify which three topologies fit these three descriptions.

_____

_____

_____

**Step 3.** In the tutorial at the Wellington Institute site, find and read the description of star topology and examine the diagram of a star topology network. At the Webopedia site read the information on star topology. Answer the following questions:

a. The Wellington Institute tutorial has a table that lists advantages and disadvantages. However, there is one other fact included in the article that could be listed as a disadvantage. What is this "disadvantage?"

_____

_____

b. Both sites describe a device as being at the center of a star network. What is the name of this network device?

_____

_____

**Step 4.** Switch to the Wellington Institute page and navigate to the information on bus topology. Read this information being sure to examine the graphic of a bus topology network. Switch to the Webopedia site and select the "Bus network" link. Read the definition, then click the "Network Topology Diagrams" link, and look at the bus topology diagram. In the related terms box click the "Terminator" link, and read about the function of a terminator in a bus network. Based on what you have learned from these two sites, answer the following questions:

a. A message traveling on a bus network is visible to which nodes on the network?

_____

_____

b. What is the purpose of a terminator in a bus network?

_____

_____

**Step 5.** Switch to the Wellington Institute tutorial page and navigate to the information on ring topology. Read this information, being sure to examine the graphic of a ring topology network. Switch to the Webopedia site and select the "Ring Network" link. Read the definition and then click the "Network Topology Diagrams" link and look at the ring topology diagram. The Webopedia site has a ring topology diagram that is truly a generic ring topology. The Wellington Institute site has a ring topology diagram that shows a common implementation of a ring topology in a LAN—token ring. IBM's token ring network uses a special packet, called a token. At the Wellington Institute site find the link labeled "Token-ring Network" and read about this type of ring network. Do the same for the term "Token Passing."
Based on what you have learned from these two sites, answer the following questions:

a. What is a generic definition of a ring topology network?

_____

_____

b. How does a computer get access to put data on a token ring network?

_____

_____

c. What is the significance of the capitalized term "Token Ring?"

_____

_____

**Step 6.** Return to the tutorial at the Wellington Institute site and find the discussion of the differences between logical and physical networks. Read the explanation and study the graphic. The example they give of a physical star, logical bus network describes an Ethernet network. When you look at such a network you can see that the computers, cables, and hubs are clearly connected as a physical star. However, an Ethernet hub actually contains an Ethernet bus within it. Connecting to the hub connects each node to the bus. Therefore, it is said that such a configuration has a logical bus.

Remain in the Wellington Institute tutorial and look at the diagram of a ring topology network. Notice that the ring is labeled "Token Ring." In a token ring network, a special network hub device, actually called a MAU (Multiple Access Unit) is used. (There are other terms used for a MAU—such as MSAU, which means Multi-Station Access Unit. For simplicity we will use the term MAU to represent all token ring hub-like devices.) All the nodes on the network connect to one or more MAU(s). Therefore, a token ring network is physically a star, but, like the Ethernet network, a logical topology is "hidden" within the MAU. Each node connected to a MAU is connected to the ring within the MAU. The cabling and NICs for a Token Ring network are also special, containing separate wires to carry the incoming and outgoing signals.

**LAB EXERCISE 7.02**

# Identifying Common Network Protocols

**I Hour**

A protocol is a set of rules. When we network computers, they must have protocols in common in order to communicate. When two computers use the same set of rules they can communicate. In human communications, if you understand and speak only French, and I understand and speak only English, we will not be able to communicate. Even if both parties understand and speak both languages, we will need to agree on which language we will use for our communications.

Networks have protocols at all levels for how they communicate, beginning with the hardware. The most common low-level LAN protocols are Ethernet and Token Ring. Ethernet and Token Ring rules cover how networks communicate at the lowest level where the data is placed onto the network and picked up from the network. These protocols include the cabling, the connection devices on the network (hubs and switches), the NICs, the firmware on the NICs, and the device drivers used to transfer messages to and from the network through the NICs. Whether you are using an Ethernet or Token Ring (or other) network, there are a few standard protocols that sit on top of these lower level protocols.

From bottom to top, these are all network protocols. But when network professionals talk about "network protocols," they are usually talking about the protocols sitting on top of the lower level protocols. In LANs, the most common of these network protocols are NetBEUI (NetBIOS Enhanced User Interface), IPX/SPX (Internetwork Packet Exchange/Sequenced Packet Exchange), and TCP/IP (Transmission Control Protocol/Internet Protocol). NetBEUI is a very simple protocol, practical only in a very small network, but the other two are actually very sophisticated—each of them including many protocols and utilities. In spite of including many protocols, we often refer to TCP/IP and IPX/SPX in the singular, saying that we are using the TCP/IP protocol or the IPX/SPX protocol. We also refer to these protocols as "stacks" because they each include many protocols, logically stacked into layers.

cross
**Reference**

*To best prepare for this lab, you should read the "Protocols" section in Certification Objective 7.01 in Chapter 7 of the A+ Certification Study Guide.*

## Learning Objectives

In this lab you will explore the three popular network protocols. After you've completed this lab, you will be able to:

■ Identify common Windows network protocols

## Lab Materials and Setup

For this lab exercise, you'll need:

■ A PC with Windows 95 or later version installed
■ Internet access and a web browser

## Getting Down to Business

In this exercise, you will continue to use the Internet to do research, but this time your research will focus on network protocols rather than on network topologies. You will be given less detailed guidance in this exercise so you can hone your research skills. Although the questions you will be asked in this lab are important,
it is even more important that you use the opportunity to really study the material you discover on the Internet in order to truly understand how network protocols work.

**Step 1.** Use your Internet browser to connect to the Webopedia site at www.webopedia.com and search on NetBEUI. This will give you a basic definition of NetBEUI, much like that in the A+ Certification Study Guide. One of the best explanations of NetBEUI we have found is in an older (April 1998) article at the Windows 2000 Magazine site at www.win2000mag.com titled, "Windows NT Protocols." Go to this site and search for this title. If this article is not available, look for other articles on NetBEUI. Based on the information on NetBEUI from all the sources at your disposal, answer the following questions:

a. Do you expect to find NetBEUI in many networks in the workplace? Explain your answer.

b. Could you use the NetBEUI protocol to communicate between UNIX and Windows computers?

**Step 2.** Search for the definition of IPX/SPX at the Webopedia site and at another site. We suggest that you look at the web site of the Computer Technology Documentation Project at www.comptechdoc.org and look at the link under "Networking," then select the "Beginning Networking Guide" document. (You will want to add this document to your list of resources.) For now, look for IPX/SPX and read the page on this protocol. Using the information you have found at these sites, and other references at your disposal, answer the following questions:

a. How is this protocol essentially different from NetBEUI?

b. What network operating system has traditionally used this protocol?

    c. Is this protocol used on the Internet?

_____

_____

    d. Why is it important that the IPX/SPX frame types match on an Ethernet network?

_____

_____

**Step 3.** Let's now take a look at the world's most popular network protocol suite: TCP/IP. This is a huge topic which you will revisit in Chapter 11 and in your career. For now, we will just take a very general approach to this topic. Use Internet sites or other references available to you to find a basic definition of TCP/IP and learn about the general characteristics of TCP/IP. Webopedia and the TechEncyclopedia at www.techweb.com/encyclopedia are great places to begin learning about TCP/IP. Find definitions of TCP/IP and then answer the following questions.

    a. True or false? The TCP/IP protocol suite consists of exactly two protocols, TCP and IP.

_____

_____

    b. How many bits are in an IP address?

_____

_____

    c. In one or two sentences, give a brief history of TCP/IP.

_____

_____

## LAB EXERCISE 7.03

# Working with Network Media

**30 Minutes**

There are a number of different types of media that can be used in a network. ("Media" refers to the physical pathway used to transport data from one place to another.) Media can include copper cable, fiber optic cable, wireless transmission, etc. Because it is important to understand the various media you will run into in your career as a certified technician, this lab will help you understand the characteristics and advantages and disadvantages of the most common media.

cross
Reference

*To best prepare for this lab, you should read the section titled "Cabling" under Certification Objective 7.01 in Chapter 7 of the A+ Certification Study Guide.*

## Learning Objectives

After you complete this lab you will be able to:

- Identify twisted-pair cable standards and features
- Identify the features, advantages, and disadvantages of coaxial cabling
- Identify the features, advantages, and disadvantages of fiber optic cabling

## Lab Materials and Setup

The materials you need for this lab are:

- A PC with Windows 95 or later installed
- Internet access and a web browser
- Acrobat Reader (free download at www.adobe.com/products/acrobat/readstep.html)

## Getting Down to Business

The following steps will guide you through the process of researching network media. You will be given the names of web sites, some of which are provided by individuals. Such sites may come and go. If a site referenced in this steps is not available to you, use your favorite search engine (ours is www.google.com) to search on the key words.

**Step 1.** Table 7-1 in the *A+ Certification Study Guide* provides twisted pair cable standards. These standards are defined by an organization known as ANSI/TIA. The last entry in the table is CAT5, however there are now more categories of twisted pair cable. Using the Internet or other references available to you, research ANSI/TIA and answer the following questions:

a. What does ANSI/TIA stand for?

_____

_____

b. In the table below provide information on the newer ANSI/TIA cable standards not shown in Table 7-1 of the *A+ Certification Study Guide.*

| Type | Speed | Common Use |
|------|-------|------------|
| CAT5e | | |
| CAT6 | | |
| CAT7 | | |

**Step 2.** In this step you will locate references on the Internet for cabling. The two sites we suggest are net21.ucdavis.edu/100bt.htm and www.helmig.com.

Connect to the first site, which is at the University of California at Davis and review the table for Fast Ethernet Standards.

Use your web browser to connect to www.helmig.com, and click the button labeled "Basics/Cabling." This will take you to the Network Basics/Cabling page. If you scroll down, you will find a list of topics. All of these topics contain good information, however, for the sake of this lab, you should read all the articles on twisted pair cabling.

Table 7-2 in the *A+ Certification Study Guide* is an excellent reference for a service technician to have on the job. It is also valuable in preparing for the A+ Core Hardware Service Technician Exam. There is one more piece of information that is useful in both situations—the number of wires used for the various implementations of twisted pair (yes, a pair means "2," but how many pairs?). All data quality cable categories from Cat 2 through Cat 6 have 8 wires (4 pairs), but not all the wires are necessary for all network implementation. Search the UC Davis site, the Helmig site, and/or other sources to find the information needed to complete the following table.

| Type | Actual # of Wires Used | Cable Category |
|------|------------------------|----------------|
| 10BaseT | | |
| 100BaseTX | | |
| 100BaseT4 | | |

Now you have an additional reference. It is important to remember that 100BaseTX and 100BaseT4 need wiring that can handle the higher speed. While it allows for two types of wiring, if you want to take advantage of the duplex mode of 100BaseTX or 100 BaseT4 only one of these wiring types will work.

lab
(h)int

*You probably do not need to be reminded that technology advances at the speed of light (or something like that), especially when it comes to speed! This sometimes makes us wish we had gone into a more stable field such as geology. Here is an example of how fast technology advances. We actually have faster Ethernet standards than those discussed above—one is called 1000BaseT (fondly called Gigabit Ethernet). Gigabit Ethernet is now one of the common choices for a new network backbone (the high speed central network of a large internetwork). There is also a faster standard (in the works at the moment) called 10 Gigabit Ethernet. If you use an Internet search engine and query on "gigabit" your search results will include information on both of these standards and maybe even something faster yet!*

**Step 3.** Using the Internet references you used above, or others which you have found, answer the following questions about coaxial cable:

lab
(h)int

*The Helmig site has an article on Thin Ethernet (10Base2). Another site to try is that of the Free On-Line Dictionary of Computing at foldoc.doc.ic.ac.uk/foldoc.*

a. How many wires are in a coaxial cable?

_____

_____

b. What type of connector is used with 10Base2 coax cables?

_____

_____

c. What is the maximum cable length of 10Base2 cables?

_____

_____

d. Provide one advantage and at least one disadvantage of coaxial cable.

_____

_____

e. What are the most common cabling types that you should expect to find in a corporate network?

_____

_____

**Step 4.** In this step research fiber optic cable by looking for the definition of this type of cable at a site that contains technical definitions, such as Webopedia. Then answer the questions below:

lab
**ⓘint**

*When searching for information on the Web you may have to search both with and without hyphens in words. If you can't find a reference to "fiber optic" try a search on "fiber-optic."*

a. Provide at least three advantages of fiber optic cable.

_____

_____

**b.** Provide two disadvantages of fiber optic cable.

_____

_____

**LAB EXERCISE 7.04**

# Exploring Network Access Methods

**30 Minutes**

In order to transmit data across a network, a computer must have some way to determine when data can be sent and how messages are to be sent. It must also know what to do if other computers are sending data at the same time, and the data it is sending collides with the data being sent from other computers. There are various network access methods in use to solve these problems. In this lab you will explore the two most common network access methods: CSMA/CD and token passing.

***To best prepare for this lab, you should read the section titled "Network Access" under Certification Objective 7.01 in Chapter 7 of the A+ Certification Study Guide.***

## Learning Objectives

Once you've completed this lab, you will be able to:

- Understand and explain CSMA/CD
- Understand and explain token passing

## Lab Materials and Setup

The materials you'll need for this lab are:

- A PC running Windows 95 or later installed
- Internet access and a web browser

## Getting Down to Business

The following steps will guide you through your own research into the most common network access methods. You are now skilled enough to be able to find appropriate reference sites on your own. Remember, the more you read and learn, the more comfortable you will be with the concepts. Good luck!

**Step 1.**   Use your web browser to connect to two web sites where you can research the term: CSMA/CD. Answer the following questions:

a. Provide a definition for CSMA/CD, including the actual words represented by the acronym.

_____

_____

b. Define the word "collisions" in a network context (as opposed to an automotive context).

_____

_____

c. Why is CSMA/CD considered a contention protocol?

_____

_____

**Step 2.**   Use your web browser to connect to two web sites where you can research the term: "token passing." Answer the following questions:

a. Token passing can be used with which types of topologies?

_____

_____

b. What token passing protocol suite did IBM develop?

_____

_____

c. True or false? Token passing is a contention network access method.

_____

_____

**LAB EXERCISE 7.05**

**15 Minutes**

# Identifying the Difference Between Full-Duplex and Half-Duplex

The concepts of full-duplex communication and half-duplex communication are important ones to understand. This lab will give you a chance to explore these concepts further.

cross
**Reference**

*To best prepare for this lab, you should read the section "Full- and Half-duplex Transmission" under Certification Objective 7.01 in Chapter 7 of the A+ Certification Study Guide.*

## Learning Objectives

After you complete this lab you will be able to:

■ Explain the differences between full-duplex and half-duplex

## Lab Materials and Setup

The materials you need for this lab are:

■ A PC with Windows 95 or later installed
■ Internet access and a web browser

## Getting Down to Business

In the following step you will use the Internet to access different explanations of the terms. Again, different sources can emphasize different aspects of a concept. It makes sense to get several different versions in order to synthesize your own definition.

**Step 1.** Use your web browser to connect to two web sites where you can research the terms: half-duplex and full-duplex. Answer the following questions:

a. Provide a definition for half-duplex, including a non-computer example of this type of communication.

_____

_____

b. Provide a definition for full-duplex, including a non-computer example of this type of communication.

_____

_____

---

**LAB EXERCISE 7.06**

# Putting it Together—Combining Protocols and Technologies

**1.25 Hours**

So far in this chapter we have taken a very high-level view of networking, while looking at common topologies, protocols, cabling, duplex communications, and network access methods. These are all pieces of the whole, which can be combined in many variations to provide network solutions. Now we will look at the common combinations of these technologies that you may encounter on the job.

**cross Reference**

*To best prepare for this lab, you should read "Ways to Network PCs" under Certification Objective 7.01 in Chapter 7 of the A+ Certification Study Guide.*

## Learning Objectives

After you complete this lab you will be able to:

- Define the basic characteristics of an 802.3 Ethernet network
- Define the basic characteristics of an 802.5 token ring network
- Define the basic characteristics of a Fiber Distributed Data Interface (FDDI) network
- Define the characteristics and requirements of Dial-Up Networks
- Identify the cable options for Direct Cable Connection

## Lab Materials and Setup

The materials you need for this lab are:

- A PC with Windows 95 or later installed
- Internet access and a web browser

## Getting Down to Business

In the following steps you will research the most common ways the technologies you have studied are combined and applied in our networks today.

**Step 1.**   Use your web browser to connect to two web sites where you can research IEEE 802.3 and IEEE 802.2. Answer the following questions:

a.  The 802.3 standard is often informally referred to by the name of the technology that existed before the IEEE committee standardized it in 802.3. What is this name?

_____

_____

b.  What is the access method used by 802.3?

_____

_____

c. True or false? The 802.2 standard is identical for all network topologies and provides a general interface between the network protocols and the underlying network (802.3 Ethernet, 802.5 Token Ring, etc.)

_____

_____

d. Parse 100BaseF, describing what each portion of its name defines.

_____

_____

**Step 2.** Use your web browser to connect to web sites where you can research the term: IEEE 802.5. Answer the following questions:

a. The 802.5 standard is often informally referred to by the name of the technology that existed before the IEEE committee standardized it in 802.5. What is this name?

_____

_____

b. What is the access method used by 802.5?

_____

_____

c. The data path on an 802.5 network is (select the one that applies).

    1)   full-duplex

    2)   unidirectional

    3)   half-duplex

**Step 3.** Use your web browser to connect to web sites where you can research the term: Fiber Distributed Data Interface (FDDI). Answer the following questions:

a. What are the speed and distance limits of FDDI?

_____

_____

b. What is the topology of FDDI?

_____

_____

c. Contrast FDDI to another network technology that uses the same topology.

_____

_____

d. What organization sets the standards for FDDI?

_____

_____

**Step 4.** Dial-up networking is yet another way to network PCs. Use Internet sites or other books and resources to research the following questions:

a. When you connect to a network with dial-up networking, the modem takes the place of what network device?

_____

_____

b. What are the minimum requirements to perform dial-up networking?

_____

_____

c. When you connect to a server with dial-up networking, how are you able to access the network to which the server is connected?

_____

_____

**Step 5.** Use your web browser to connect to web sites where you can research the term "Direct Cable Connection." We will give you a little help on this one: www.helmig.com has a nice article with this title. But search other references and sites also. Answer the following questions:

    a. What are the cable options for direct cable connection?

_____

_____

    b. Give the advantages and disadvantages of each type of cabling and connections.

_____

_____

    c. True or false? It is possible to use only direct cable connections between two PCs. If you need to connect more than two PCs you need to purchase networking hardware (NICs, cables, and hubs).

_____

_____

**Step 6.** Most organizations prefer to make changes to their computing environment gradually. This is especially true of the physical network infrastructure. You have a customer who wants to upgrade a 10BaseT Ethernet network to 100BaseT, but they would like to do this gradually—perhaps beginning with the hubs, then gradually upgrading to 100BaseT NICs. Research the feasibility of this approach and write your response to the customer below:

_____

_____

_____

_____

_____

**LAB EXERCISE 7.07**

# Troubleshooting Common Network Problems

**1.5 Hours**

No one lives in a vacuum. We are all affected by what is happening around us, and that is also true of computers. Since the vast majority of computers in the workplace are networked, we cannot ignore the network when servicing a computer. A user's unhappiness with his or her computer may be related to the performance of the system itself, or the performance of the network to which the computer is connected. Therefore you must be capable of recognizing and troubleshooting common network problems.

## Learning Objectives

After you complete this lab you will be able to:

- Troubleshoot a network card configuration
- Troubleshoot common bandwidth problems
- Troubleshoot loss of network connectivity
- Troubleshoot common causes for network slowdowns
- Minimize loss of data on a network
- Troubleshoot network slowdowns

## Lab Materials and Setup

The materials you need for this lab are:

- A PC with Windows 95 or later installed
- Internet access and a web browser

# Getting Down to Business

In some of the following steps you will be asked to suggest the possible causes for a common network problem. You can use an Internet-based network troubleshooter to research these answers. There is a fairly simply one titled "Interactive Ethernet Network Troubleshooting" which is part of the *Network Design Manual*, available on the Network Computing web site at www.networkcomputing.com/netdesign/troubleintro.html. If this page is no longer there, connect to www.networkcomputing.com/netdesign and search the page for a link to "Interactive Ethernet Network Troubleshooting," or another similarly titled link. If this is no longer available, you can use a search engine to search on "network troubleshooting." Use one of these tools to provide possible resolutions when you are asked to do so in the steps below.

**Step I.** Flamingo Furriers have called you to their main office where a new desktop computer was installed for the use of the accounts payable clerk. She is not able to access anything on their Ethernet network which is running TCP/IP. Other desktops and servers on the network are working fine. This is a big problem because she must access the accounts payable system on the network in order to process the week's checks. What are possible solutions that you will explore when you visit Flamingo? In this step you research the Flamingo problem before you leave for the client's site. Record the troubleshooting steps that your research suggests you do to resolve this problem and get the accounts payable clerk up and running.

_____

_____

_____

_____

_____

**Step 2.** You are at Flamingo Furriers where you have used the list of steps you created from your research in Step 1. You have eliminated network hardware outside the computer as being the source of the problem. In this step you will use a few common utilities to check out the software and hardware configuration of a networked computer.

Open a command prompt and type: IPCONFIG /ALL (if you are using Windows 9x type: WINIPCFG /ALL).

You should see output similar to that in Figure 7-1, which is the result of running the IPCONFIG /ALL command on a Windows 2000 computer.

Perhaps you were not born knowing what all the data in this screen means. For now, that level of network knowledge is not expected of you. You might have to ask a network administrator if this information is correct for this computer. What you want to watch for is the inability to run the command at all, which would mean that you do not have TCP/IP installed on your computer, perhaps because there is no network card. Yes, you would have noticed that in Step 1 when you swapped the network cable, but perhaps the network card has failed.

Another important sign to watch for is an empty IP address. If you look at the line that begins with IP Address and the value on the right is 0.0.0.0, then the NIC did not receive an address and it is time to find out why. Should this machine have a "static" address, which means that someone must manually enter the address in network settings, or should this NIC receive an address automatically from a special network server that gives out IP addresses? If the IP address is empty, call a network administrator and discuss the problem with her. If you determine that the NIC and the protocol were configured properly, the problem might be the NIC. If the NIC has a utility that you can use to perform diagnostics, you could test it.

**FIGURE 7-1**

The results of running IPCONFIG in Windows 2000 Professional

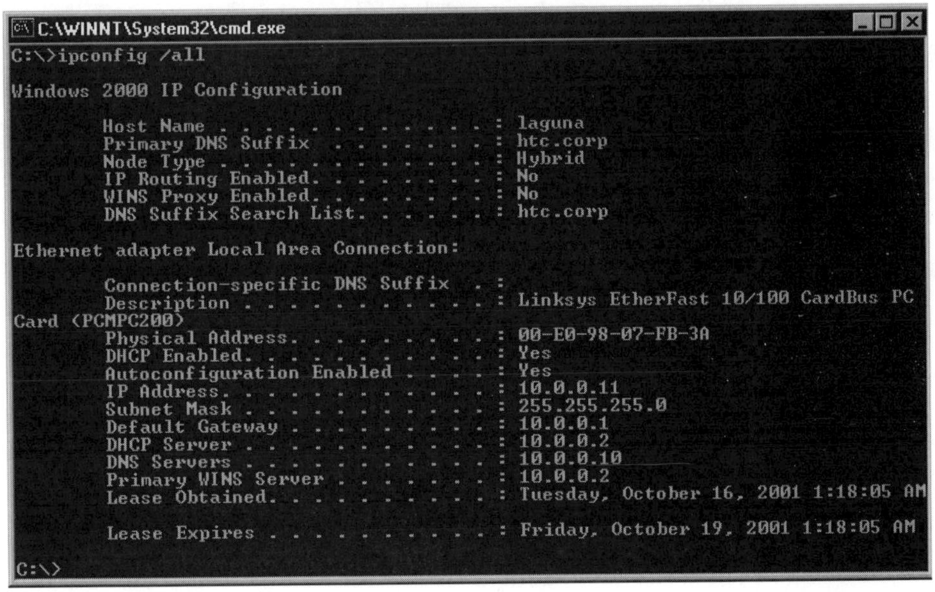

In many of these steps we have at least stood square on the line (and maybe stumbled across) between playing the roles of a hardware service technician and a network support technician. At this point in your career, you are not expected to do the job of a network engineer, but you are expected to look for the common solutions and call in a network engineer or administrator when you cannot fix the problem.

**Step 3.** You can also use Control Panel tools to check on the NIC and protocol configuration. Most experienced network troubleshooters first use the IPCONFIG (WINIPCFG for Windows 9x) utility to see if the protocol was configured properly. Then, if they must make a change or look at the manual configuration, they use the Control Panel tools.

If you are using Windows 9x, open the Network program in Control Panel and verify that the TCP/IP protocol is listed. If it is not listed, check that a NIC is listed. If a NIC does not show as being installed, but you know that it is physically present, then the driver has not been installed. You will need to install the driver for the NIC, then install the protocol. Both can be done from this program. Once the NIC is recognized with the proper driver, you will have to configure the protocol. If you need to do this you can follow the steps in Exercise 7-2 in the *A+ Certification Study Guide.*

If you are using Windows 2000 you will use the Network and Dial-up Connections in Control Panel to do most of the steps in the previous paragraph. If you have physically installed a new PnP NIC, the operating system will discover it when you boot up. If it is not discovered by the operating system you will have to use the Add New Hardware wizard from the Control Panel. If you need to upgrade the NIC driver, you can do that from the properties dialog of the Local Area Connection object for that NIC in Network and Dial-up Connections. Figure 7-2 shows the Local Area Connection Properties dialog for a Linksys EtherFast 10/100 NIC.

If you click Configure, you can access the properties of the NIC, as shown in Figure 7-3. From this dialog box you can verify the status of the NIC, modify special properties through the Advanced tab, update the driver through the Driver tab, and view the resources in use by the NIC in the Resources tab.

In the Local Area Connection Properties dialog box you can also access the properties of the Internet Protocol (TCP/IP) and verify that the settings are correct. Once again, you may need to check with a network professional to determine the proper settings. For our scenario, we will assume that the problem was in the configuration of the TCP/IP protocol for the NIC, which you corrected after talking to your LAN administrator.

**FIGURE 7-2**

Windows 2000
Local Area
Connection
Properties

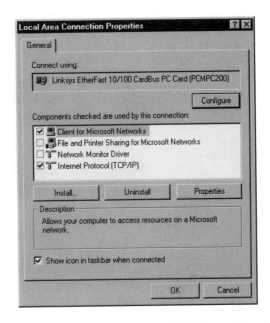

**Step 4**  After solving the network connection problem at Flamingo, you are sent to the Valley Town Clinic to solve another problem. The network is slow. Use an

**FIGURE 7-3**

Windows 2000
Properties of
a NIC

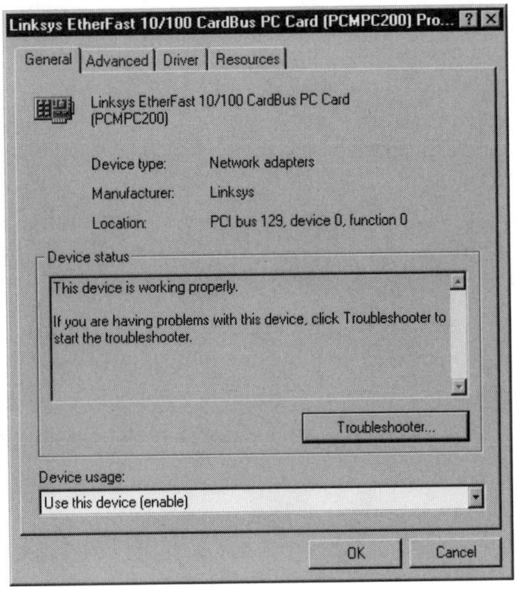

Internet site or another reference of your choice to research possible causes, and steps you should take to troubleshoot. Describe your findings below.

lab

**Warning**    *Do not spend too much time researching all the analyses you will find for troubleshooting a slow network. It is enough for now for you to know that there are a few common causes of slowness on networks.*

_____

_____

_____

_____

_____

**Step 5.**    You are on site at Concurrent Heating Controls when the Production Manager calls you over to his desk. He received the  error message "Unable to Browse Network" when he attempted to open Network Neighborhood. Use the sources available to you to determine what steps you should take to discover the problems, and what the possible problems and solutions may be?

_____

_____

_____

_____

_____

**Step 6**    Carly's Craft Supplies, a national chain with many retail stores and a fast-growing Internet e-commerce business, has inquired about the steps they can take to prevent loss of data. They are presently doing rigorous backups of all their servers, testing the backups every three months. As they grow and become more successful, especially with a 24x7 Internet presence, a loss of data looms as a bigger and more costly possibility. They also cannot afford to be down for even a brief time. You know that they are ready to hear about other, more sophisticated ways to prevent data loss. Research ways to prevent data loss on a network and provide a paragraph on the options you will discuss with this client.

_____

_____

_____

_____

_____

# LAB ANALYSIS TEST

1. You have gone along on a sales call to a potential customer to answer the customer's technical questions about the services provided by Nerd Matrix. You are also gathering information about the client's present computing and network environment to help your company design a support package for this client. Early in the meeting, the Information Services Manager states that they are an IBM shop as far as all computing hardware and networks are concerned. What network topology do you expect to find at this site?

   _____

   _____

2. You are setting up a computer that will be connected to a large, routed corporate network with Internet access. The company also hosts its own private Internet services within the corporate intranet. What network protocol stack should you expect to install?

   _____

   _____

3. A former classmate of yours works at a large high school that installed their first Ethernet network around 1990. They have gradually upgraded their hubs and NICs to 100Mbps by using all 10/100 devices. Now that all hubs and NICs are at this level, they are disappointed to find out through testing, that the network is still running at 10Mbps. He has asked you for your opinion of what might be causing this problem. Give your answer below.

   _____

   _____

4. You have been called to a biological research station located in a state park in Northern Minnesota. They have a special networking problem. They have Ethernet networks with CAT5 cabling in all classrooms and labs. The instructors are housed in cabins that are grouped around a clearing within sight of the classroom and lab buildings. They would like to provide network access for the instructors from their cabins, but it would be very expensive to run cabling from each cabin to the network in the classroom and lab buildings, especially for just one or two people per cabin. What solution will you suggest exploring for this network?

   _____

   _____

5. List some common causes of a slow network.

   _____

   _____

# KEY TERM QUIZ

Use the following vocabulary terms to complete the sentences below. Not all of the terms will be used.

>carrier sense multiple access/collision detection (CSMA/CD)
>
>star
>
>ring topology
>
>token passing
>
>twisted pair
>
>direct cable connection
>
>contention
>
>fiber optic
>
>Transmission Control Protocol/ Internet Protocol (TCP/IP)
>
>Internetwork Packet Exchange/Sequenced Packet Exchange (IPX/SPX)

1.  Ethernet is based on a logical bus topology, with a _____ physical topology.

2.  Today the most important protocol suite in computer networking is the _____ suite.

3.  The most common cabling found on a LAN is _____.

4.  CSMA/CD is a _____ access method.

5.  If you need to connect only two PCs, consider using _____.

# LAB WRAP-UP

In this chapter you have rounded out your knowledge of hardware needed by a service technician both on the job, and to prepare for the CompTIA A+ Core Hardware Service Technician exam. You researched and explored many basic networking topics, such as topologies, protocols, cabling, network access methods, full- and half-duplex, ways in which technologies are combined for networking, and troubleshooting of common network problems.

# LAB SOLUTIONS FOR CHAPTER 7

## Lab Solution 7.01

### Step 1.

a. Network topology is defined as being the shape, or layout of a network, including all connected devices.

b. This site lists five network topologies: mesh, star, bus, ring, and tree.

### Step 2.

a. Yes, the definitions agree, even if they do not use the exact same words.

b. This site lists four major topologies: bus, ring, star, and FDDI.

c. The topologies listed at both sites are bus, ring, and star.

d. The tree topology, as described at the Webopedia site, is a hybrid of the star and bus topologies. FDDI is actually an implementation of a ring topology, with two counter rotating rings. The mesh topology is a unique network topology, although it is often overlooked in discussions of LAN topology because most actual LAN implementations do not include a complete mesh topology. If they did, this would be the topology using the most cable!

### Step 3.

a. Star topology uses the greatest amount of cable, a fact that could be construed as a disadvantage. This is important to remember because it adds to the cost of a star network.

b. The network device at the center of a star network is a hub.

### Step 4.

a. A message traveling on a bus network is visible to all nodes on the network. A node will only process it if it is addressed to that node.

b. The purpose of a terminator in a bus network is to absorb signals so that they do not reflect, or bounce, when they reach the end of the bus, which would cause confusion and unnecessary traffic. An Ethernet bus network requires termination on both ends. A SCSI network requires termination at one end.

## Step 5.

a. The physical connections are arranged in a ring, and messages travel around the ring. Each node regenerates the signal so that it can span longer distances than a bus or star network.

b. On a token-ring network a node must gain possession of the token and attach its own data to the token.

c. The capitalized term "Token Ring" refers to the network protocol developed by IBM. The Institute of Electrical and Electronics Engineers (IEEE) has also standardized this in the IEEE 802.5 standard.

**Step 6.**  There are no questions to be answered in Step 6.

## Lab Solution 7.02

## Step 1.

a. You will not find NetBEUI in many networks in the workplace because it is best for small, non-routed networks. Therefore it may be found in small businesses, or within small departments in larger organizations.

b. NetBEUI is supported only by Microsoft DOS, IBM OS/2, and Windows operating systems prior to Windows XP. Therefore, you could not use it to communicate between Windows and UNIX systems.

lab
ⓗint  *While NetBEUI is not officially supported for Windows XP, it can be manually installed from directions and files found under the VALUEADD\MSFT\NET\NETBEUI folder of the distribution CD.*

## Step 2.

a. This protocol is essentially different from NetBEUI in that it is routable and offers connection services similar to TCP/IP.

b. This protocol was developed by Novell and has traditionally been used by Novell's NetWare operating systems. It is also supported by Windows operating systems but employed primarily for connectivity to Novell servers. Microsoft's version of IPX/SPX is NWLink.

c. Though routable, the IPX/SPX suite is not used on the Internet.

d. If the frame types do not match on an Ethernet network, the computers will not be able to communicate. That is, any two computers using IPX/SPX that do not have a frame type in common will not be able to communicate. The issue here is between the 802.3 and 802.2 frame types.

## Step 3.

a. False. The TCP/IP protocol suite consists of many protocols. A short list includes TCP, IP, UDP, ARP, ICMP, RARP, FTP, SMTP, DNS, and Telnet.

b. There are 32 bits in an IP address. If you find a source that gives 128-bits, this is not true of IP version 4 used on the Internet (IPv4), but it is true of IP version 6 (IPv6), which is used on Internet 2. (Point your browser to internet2.org.)

c. TCP/IP has it origins in the early days of the Internet when it was developed by Vinton Cerf and Bob Kahn as part of a U.S. Department of Defense project to internetwork dissimilar systems.

# Lab Solution 7.03

## Step 1

a. ANSI/TIA stands for American National Standards Institute and Telecommunications Industry Association. These two organizations often work together to provide standards. ANSI creates standards for the computer industry, while TIA is a trade association of communications and information technology organizations. Since 1988 TIA has sponsored engineering committees to set standards.

b. Newer ANSI/TIA cable standards (since CAT5)

| Type | Speed | Common Use |
|------|-------|------------|
| CAT5e | 100Mbps | 100Mbps TPDDI<br>155Mbps ATM |
| CAT6 | 200-250 MHz | Super-fast broadband applications |
| CAT7 | In process | In process |

## Step 2.

| Type | Actual # of Wires Used | Cable Category |
|------|------------------------|----------------|
| 10BaseT | 4 wires (2 pairs) | Cat3 or Cat5 |
| 100BaseTX | 4 wires (2 pairs) | Cat5 only |
| 100BaseT4 | 8 wires (4 pairs) | Cat5e or greater |

## Step 3.

a. A coaxial cable contains a single wire.

b. BNC connectors are used with 10Base2 cables.

c. The maximum length of a 10Base2 cable is 185 meters. A meter is 1.09 yards. 185 meters equals 202.318 yards. Therefore, some people remember this length by thinking of it as being about 200 yards, and relating it to the "2" in 10Base2.

d. An advantage of coaxial cable is that it is less susceptible to interference than twisted pair cable. Coax cable is used in a bus topology and has the disadvantages of the bus topology, in that it must be terminated. If one node fails, it can bring down the entire bus. Coax cable, especially 10Base5, is less physically flexible to work with than unshielded twisted pair cabling.

e. Twisted pair cabling, usually Cat5, is the most common cabling type that you should expect to find in corporations.

**Step 4.**

    a.  Advantages of fiber optic cable include:

- greater bandwidth
- less susceptible than copper to interference (not at all susceptible to EMI interference)
- fiber optic cables are much thinner and lighter than metal wires (however, usually there are MANY bundled together)
- signals can be carried digitally rather than as analog signals as on copper wire

    b.  Disadvantages of fiber optic cable include:

- it is expensive to install
- it is physically more fragile than copper wire and difficult to join or split

## Lab Solution 7.04

**Step 1.**

    a.  CSMA/CD is short for Carrier Sense Multiple Access/Collision Detection. This is a protocol for network access in which a device that wants to place traffic on a network first listens for other traffic. This is the "carrier sense" part of the name. It is sensing, or listening for, a carrier, or signal, on the wire. If it does not detect any traffic, it will place a signal on the wire, and continue to listen for a collision. Now, another device may have also made the same discovery and placed a signal on the wire at the same time. This is the "multiple access" portion of the protocol. Each device continues to "listen," which is the "collision detection" part of the name. If two or more devices place traffic on the network at the same time and then detect the resulting collision, each device will wait a random length of time before repeating the process. If, on the next attempt, a device detects another collision, it will then wait twice as long as it waited previously.

    b.  A collision on a network is the garbled result of two or more devices placing traffic on the network at the same time.

   c. CSMA/CD is considered a contention protocol because it allows devices on a network to simultaneously place data on the network, which will result in a collision. It is up to the devices to then compete (or contend) for network access.

## Step 2.

   a. Token passing can be used with the bus, ring, or star topologies.

   b. IBM developed the Token Ring protocol suite.

   c. False. Token passing is not a contention network access method. Token passing is itself a network access method.

## Lab Solution 7.05

### Step 1.

   a. Half-duplex is used to describe communication which occurs in two directions, but only one direction can be used at a time. A non-computer example is two-way radio, in which only one side can communicate at a time. Two-way radio users often have a set of protocols, or behaviors, in which they give a verbal signal ("over" or "roger") when they finish talking, to signal the other person that it's his turn to speak.

   b. Full-duplex describes communications which occur in two directions simultaneously. A non-computer example of this type of communications is a phone conversation.

## Lab Solution 7.06

### Step 1.

   a. The 802.3 standard is often informally referred to as Ethernet, the technology on which the IEEE based its standard.

   b. The access method used by 802.3 is CSMA/CD.

   c. True. The 802.2 standard "links" the upper level protocols to the underlying network.

d. The "100" indicates the speed, which is 100Mbps. "Base" indicates that this cable uses baseband (single channel) signal. The "F" indicates fiber optic cabling.

## Step 2.

a. The 802.5 standard is often informally referred to as Token Ring, the technology that existed before the IEEE committee standardized it in 802.5.

b. The access method used by 802.5 is token passing.

c. The data path on an 802.5 network is 2) unidirectional.

## Step 3.

a. The speed limit of FDDI is 100Mbps while the distance limit is 10 kilometers.

b. FDDI uses a ring topology.

c. FDDI and Token Ring networks both use the ring topology. But while Token Ring has a single ring with traffic going in one direction, FDDI actually has two counter-rotating rings. The first, or primary ring, is the data ring, and the secondary ring can be used for data or be held in reserve to provide fault tolerance. When a fault occurs, the FDDI nodes can use the secondary ring to route traffic around the fault. FDDI stations automatically incorporate this secondary ring into the data path to bypass the fault. If a FDDI network is configured to use both rings for data, the bandwidth is effectively doubled.

d. The American National Standards Institute (ANSI) is the organization that sets the standards for FDDI.

## Step 4.

a. When you connect to a network with dial-up networking the modem takes the place of the network interface card (NIC).

b. The minimum requirements to perform dial-up networking are a client computer with dial-up networking software (built into Windows 95 and later) and a modem properly connected to both it and a phone line. That client will connect to a remote server that has a modem connected to both it and a phone line. The client must be configured with the phone number of the server. The server must be configured as a remote access server, set to answer incoming calls.

c. In order for a client computer to be able to access the network to which the host computer is connected, the host computer must be configured to allow that access.

**Step 5.**

a. The cable options for direct cable connections are parallel, serial, and USB. With parallel or serial connections, the cables must be wired as crossover cables. With USB connections, the cable must have special electronics to switch the signals. Infrared is often overlooked, as it is certainly not a cable, but a wireless technology that uses light waves in the infrared range of the light spectrum to carry signals. It is used for direct connection between computers, especially personal digital appliances (PDAs).

b. A limit to both serial and parallel connections is that they will allow you to directly connect only two computers, while USB allows you to connect several computers. Serial is common and easy to use, but it is the slowest of these three options at a maximum speed of 10KB per second. A basic parallel cable will allow only about 60-80KB per second, and a special parallel cable designed just for direct cable connections (for example, the DirectParallel Universal Fast Cable by Parallel Technologies) works at speeds of up to 500+KB per second on EPP/ECP ports. A USB connection has similar speeds, but has the added benefit of allowing more than two computers to connect. The disadvantage of the USB connection when you are connecting more than two computers is the additional cost of a USB hub or hubs through which to make the multiple connections, and the incremental cost of the special USB cables. Also, USB is not available in all PCs, especially older PCs, and was not supported until Windows 95 OSR 2.1 (or Version B). Infrared is also not supported by all versions of Windows and is in few PCs, although it is in a high percentage of personal data assistants (PDAs) and many notebook computers. The most commonly supported infrared standard is from the Infrared Data Association and is simply referred to by its acronym, IrDA. This standard has a transmission speed of 4Mbps, while another infrared standard, IEEE 802.11, is an Ethernet standard with speeds up to 20Mbps.

c. False. USB allows more than two computers to be directly connected.

**Step 6.** It is very feasible to upgrade the hubs on a 10BaseT network to what are called 10/100 hubs, which can support both 10BaseT and 100BaseT on the same network. You would also use 10/100 NICs, which provide the same support. It would be a good idea to test the cabling before proceeding to see if it needs upgrading. It probably does not, but it doesn't hurt to be sure.

## Lab Solution 7.07

**Step 1.** The network computing "Interactive Ethernet Network Troubleshooting" section of the *Network Design Manual* presents a list of possible symptoms from which to choose. The one that most closely matches this problem is "An Ethernet station node or network peripheral cannot be used or accessed." By clicking "Ethernet station node" you walk through several pages in which you answer questions. As you go through the questions, the following suggestions are offered:

Move the Ethernet station to another port on the repeater or wiring hub and recheck the node operation. If this does not solve the problem, check out the cable to the computer by swapping it with one that you know works, or by testing it with a cable tester. If the cable checks out, then check out the network software and hardware configuration on the computer.

Look for a hub that is malfunctioning or not up to the job. A network can also be brought to its knees by excessive electromagnetic interference (EMI), so you will want to have network technicians check out any cabling that may be exposed to sources of EMI.

**Step 2.** The instructions for Step 2 are complete, and no response is required.

**Step 3.** The instructions for Step 3 are complete, and no response is required.

**Step 4.** Using the network computing "Interactive Ethernet Network Troubleshooting" section of the *Network Design Manual,* the closest match for our problem from the symptoms list was "The whole network is operating slowly." When this was selected, it recommended using a protocol analyzer or network monitoring tool to monitor the network bandwidth utilization and compare with a previously established baseline for the network. Well, this is certainly a job for a network professional. If you work for a larger organization in which technical support jobs are very specialized, you may not have an opportunity to perform this kind of test. In that case, you would call in a person who is responsible for such analysis of the network. In a smaller company, you may well be expected to perform such diagnostics because, in a small company, a small number of people are performing a wider range of jobs. A network that gets slower and slower over time may be a victim of its own popularity—traffic has increased and the bandwidth has become inadequate.

In general, a slow network can be caused by reduced bandwidth, which, in turn, may be caused by increased traffic or a network connection device not functioning or not being up to the standards of the rest of the network (can you say "weakest link?"). Increased traffic may simply be caused by increased normal use of the network, but it can also be caused by unauthorized use of the network—perhaps there are users playing network games, surfing the Internet and downloading large files that are not required for their work. In addition, there can simply be too many protocols on the network. You can install several network protocol stacks into most versions of Windows. This is not done by default, but could be done by an over enthusiastic, uninformed technician. Some of these protocols generate regular broadcasts, even when no one is conscious of using the protocol.

Back to hardware problems again: If you determine that there is a much higher usage of the bandwidth, you may need to upgrade the network, which can mean bringing NICs and all network connection devices up to a higher bandwidth standard—perhaps from 10Mbps to 100Mbps. Further segmenting the network to reduce the number of computers on a segment may resolve the problem without making a major upgrade to gain more bandwidth. However, to really home in on the problem and its eventual solution takes a much more sophisticated analysis of the bandwidth usage than you are expected to do as a hardware service technician.

**Step 5.** This is really a variation of the network connection problem addressed in Steps 1 and 2, and you will troubleshoot it in the same fashion. To show a second approach, the *A+ Certification Study Guide* suggests checking the NIC first, which usually has an indicator light to show that it is connected. If this checks out OK, then test the cable by swapping it for one that you have proven works on another machine, or that you have tested with a cable tester (sound familiar?). It also suggests logging off and back on with the proper network name and password.

OK, you could reboot. Sometimes rebooting resolves problems, but most of us would rather figure out exactly what the problem is than have the computer mysteriously start to behave after a reboot. The older the operating system, the more likely a reboot will "fix" it.

Also, check the configuration of the NIC in the network settings. This is very similar to the other approach, only the focus remains close to the computer whereas the strategy discussed in the solution for answers 1 and 2 looked first at other network hardware.

**Step 6**   Well, just because they say they have an adequate backup system doesn't necessarily mean that it really is, so this should be examined. Since they do perform test restores every three months, they should be able to accurately predict how long it would take to bring up a server if a drive failed, was replaced, and the data restored. This is something that can take from a few hours if everything goes well, to days if the right procedures are not in place. Or the hardware, such as a slow tape backup system, could be inadequate for the job.

In addition, mirroring of drives and other fault-tolerant options such as RAID 5 should be considered. There are also some sophisticated configurations of network servers, such as clustering, in which multiple servers provide a service that appears to be hosted on just one server. If one of the servers fails, another replaces it in automatic "fail over" to the replacement server.

# ANSWERS TO LAB ANALYSIS TEST

1.  The client's statement that this company is an IBM shop for computing and networks indicates that they are using IBM Token Ring, which has a ring topology with special cabling and NICs.

2.  A large routed network hosting Internet services to internal clients will use the TCP/IP protocol stack, and that is what should be installed on the computer.

3.  A ten-year-old network may still have CAT3 cabling, which could account for the slower speed. It should be upgraded to at least CAT5.

4.  For a situation in which running cable from the cabins is not desirable, consider using wireless communications. The *A+ Certification Study Guide* provides information on infrared, but there are also radio wave options.

5.  If users are reporting that the network seems slow, investigate the following possible causes:

    a.   Bandwidth reduced by increased traffic, whether by valid use or by unnecessary traffic

    b.   Inadequate network connection hardware

    c.   EMI interference

# ANSWERS TO KEY TERM QUIZ

**1.** star

**2.** Transmission Control Protocol/ Internet Protocol (TCP/IP)

**3.** twisted pair

**4.** contention

**5.** direct cable connection

EXERCISES • QUESTIONS • ANSWERS

# 8

# Operating System Fundamentals

## LAB EXERCISES

At Nerd Matrix you have now demonstrated your understanding of hardware concepts required for the job of service technician. However, you are still not at all comfortable with operating systems, and dread having to work with them when you are troubleshooting problems on desktop computers. You're lucky that you often can call on a more senior technician when you get stumped, but you realize that you cannot continue to depend on others for the basic skills of your job. Therefore, you have committed to take the A+ Operating System Technologies exam within 6 weeks, and you have gone to the CompTIA web at www.comptia.com, and printed out the corresponding exam objectives. Today you are beginning your study in earnest.

In this chapter you will explore the first of the areas tested in the A+ Operating System Technologies exam. The exam objectives that will be explored here are Windows operating system functions and structure. You will look at basic file and directory management, and the utilities that are useful tools for service technicians.

**LAB EXERCISE 8.01**

# Identifying the Common Windows Components

**1 Hour**

A user interface is the visual component of the operating system through which the user communicates with the OS and the computer. Notice that this definition does not say that a user interface is graphical; some system interfaces use non-graphical characters, but they are still visual. In Windows, the predominant user interface is graphical—known as a Graphical User Interface (GUI)—and includes windows, icons, and other symbols. The graphical surface on which these items are displayed is called the desktop. In this lab you will identify the common Windows graphical components. In later labs you will use the secondary user interface provided in Windows: the Command Prompt—a non-GUI character mode interface.

cross **Reference**

**To prepare for this lab, read the section titled "Common Windows Components" in Certification Objective 8.01 in Chapter 8 of the A+ Certification Study Guide.**

## Learning Objectives

After you've completed this lab, you will be able to identify and explain the characteristics of the common Windows user interface components.

## Lab Materials and Setup

The materials you need for this lab are:

- A PC with Windows 95 or later installed
- Internet access and a web browser

## Getting Down to Business

The following steps will guide you as you research the many elements of the Windows user interface. The lab suggests that you use the Windows Help program, which is accessed from the Start menu—it's called Help and Support in Windows XP Professional). You may also use other sources that are available to you. Several of the most basic components of Windows are not documented in the Help program in most versions of Windows. The term "window" is a good example. If you experience this, try a technical encyclopedia, such as Webopedia at www.webopedia.com.

**Step 1.** Log on to your computer. From the Start Menu select Help.

In the Help program, notice that there are three tabs: Contents, Index, and Search (called Find in Windows NT). Contents and Index are organized much like the Table of Contents and Index of a book. The Search tab lets you do a search of the contents of Help. Use the Help program to look up the definitions of the following components of the Windows user interface, and record them below:

a. Command Prompt

_____

_____

b. Control Panel

_____

_____

c. desktop

_____

_____

d. folder

_____

_____

e. icon

_____

_____

f. My Computer

_____

_____

g. Recycle Bin

_____

_____

h. shortcut

_____

_____

i. shortcut menu

_____

_____

j. taskbar

_____

_____

k. window

_____

_____

l. Windows Explorer

_____

_____

In this lab you researched the common user interface components found in Windows operating systems.

**LAB EXERCISE 8.02**

# Identifying the Differences Between Windows Operating Systems

**30 Minutes**

On a typical day at Nerd Matrix, you may visit several client sites where you are expected to solve problems on desktop computers regardless of which Windows operating system is installed. For this reason, you have decided to learn more about the differences among the versions of Windows you are most likely to encounter: Windows 9x, Windows NT, Windows 2000, and Windows XP. Your friends who have taken the A+ Operating System Technologies exam have told you that you do not need to know anything about XP to pass the exam. However, you have included XP in your research for two reasons: 1) you will encounter it on the job, and 2) the CompTIA exams do get revised on a regular basis to keep up with new technologies, and Windows XP will eventually be included.

*To prepare for this lab, read the section titled "Contrasts Between Windows 9x and Windows 2000" in Certification Objective 8.01 in Chapter 8 of the A+ Certification Study Guide. Be sure to complete Exercise 8-1.*

## Learning Objectives

The Windows operating systems are very complex, and you know that only hands-on experience will acquaint you with the idiosyncrasies of the various versions. Your current objective is to understand the general differences among these operating systems. Once you've completed this lab, you will be able to:

■ Identify the common Windows operating systems

■ Identify the major security differences between Windows operating systems

■ Identify the major network configuration differences between Windows operating systems

## Lab Materials and Setup

The materials you'll need for this lab are:

- ■ A PC with Windows 95 or greater installed
- ■ Internet access and a web browser

## Getting Down to Business

In this lab you will use the Internet to find information on Windows operating systems.

**lab**
**Hint**   *All references to Windows XP refer to Windows XP Professional, although it is not always stated in the text.*

**Step I.**   For this step we recommend two resources: the Windows pages at the Microsoft web site (www.microsoft.com/windows) and Microsoft's online TechNet database at www.microsoft.com/technet. Using these and other sites, find the answers to the questions below.

a. What are the Windows 2000 operating systems and their features?

_____

_____

b. Which Windows 2000 product should a PC service technician expect to encounter on desktop computers in medium to large organizations?

_____

_____

c. How do Windows NT, Windows 2000 and Windows XP differ from Windows 9x?

_____

_____

d. Can you expect to find Windows 9x on desktop computers in medium to large organizations?

_____

_____

**Step 2.** Determine the version of the operating system residing on your classroom computer and record it below. One place to find this information is on the General tab of the System Properties dialog box.

---

**LAB EXERCISE 8.03**

# Identifying the Major System Files—Their Locations, Functions, and Content

I Hour

You are making good progress in learning the fundamentals of operating systems. The next step is to learn about some special files in each of the Microsoft operating systems. These are files that are critical to the functioning of the operating system. These files have a wide range of control over the operating system, and we lump them together under the category of "system files." CompTIA lists several of these files in their exam objectives for the A+ Operating System Technologies exam.

## Learning Objectives

In this lab you will research the location of and the functionality that individual system files provide to the operating systems that use them. After you complete this lab you will be able to:

- Locate key system files for Windows 9x, Windows NT, Windows 2000, and Windows XP

- Define the function of key system files for Windows 9x, Windows NT, Windows 2000, and Windows XP

- Identify Common Utilities for Windows 9x, Windows NT, Windows 2000, and Windows XP

## Lab Materials and Setup

The materials you need for this lab are:

■ A PC with Windows 95 or later installed

■ Internet access and a web browser

## Getting Down to Business

In the following steps you will research key system files and utilities to identify their location on disk, their purpose to the operating system, and their importance to you as a service technician.

cross
**Reference**

*To prepare for this lab, read Certification Objective 8.02 in Chapter 8 of the A+ Certification Study Guide up to the section titled "Command-Line Files." Be sure to complete Exercise 8-2 and to review each Scenario & Solution.*

**Step 1.** These important system files are often hidden, which means that a special attribute of the file, the *hidden* attribute is turned on. In addition, they often have another special attribute, the *system* attribute, which further identifies them as being special to the operating system. Special attributes allow the user interface to protect these files from damage due to carelessness. Imagine someone noticing a file with a strange name, and deciding to delete it because he doesn't know what it does. Then the operating system loses the functionality provided by that file, and perhaps is totally disabled. For this reason the default setting for viewing folders in My Computer and Explorer is not to allow either hidden files or system files to be visible. However while learning about these system files, you will want to browse your hard drive and look for the system files for your operating system. In this step you make such files visible in the user interface.

In Windows 2000 and Windows XP access Folder Options in the Control Panel. In XP, you will have to browse through the categories in Control Panel, or switch it to Classic View, which will allow you to view the Control Panel icons directly without searching through the categories. In all cases, you will also want to deselect the setting *Hide file extensions for known file types* and *Hide protected operating system Files.* In Windows XP you will also want to select the setting *Display the contents of system folders.* Figure 8-1 shows the Folder Options dialog box on a Windows 2000 Professional computer with these View settings.

Folder Options
View settings in
Windows 2000
Professional

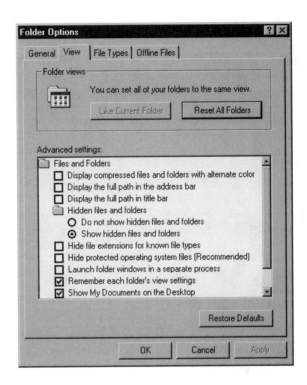

**lab**
**Warning** *These settings are not recommended for every user or every situation. Use these settings only when it is critical that you see all the files—including the system files. In general, that would be when learning—as now—or when troubleshooting. If you change settings on any computer for this exercise, be sure to change them back to a more secure setting when you are finished.*

**Step 2.** Using a reference source such as the *A+ Certification Study Guide* or one of the Internet sites you have used previously, fill in Table 8-1. It contains a list of Windows 9x system files. For each file fill in the location and function of the file.

**Step 3.** Windows 9x also has several utilities that are handy for system recovery and troubleshooting. Using a reference source such as the *A+ Certification Study Guide* or one of the Internet sites you have used previously, fill in Table 8-2. It contains a list of Windows 9x utility files. For each utility fill in the function.

**TABLE 8-1**     Windows 9x System Files

| Filename | Location | Function |
|---|---|---|
| IO.SYS | | |
| MSDOS.SYS | | |
| WIN.COM | | |
| SYSTEM.DAT | | |
| USER.DAT | | |
| WIN.INI | | |
| SYSTEM.INI | | |
| CONFIG.SYS | | |
| AUTOEXEC.BAT | | |

| TABLE 8-2 | Windows 9x Utilities |

| Utility name | Function |
|---|---|
| Automatic Skip Driver | |
| Device Manager | |
| WINDOWS 98 System Configuration Utility (MSCONFIG.EXE) | |
| REGEDIT.EXE | |
| SCANREG.EXE | |
| System Configuration Editor (SYSEDIT.EXE) | |
| Windows Scripting Host (WSCRIPT.EXE) | |

**Step 4.** Using a reference source such as the *A+ Certification Study Guide* or one of the Internet sites you have used previously, fill in Table 8-3. It contains a list of system files unique to Windows NT/2000/XP. For each file fill in the location and function of the file.

**Step 5.** Windows NT, Windows 2000, and Windows XP also have several utilities that are handy for system recovery and troubleshooting. Using a reference source such as the *A+ Certification Study Guide* or one of the Internet sites you have used previously, fill in Table 8-4. It contains a list of utility files that are listed in the A+ Operating System Technologies exam objective. Computer Management is not included in Windows NT. At this writing Windows XP is not on the exam, but we mention it here because these utilities are available in that operating system. For each utility fill in the function.

**TABLE 8-3**  Windows NT/2000/XP System Files

| Filename | Location | Function |
|----------|----------|----------|
| BOOT.INI |  |  |
| NTLDR |  |  |
| NTDETECT.COM |  |  |
| NTBOOTDD.SYS |  |  |

**TABLE 8-4**  Windows NT/2000/XP Utilities

| Utility name | Function |
|--------------|----------|
| Computer Management |  |
| Device Manager |  |
| REGEDIT.EXE |  |
| REGEDT32 |  |
| Windows Scripting Host (WSCRIPT.EXE) |  |

**Step 6.** The published A+ Operating System Technologies exam objectives list several terms under the category of "memory management." Therefore, you can count on at least one question involving memory management. What is it? Something that, for the most part, we have not cared about since before Windows 95. This is only a small exaggeration. Actually, advanced operating systems do a great deal of memory management, but it is not something we typically have to configure and control as we did in the DOS and Windows 3.X days. There is, however, one term under memory management that is still viable in operating systems today: virtual memory. Once again, using a reference source such as the *A+ Certification Study Guide* or one of the Internet sites you have used previously, fill in the definitions in Table 8-5. It contains a list of memory management terms that may appear on the exam. It also doesn't hurt (too much) to understand some of the technologies that preceded our current versions of Windows.

**TABLE 8-5**     Memory Management Terminology

| Term | Description |
| --- | --- |
| Conventional Memory | |
| Upper Memory | |
| Extended and High Memory | |
| Expanded Memory | |
| Virtual Memory | |

# Exploring Command Prompt Commands and Their Syntax

I Hour

In Windows when you open a command prompt you are accessing a DOS command shell. You can call this up in Windows 9x from Start Menu | Programs | MS-DOS Prompt or by entering **command** at the Windows Run command.

In Windows NT, Windows 2000, and Windows XP there are actually two command prompt environments. The one that is accessed from the Start Menu | Programs | Accessories | Command Prompt is a 32-bit character-mode environment. Another way to open this same 32-bit command shell is by entering **cmd** at the Start Menu | Run command. Opening up this command prompt does not open a virtual machine. (New term to you? Look up "virtual machine" at www.webopedia.com.)

However, if you start a command prompt in NT, Windows 2000, or Windows XP by using the COMMAND.COM program, say by opening Start | Run and typing **command**, you *are* in a virtual machine. If you do not see the difference here, please be patient. We will try to demonstrate it for you. Figure 8-2 shows two command prompt windows in Windows XP. The one on the top was opened by selecting Start | All Programs | Accessories | Command Prompt. Notice it gives the version as "Microsoft Windows XP" (please ignore the numerical version). Notice that in this version of the command prompt the entire long filename for the folder "Documents and Settings" is displayed.

**FIGURE 8-2**

Two Command Prompt windows

The bottom window was opened with the second method. Notice the version is "Microsoft® Windows DOS" and that the long filename for the folder is converted to a short filename. There are also other results you may get depending on the version of Windows you are running. As you can see, Windows XP opened focusing on the Documents and Settings folder of the current user. NT 4.0 and Windows 2000 focus on the root folder of the drive on which the operating system is installed. For instance, if your operating system is installed in C:\WINNT, the command prompt in NT 4.0 and Windows 2000 would open focused on C:\. However, you would see similar version differences, with the second method showing up as DOS. We will also demonstrate the virtual machine aspects of the second method in the steps below.

Why should you care about this difference? A virtual machine takes up more memory and may limit the scope of certain commands to just that virtual machine, some commands behave differently in a virtual machine, and others will not run in a virtual machine.

## Learning Objectives

After you complete this lab you will be able to:

- Distinguish between the two command shells supported by Windows NT, Windows 2000 and Windows XP
- Understand the basic command syntax for shell commands
- Work with common shell commands

## Lab Materials and Setup

The materials you need for this lab are:

- A PC with Windows 95 or later installed

## Getting Down to Business

In the following steps you will work with the two types of command shells to learn how to:

- Distinguish between the two command shells supported by both Windows 2000 and Windows XP
- Work with common shell commands

cross
**Reference**    *To prepare for this lab, read the section "Command-Line Files" in Chapter 8 of the A+ Certification Study Guide.*

**Step 1.**    If you are running Windows 2000, Windows NT, or Windows XP, do this step. If you are running Windows 9x, skip this step, but take time to read through it before moving on to Step 2.

Make sure that all windows are closed, not just minimized. Open Task Manager on the desktop. Click the Options menu and clear the check next to *Always On Top.* Click on the **Processes** tab and ensure that NTVDM is not listed. NTVDM is the code that supports NT Virtual DOS Machines in Windows 2000, Windows NT, and Windows XP. Leave Task Manager open on the desktop.

Open a command prompt by clicking Start I Run and entering **cmd**. Leave this window on the desktop and switch to Task Manager.

    a.  Is NTVDM showing as a new process?

    _____

    b.  What new process appears in Task Manager?

    _____

Leave the first command prompt open on the desktop. Open the second command prompt by entering **command** in the Run box. Switch to Task Manager.

    c.  What new process appears in Task Manager?

    _____

Click on the Applications tab in Task Manager and notice that the two command prompts appear there with their full path and filenames. Close all the windows on the desktop.

lab
  **Hint**    *In the following steps you will be working with various command prompt commands. If you do not know the syntax for a command, simply type the command name followed by /? and help information for the command will appear. To see a list of commands and their descriptions, simply type **help** at the command prompt.*

**Step 2.**   In this step you will create a new folder by running a command from the command prompt. From the start menu, navigate to the shortcut for the Command Prompt, and click on it.

From the Command Prompt use the Make Directory (MD) command to create a folder named MYFOLDER.

Now use the DIR command to verify that your folder was created. Figure 8-3 shows the use of the MD command, followed by the result of the DIR command, which confirmed that the new folder, MYFOLDER, was created.

**Step 3**   Use the CLS command to clear the screen of the output from the previous commands (just to be tidy), then use the Change Directory command (CD) to change to the new folder, as shown.

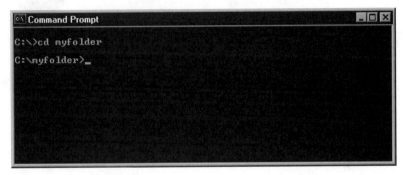

**Step 4**   Open Windows Explorer and browse to your new folder. Open MYFOLDER in Windows Explorer, and create 5 new text documents named ONE.TXT, TWO.TXT, THREE.TXT, FOUR.TXT, and FIVE.TXT. (If you right-click in the details pane containing the contents of MYFOLDER, you can select New | Text Document from the shortcut menu. The document will be created, given the name New Text Document.txt, which you can rename to ONE.TXT. Repeat these steps for each file.)

**Step 5**   Switch to the command prompt and use the DIR command to see the new files in MYFOLDER.

**FIGURE 8-3**

Using the MD and
DIR commands

```
Command Prompt                                                        _ □ ✕

C:\>md myfolder

C:\>dir
 Volume in drive C has no label.
 Volume Serial Number is 407B-B9E1

 Directory of C:\

01/17/2001  02:13p       <DIR>          CanonBJ
10/22/2001  03:35p       <DIR>          captures
08/02/2001  03:24p       <DIR>          collwin
10/23/2001  10:13a       <DIR>          data
05/19/2001  10:00a       <DIR>          DeLorme Docs
09/04/2001  12:30a       <DIR>          Documents and Settings
08/04/2001  12:26p       <DIR>          Downloads
07/05/2000  04:11p       <DIR>          drivers
10/23/2001  10:00a       <DIR>          folder
06/21/2001  05:45p       <DIR>          Inetpub
06/21/2001  05:44p       <DIR>          MSSQL7
05/31/2000  04:43p       <DIR>          My Music
10/23/2001  10:17a       <DIR>          myfolder
09/08/2001  08:06a       <DIR>          PerfLogs
10/22/2001  07:00a       <DIR>          Program Files
01/04/2001  07:03p       <DIR>          technet
10/20/2001  02:43p       <DIR>          temp
10/02/2001  08:25p       <DIR>          Windows Update Setup Files
10/22/2001  08:59p       <DIR>          WINNT
               0 File(s)              0 bytes
              19 Dir(s)   1,559,228,416 bytes free

C:\>_
```

Use the ATTRIB command to view the attributes on these files. You should see a listing similar to this one, which shows the results of the DIR command and the ATTRIB command.

```
Command Prompt                                                        _ □ ✕

C:\myfolder>dir
 Volume in drive C has no label.
 Volume Serial Number is 407B-B9E1

 Directory of C:\myfolder

10/23/2001  10:31a       <DIR>          .
10/23/2001  10:31a       <DIR>          ..
10/23/2001  10:31a                    0 five.txt
10/23/2001  10:31a                    0 four.txt
10/23/2001  10:30a                    0 one.txt
10/23/2001  10:31a                    0 three.txt
10/23/2001  10:31a                    0 two.txt
               5 File(s)              0 bytes
               2 Dir(s)   1,558,466,560 bytes free

C:\myfolder>attrib
A            C:\myfolder\five.txt
A            C:\myfolder\four.txt
A            C:\myfolder\one.txt
A            C:\myfolder\three.txt
A            C:\myfolder\two.txt

C:\myfolder>
```

Use the ATTRIB command to turn on (or "set") the read-only and hidden attributes on the file ONE.TXT. Then, use the ATTRIB command to confirm that these attributes were set, as shown.

Now, we aren't going to help you with this next use of ATTRIB (unless you peek at the Lab Solutions). Use the ATTRIB command to turn off the Read-only and Hidden attributes on the file ONE.TXT. Then use the ATTRIB command to confirm that the command worked.

**Step 6**  Still working in the command prompt, enter the following: EDIT.EXE. Record the result of entering this command:

_____

_____

**Step 7**  Still working in the command prompt, enter the following: EDIT.COM. Record the result of entering this command:

_____

_____

Exit and return to the command prompt.

**Step 8**  Still working in the command prompt, enter the following: EDIT. Record the result of entering this command:

_____

_____

On your own, repeat steps 6, 7, and 8 using CMD.COM and CMD.EXE.

lab
ⓗint

*In steps 5 and 6 you provided both the filename and extension (EDIT.EXE, for example). So Windows searched for a file named EDIT.EXE. When it could not locate that file in the paths in which it searches for executables, it gave you an error message. More often we start commands using only the filename of an executable file, without specifying the extension. Windows (and DOS) attempts to locate an executable that has the filename you have provided.*

*When you enter a string of characters that does not include an extension, the operating system searches in memory for a command that is always in memory (like the COPY command—it does not run from an executable file, but from code stored in memory). Next, the operating system searches in the current directory for a file with that filename, but with various extensions (COM, EXE, BAT, CMD, etc.). If it finds a match, then it executes the program code in the file it found. If it does not find a match, it searches elsewhere, going through directory paths that are held in memory as the environment variable PATH.*

When you have completed this lab, close all open windows on the desktop.

In this lab you worked with the Windows command prompt using several commands to perform file management. You have also explored the mechanism of executing commands from the command prompt.

## LAB EXERCISE 8.05

I Hour

# Perform File and Folder Management and Other Tasks

Sometimes, after you have delivered and set up a computer for a customer, you need to add or modify drivers or customize the desktop for the customer. Perhaps you are asked to provide an easy way to open a frequently used program. Such a simple request! You may also be called upon to do some simple file management tasks. Although you have become quite competent with the hardware, do you choke when it comes to using the operating system in front of a customer? Then you need to become comfortable with using the Windows operating systems so that you can do tasks related to your job. Practice working with Windows so that you can do several typical tasks without having to search around and experiment in front of the customer. This lab will give you opportunities to navigate the Windows operating system while performing some typical tasks.

## Learning Objectives

After you complete this lab you will be able to:

- Create shortcuts for programs
- Map a network drive and create a shortcut
- Create a folder from the GUI
- Perform several file management tasks

## Lab Materials and Setup

For this lab exercise, you'll need:

- A PC with Windows 95 or later installed
- A shared folder on another computer on the classroom network with permission to access it

## Getting Down to Business

In this exercise, you will practice some basic tasks. The instructions in the steps will give some detail, but if you need more instructions on how to do any of these, use the Help program of your operating system, or other resources, to discover the exact steps you must take.

**cross
Reference**

*To prepare for this lab, read Certification Objective 8.03 in Chapter 8 of the* **A+ Certification Study Guide** *in its entirety. Be sure to do the exercises and review each Scenario and Solution.*

**Step 1.** First, let's take care of the client's request for an easy way to open a frequently used program. One way to do this is to put a shortcut to the program on the desktop or place it on the top of the Start Menu. You will practice this below. Another little productivity enhancement is to place a shortcut to a mapped network drive on the desktop. This way the user doesn't have to open up My Computer to get to Explorer to access the network resources. This also requires knowing how to map network drives. Below, we list the three tasks you should practice. If you have not done this before, use Windows Help to find out the steps that you have to perform. We also provide these steps in the Lab Solutions.

    a. Create a shortcut on the desktop to a word processing program such as MS Word or WordPad.

    b. Create a shortcut on the Start Menu to the Calculator program.

    c. Create a shortcut on your desktop to a mapped drive. (This requires a network share on another computer that you are given permission to access.)

**Step 2.**   Right-click on My Computer and click Open or Explore (we prefer Explore). Navigate to your C: drive and create a folder using your first name as the folder name.

**Step 3.**   Copy two files from the folder MYFOLDER into the new folder. Be very careful not to Cut the files, which will delete them from the source location after copying them to your folder.

**Step 4.**   Click on one of the copied files to select it. Then press the Delete key. You will receive a message similar to the one shown here. Click Yes to delete the file. Leave the folder window open while you proceed to the next step.

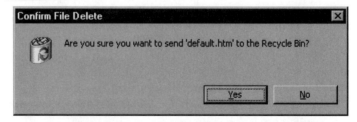

**Step 5.**   Open the Recycle Bin, find the file you just deleted, right-click on the file, and select Restore. Switch back to the Windows Explorer and verify that the file was restored to the folder.

Now you will delete it permanently, so that it is not saved in the Recycle Bin. Select the file once again. Then press and hold the Shift key while you press the Delete key. You will see the Confirm File Delete message box:

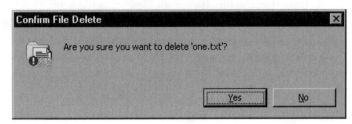

Open the Recycle Bin and confirm that the deleted file is not in the Recycle Bin. If there are other files here that you know you want permanently deleted, you can do it right in the Recycle Bin. After all, that is what it is for. It allows us to have second thoughts about files we may have deleted in error, but you should look into it frequently—perhaps once a week—to see if there are files that should be permanently deleted.

**Step 6.** Return to the window containing your folder, and right-click on the remaining file. Open the Properties dialog box for the file. Notice the file attributes on the general tab. Add a check to Read-only and Hidden to turn on these attributes. Click the OK button to close the Properties dialog box. Notice the change to the icon for the file. Try to delete the file. Notice the message that appears, but do not continue with the delete.

Open the Properties dialog box for the file and remove the Read-only and Hidden attributes. Then click OK to close the Properties dialog box.

Try to delete the file again, and notice the difference in the message that appears.

**Step 7.** File extensions (the 3-character portion of the file name after the period) have special meaning to your operating system. You could say that a file extension creates an expectation that the file is of a certain format. For instance, an EXE file extension indicates that a file is an executable with a certain file structure. But simply giving a file an EXE extension does not make it an executable. There are many other file structures for files that contain program code, like COM and DLL files.

Similarly, there are certain file structures for data files. Perhaps the most simple data file is what we call a "text" file. This is a file that can be read and edited with a simple text editor (like Notepad), a graphical program, or the command line text editor, Edit. The file extension is the operating system's first clue as to how it should handle a file. If you double click a file with an EXE extension Windows will attempt to execute the code within the file. If you double-click a file with a TXT extension, Windows will attempt to load the default program it has associated with that type of file, and it will open the file in that program so that the file is ready to edit.

When you created your files, you created them as text files, and they were given TXT extensions. If the remaining file in your new directory still has its TXT extension, you should be able to double-click the file, and it will open in a text editor. In Windows, this is usually Notepad.

Double-click the text file you created. The file is empty, because you were not told to add any text to the file. Type a message into the file, save it, and close the text editor.

**Step 8.** Rename the file you edited, removing the TXT extension. Double-click on the file again.

Can you still load this file in Notepad? Record the result below:

---

# Preparing New Hard Disks

**1 Hour**

The last area of operating system fundamentals is disk management. For your job and for the exam, you need to understand how a hard disk is prepared for use. A brand new hard drive needs to first be partitioned, which is the process of defining the boundaries of one or more logical volumes (partitions) on the drive. Each partition is assigned a logical drive letter. Then each partition must be formatted, which involves placing onto the drive the logical structure that a file system uses to organize data.

## Learning Objectives

After you've completed this lab, you will be able to:

- Describe the process of preparing a hard drive for use
- Identify the common file systems in use by Windows operating systems

## Lab Materials and Setup

The materials you need for this lab are:

- A PC with Windows 95 or later installed
- Internet access and a web browser

## Getting Down to Business

Your boss at Nerd Matrix has suggested that you need to be able to prepare hard drives for use in any of the common operating systems. Up to now you have been using pre-prepared hard drives when you made a hard drive installation. It is time for you to research the processes involved in appropriately configuring hard drives right out of the box to be used in any of the computer systems you are likely to encounter. The following steps will help you find your way.

cross **Reference**

*To prepare for this lab, read the section "Certification Objective 8.04" in Chapter 8 of the* **A+ Certification Study Guide**.

**Step 1.** Use your Internet browser to connect to the Microsoft TechNet site at www.microsoft.com/technet and research which tool you would use to partition a disk and prepare it for use with each of the following operating systems.

    a. DOS _____

    b. Windows 9x_____

    c. Windows 2000_____

    d. Windows XP _____

**Step 2.** In this step you will determine the file system in use on your lab computer. One way to do this is to use My Computer or Windows Explorer and look at the Properties dialog box of each of the disk drives. Record below the file system(s) in use on your computer:

a. Drive C: _____

b. Drive D (if present as a hard drive partition): _____

**Step 3.** Find a classroom lab computer that has the NTFS file system on a drive. Find another classroom lab computer (it could be the same one) that has a drive with either FAT16 or FAT32. On each of these drives, select a file or folder, and look at the properties dialog for that file or folder. What is the main difference between a FAT file system and the NTFS file system? Record your observation below:

_____

_____

**Step 4.** Microsoft introduced a new version of the NTFS file system with Windows 2000, NTFS version 5 (NTFS5). This is also the same version used by Windows XP. In fact, if you install either of these operating systems on a hard drive with an existing NTFS file system, the install program will upgrade NTFS to NTFS5. While it is true that only these operating systems can use the new capabilities of this version, the Microsoft team had to allow for those who would want to dual-boot between NT 4.0 and Windows 2000 or Windows XP. Therefore, in one of the NT 4.0 service packs, they cleverly added compatibility (not support—just the ability to exist on NTFS5 without breaking). If an NT 4.0 computer with an NTFS drive on it has this level service pack or greater, one of these newer operating systems can be installed in a dual boot configuration and you can successfully run NT 4.0 after the installation. Using your favorite source of Microsoft technical information, determine which NT 4.0 service pack added compatibility with NTFS5.

_____

_____

**Step 5.** NTFS (in either version) sounds pretty nifty, but what if you install Windows 2000 or Windows XP onto a FAT drive. Are you stuck with it? Actually no.

There is a command that has been available since NT 4.0 to allow an administrator to convert a FAT volume to an NTFS volume, which the current operating system supports. Research this command, and enter below the exact command line syntax you would use to convert drive D: from FAT to NTFS.

_____

_____

# LAB ANALYSIS TEST

**1.** Algonquin Antique Auctions is moving to new offices and buying all new desktop computers. The office manager, Alexis, is very concerned about security because they had an incident with their old system involving someone accessing confidential data on a Windows 95 computer. What can you tell Alexis about the Windows operating systems in regard to their security needs?

_____

_____

**2.** Nerd Matrix has received a call from a client who is concerned that he may have deleted an important system file from his Windows 2000 Professional computer. It took some effort, but he finally deleted the IO.SYS file while in Windows Explorer. Now he is wondering whether this was an important file and is afraid to shut down his computer. He adds that he saw plenty of others to delete that he doesn't use—like that file, BOOT.INI—it sure sounds like something a virus must have put on his hard drive. How can you help this client?

_____

_____

**3.** You have been called to a site where a Windows 98 computer will start, but it is slow and some of the programs will not run. After many questions, the customer admits that a friend had visited him and installed some new software. His friend made some changes  to make his computer run better. He saw his friend edit some files—"config-something" and "auto-something." What utility can you use to test various configuration options on a Windows 98 computer?

_____

_____

**4.** A customer has complained to you that she dislikes using My Computer because she cannot see the "big picture." What can you suggest to this customer?

_____

_____

**5.** Algonquin Antique Auctions has decided to use Windows XP Professional on their desktop computers, thanks to your recommendation. However, Alexis installed it on one computer and is disappointed that she does not have file security. She shares the computer with a part-time appraiser, and they find that they can both see each other's files. What can you suggest to them?

_____

_____

# KEY TERM QUIZ

Use the following vocabulary terms to complete the sentences below. Not all of the terms will be used.

Device Manager

BOOT.INI

virtual memory

CONFIG.SYS

attribute

conventional

file extensions

upper memory

components

REGEDIT

1. The _____ utility that comes with Windows 9x, Windows 2000, and Windows XP allows you to directly edit the registry.

2. On Windows NT, Windows 2000, and Windows XP computers, the _____ file provides information about the location of operating system files during bootup.

3. The Hidden file _____ is a simple means of protecting important files so that they are either not visible or are greyed out in the GUI.

4. The DOS operating system limited the memory used by an application to an area called _____ memory.

5. Windows operating systems are able to load more programs and data into memory than the physical memory can hold because they use _____ .

# LAB WRAP-UP

It certainly is good to have the fundamentals behind us that help us understand what an operating system is and how it works. Now we can move on to the things that a service technician will actually do like installing, configuring, upgrading, and troubleshooting. As you do those tasks it will certainly help to understand the things you learned in this chapter, like the functions of operating systems, the system files, command prompts, and file systems.

# LAB SOLUTIONS FOR CHAPTER 8

In this section, you'll find solutions to the lab exercises, Lab Analysis Test, and Key Term Quiz.

## Lab Solution 8.01

**Step 1.**    Answers may vary, but should generally agree with the following:

a. The *Command Prompt* in Windows 2000 is a non-GUI character mode window from which you can launch any program that will run in Windows 2000. One value of the command line interface is that there are many useful command line utilities that technical support personnel frequently use. Also, technical support people often create "shell scripts" (also called batch files) to automate repetitive administrative tasks. [This definition was mainly derived from experience and knowledge of Windows. We disagree with the definition we found in the Windows 2000 Help Glossary, which defines a command prompt window as a window displayed on the desktop to interface with the MS-DOS operating system. This is *not* exactly true, especially for any version of Windows after Windows 95 and Windows 98. Windows NT, Windows 2000, and Windows XP actually have two versions of the Command Prompt. We will explore this in Lab 8.04.]

b. The *Control Panel* is a special folder in Windows that contains icons for programs to configure various components of the operating system, such as the clock, video display, folders, game controllers, keyboard, mail, mouse, network, and printers. There are also icons for adding and removing software and hardware. Settings created and modified in Control Panel are saved in the registry—a central database of all Windows settings. [This definition was not available in Windows 2000 Professional Help, but was included in Windows XP Professional Help.]

c. The *desktop* is the area that first appears on the screen after you start Windows. This is your workspace, much as your physical desktop is a workspace. [This definition was found in Chapter 4 of Windows 2000 Help in an article titled "What is the Desktop?"]

d. A *folder* is a container for documents and programs.

e. An *icon* is a small graphic that represents files, folders, or programs. Double-clicking on an icon will cause an action appropriate to the type of object it represents. If you double-click on a file that is associated with a program (a special relationship that the operating system understands), the program will run, and the file will be opened by the program. If you double-click on a folder, the folder will open. If you double-click on a program, the program will run.

f. *My Computer* is an icon on the desktop that, when double-clicked, displays the local and mapped drive icons. You can then open each of the drive icons and browse the contents of the drives.

g. The *Recycle Bin* is a special folder on the Windows desktop that stores deleted files. Deleted files in the recycle bin can be "undeleted" if you discover you have deleted them in error. Storing files in this way—so that we can second-guess ourselves—does come with a price: disk space. You will want to clean out the Recycle Bin on a regular basis to keep from eating up too much disk space.

h. A *shortcut* is a special icon that acts as a pointer to a file, folder, or program. Double-clicking a shortcut icon will produce the same results as double-clicking on a normal icon, as described above. Deleting, moving, or renaming a shortcut will not affect the object it represents because the shortcut is only a pointer to the object. The location of the object it represents is not changed by the creation of the shortcut. A small bent arrow on its lower left corner identifies an icon as a shortcut.

i. A *shortcut menu* is a menu that appears when you right-click on an object in Windows. This menu lists common commands for the object selected.

j. The *taskbar* is a graphical bar, normally at the bottom of the Windows desktop (although it can be moved elsewhere) that contains the Start Button, buttons for active programs, and Taskbar Toolbars (only one, the Quick Launch toolbar, is on the Windows 2000 Taskbar by default).

k. A *window* is a portion of the screen where programs and processes can be run. A window has standard graphical elements, such as borders, title bars, and menus. Several windows can be open simultaneously, and they can be independently closed, resized, moved, maximized (take up the entire screen area), and minimized (reduced to a button on the task bar). [We found this definition in the Windows XP Professional Help Glossary; there was no definition for "window" in Windows 2000 Professional Help.]

l.  *Windows Explorer* is a component program of Windows that allows you to view files and folders in a hierarchical structure in a single window, rather than opening disks and folders in separate windows.

## Lab Solution 8.02

**Step 1.**

a.  The actual Windows 2000 products are Windows 2000 Professional, Windows 2000 Server, Windows 2000 Advanced Server, and Windows 2000 Datacenter Server. All the Windows 2000 products are built on NT technology and they have the underlying capabilities that began with NT, but the look and functionality of the Windows 98 user interface. Windows 2000 also has full PnP support—something that was not in Windows NT—and security, reliability, and manageability enhancements over NT. Upgrading from Windows 9x to Windows 2000 Professional will bring all of this to the desktop. Windows 2000 Professional is intended for the desktop.

Windows 2000 Server is the same operating system optimized for use on servers. It comes bundled with a variety of services and programs that do not come with Windows 2000 Professional and cannot be installed on a Windows 2000 Professional computer.

Windows 2000 Professional supports up to 2 processors with Symmetric Multiprocessing (SMP), the ability to deploy active threads of applications across multiple processors. Windows 2000 Server supports up to 4 processors per system. Windows 2000 Advanced Server supports up to 8 processors per system. Windows 2000 Datacenter server supports up to 32 processors per system, and is available only directly from manufacturers who bundle it with their most powerful servers. There are other differences among the server versions of Windows 2000, which are beyond the scope of this book.

b.  Of the Windows 2000 products, a PC service technician should expect to encounter Windows 2000 Professional on desktop computers. This is the most powerful operating system in this family aimed at the desktop market.

lab
①int

*Up until the Beta 2 release, Windows 2000 was supposed to be named NT 5.0. In fact, you can still find references to NT 5.0 if you dig deep enough into the files and registry.*

c. Windows 95 and Windows 98 (and all their sub-versions) do not provide the local security of Windows NT, Windows 2000, or Windows XP. A user at a Windows 95 or Windows 98 computer can log on to and participate in a Microsoft Windows NT or Active Directory domain, but the computer itself cannot be a member of that domain. Windows NT, Windows 2000, and Windows XP Professional computers can join a domain. All these computers are capable of establishing a secure trust relationship with the domain, thus enhancing the security and management of these computers.

d. Yes, you can expect to find Windows 9x on desktop computers in medium to large organizations. Many organizations stayed with these operating systems because they provided better compatibility with hardware than Windows NT. Since the advent of Windows 2000 and, more recently, Windows XP (both of which are PnP and have relatively easy installations), the Windows 9x operating systems are being phased out. This is usually done at the end of a hardware lease period, not as a major rollout of the operating systems.

**Step 2.** Answers will vary based on the version of Windows installed on the lab computer.

The result of looking at the System Properties on one Windows 2000 computer showed that it was "Microsoft Windows 2000 5.00.2195, Service Pack 2."

## Lab Solution 8.03

**Step 1.** This step does not require any response or answers.

**Step 2.** Refer to Table 8-6: Windows 9x System Files—Answers.

**Step 3.** Refer to Table 8-7: Windows 9x Utilities—Answers.

| TABLE 8-6 | Windows 9x System Files—Answers |
|-----------|----------------------------------|

| Filename | Location | Function |
|----------|----------|---------|
| IO.SYS | C:\ | Critical to the early stages of the Windows 9x boot process. It finds and loads other system files, and provides the OS with details about the hardware installed. It is a required file. |
| MSDOS.SYS | C:\ | In Windows 9x this is a text file that is read during bootup. It contains startup configuration information, including which OS to start (Windows 9x or DOS—very important on a multi-boot system), the location of required boot files, the default boot mode, and the display duration for the Windows startup screen. MSDOS.SYS is a required file. |
| WIN.COM | C:\*Windows*\* | When IO.SYS completes its duties during startup it loads WIN.COM and hands control over to it. WIN.COM loads the rest of the Windows 9x operating system. |
| SYSTEM.DAT | C:\*Windows*\* | This is the file that contains the computer-specific registry settings that determine how the OS and hardware interact. These settings include the names and locations of drivers and their configuration settings. Windows 9x saves all computer setting changes of the registry to this file, saving the previous version of the file in a file named SYSTEM.DA0 (zero). If SYSTEM.DAT is missing or corrupt during bootup, the operating system will use SYSTEM.DA0. SYSTEM.DAT is a required file. Windows 9x will not run if it cannot find either it or the backup file. |
| USER.DAT | C:\*Windows*\* | This is the file that contains the user-specific registry settings including preferences for installed applications and user desktop settings. By default this file is stored in the Windows directory, and used by all users who log on to the Windows 9x computer. If user profiles are enabled on a Windows 9x computer, the USER.DAT file is stored locally with the user's profile, which is a folder containing files, folders, and shortcuts that make up the user's Start Menu, registry settings (USER.DAT), and other files and folders. The previous version of USER.DAT is saved in a file named USER.DA0 (zero), and is done every time Windows shuts down. If USER.DAT is missing or corrupt during boot up, the operating system will use USER.DA0. USER.DAT is a required file and Windows 9x will not run if it cannot find either it or the backup file. |

| TABLE 8-6 | Windows 9x System Files—Answers *(continued)* | |
|---|---|---|
| **Filename** | **Location** | **Function** |
| WIN.INI | C:\ *Windows** | Windows 3.x had a registry that was used for a small amount of information, mainly file associations. It used the WIN.INI file to save user settings. The WIN.INI file is included in Windows 9x for backward compatibility with older applications that require this file. |
| SYSTEM.INI | C:\ *Windows** | Windows 3.x stored most system configuration information in the SYSTEM.INI file. This included information about device drivers and configuration settings. Like WIN.INI, this file is included in Windows 9x for backward compatibility with older 16-bit applications that require this file. |
| CONFIG.SYS | C:\ | This file predates both the WIN.INI and SYSTEM.INI files. It was the main configuration file for MS-DOS. It was used to configure operating system settings and load DOS-based device drivers as the operating system was booting up. Operating system settings included the Files= setting that controlled the number of open file handles, and the Buffers= setting that controlled the number of disk-read buffers. There are many more settings. CONFIG.SYS is included with Windows 9x for downward compatibility—not for applications so much as for older device drivers. If you have a device for which you do not have a Windows 9x device driver, but for which you do have a DOS device driver, you can load the device driver in the CONFIG.SYS file using the Device= command. The downside to doing this is that it causes Windows 9x to run in DOS compatibility mode, meaning that it has less 32-bit operating system code, and more 16-bit operating system code running to accommodate the DOS device driver. You can usually notice the difference in performance. This file is not required in Windows 9x unless you need it to run a DOS device driver. In fact, unless there is a specific need as described, this file should not have any settings included. |
| AUTOEXEC.BAT | C:\ | This is another holdover from the MS-DOS days. The AUTOEXEC.BAT file contains commands that are automatically loaded as the operating system is booted up. This is also included for downward compatibility, but is not required by Windows 9x. |

\* The folder in which the Windows 9x operating system is installed. Windows is the default name, but another name can be chosen when installing Windows 9x.

**TABLE 8-7**   Windows 9x Utilities—Answers

| Utility name | Function |
|---|---|
| Automatic Skip Driver | This program (ASD.EXE) is used from the Tools menu of the System Information utility. It is used to isolate failures of device drivers during the bootup. It monitors the behavior of device drivers during the bootup and disables devices that do not start correctly. |
| Device Manager | This is not, strictly speaking, a separate utility. It is invoked through the System Properties dialog box and enables you to view and modify the hardware configuration. Device Manager is a good tool for discovering and resolving hardware configuration problems. |
| WINDOWS 98 System Configuration Utility (MSCONFIG.EXE) | This Windows 98 utility enables you to make changes to the CONFIG.SYS, AUTOEXEC.BAT, WINSTART.BAT, SYSTEM.INI, and WIN.INI settings without actually modifying the files themselves. It does this through the rather low-tech technique of renaming the original files, and creating working copies of them that it modifies so that you can experiment with various configurations, rebooting after each modification, until you find a combination of settings that works. This is the subject of several TechNet articles, and is discussed as a troubleshooting tool in the Windows 98 Resource Kit and the Windows 98 Technical Notes. |
| REGEDIT.EXE | An editor that allows you to view and modify the registry directly. |
| SCANREG.EXE | This is not truly a system file, but a useful utility you can use to backup the registry. It can be run from within Windows 98 to backup the registry. But in order to restore the registry using this utility, you must boot the computer in MS-DOS mode and run SCANREG/RESTORE from the command prompt. |
| System Configuration Editor (SYSEDIT.EXE) | This is the Windows 3.x System Configuration Editor that opens all of the Windows 3.x system configuration files at once within separate windows. This includes WIN.INI, SYSTEM.INI, PROTOCOL.INI, AUTOEXEC.BAT, and CONFIG.SYS. |
| Windows Scripting Host (WSCRIPT.EXE) | There was a time when the only scripts that could run in Windows were DOS batch files run at the command prompt. These types of scripts are now called shell scripts, but non-native scripts such as Visual Basic, Java, and Perl can also run in Windows when the Windows Scripting Host is used. |

**Step 4.**   Refer to Table 8-8: Windows NT/2000/XP System Files—Answers.

**Step 5.**   Refer to Table 8-9: Windows NT/2000/XP Utilities—Answers.

**Step 6.**   Refer to Table 8-10: Memory Management Terminology—Answers.

**TABLE 8-8**    Windows NT/2000/XP System Files—Answers

| Filename | Location | Function |
|---|---|---|
| BOOT.INI | C:\ | This file is read by NTLDR during bootup. It provides a path to the operating system files, and is critical on a dual-boot machine because it displays a boot menu from which you can select an operating system to use. The operating system can start up without this file only if the system files are installed into the default location (C:\WINNT). |
| NTLDR | C:\ | This file is the first system file loaded during boot up of Windows NT, Windows 2000, and Windows XP. It switches the processor into protected mode then locates, loads into memory, and initializes the core operating system files. This is a necessary file. |
| NTDETECT.COM | C:\ | During the boot process, this file is loaded by NTLDR. It then gathers information about the hardware and reports this information to NTLDR, which passes it on to the registry. |
| NTBOOTDD.SYS | C:\ | This file exists only if the operating system is installed on a SCSI drive with the BIOS disabled, in which case this file is the renamed SCSI driver. It is loaded into memory and initialized by NTLDR during bootup. |

**TABLE 8-9**    Windows NT/2000/XP Utilities—Answers

| Utility name | Function |
|---|---|
| Computer Management | Not available in Windows NT. This is actually a console containing several configuration and administrative utilities in three groupings: System Tools, Storage, and Services and Applications. |
| Device Manager | As in Windows 9x, this is not, strictly speaking, a separate utility. It is invoked through the System Properties dialog box and enables you to view and modify hardware configurations. As such, Device Manager is a good tool for discovering and resolving hardware configuration problems. It is not available in NT. |
| REGEDIT.EXE | An editor that enables you to view and modify the registry directly. In Windows NT and Windows 2000, this utility has some limits because it is actually the Windows 9x version. In Windows XP, REGEDIT has been updated to include support for the data types that are in the registry of the advanced versions of Windows, but were not in the Windows 9x registries. The XP version also allows you to access the permissions settings (if you have permission to do this). The version of REGEDIT in Windows NT and Windows 2000 cannot access the permissions settings on registry keys. |

**TABLE 8-9**  Windows NT/2000/XP Utilities—Answers *(continued)*

| Utility name | Function |
|---|---|
| REGEDT32 | Since Windows NT, REGEDT32 has been the "real" registry editor for the advanced operating systems. It enables you to access the permissions for registry keys, and it understands all the data types of NT and Windows 2000. Its limits are that it still has the look of a Windows 3.x application, with a separate window for each registry root key, which is awkward. It has a very limited search function. In Windows XP, REGEDT32 and REGEDIT have come together in a single, updated GUI with all the best features of the two versions. Using either executable name will bring up the same registry editor. |
| Windows Scripting Host (WSCRIPT.EXE) | See function information in Table 8-7. |

**TABLE 8-10**  Memory Management Terminology—Answers

| Term | Description |
|---|---|
| Conventional Memory | In DOS, the conventional memory occupied the first 640KB of address space. This was the only memory in which the operating system, a single application program, and the data of the application could be active. |
| Upper Memory | The total address space addressable by DOS was 1MB, but the top 384KB of this was reserved for system ROM BIOS and the RAM and ROM on expansion cards. It was not usable by programs, even if some of the addresses were unused by expansion cards. This top 384KB of address space was first referred to as reserved memory, then later as upper memory. Do not confuse upper memory with the High Memory Area, defined next. Upper Memory resides between 640KB and 1MB, while the High Memory Area is the first 64KB above 1MB. |
| Extended and High Memory Area | Both of these terms are part of schemes for making more RAM memory available for DOS applications. One of the first such schemes to gain widespread use was the Lotus Intel Microsoft (LIM) memory specification. LIM defined the terms *conventional memory* and *upper memory* (as shown above in this table), and the term *extended memory*, which is the RAM that occupies the addresses that begin at 1MB. They also developed a memory manager, HIMEM.SYS, that required at least an Intel 286 processor and 1MB of physical RAM. HIMEM.SYS would use the first 64KB of extended memory to run some of the DOS code. This memory at the beginning of the extended memory was called the High Memory Area (HMA). HIMEM.SYS had to be loaded in CONFIG.SYS. The lines that would load HIMEM.SYS and instruct it to load DOS into the HMA were:<br><br>`DEVICE=C:\DOS\HIMEM.SYS`<br><br>`DOS=HIGH` |

| TABLE 8-10 | Memory Management Terminology—*Answers (continued)* |

| Term | Description |
| --- | --- |
| Expanded Memory | On 8088 and 80286 computers you could buy specialized boards that would enable you to access yet another type of memory—expanded memory. The expanded memory scheme on these computers did not use extended memory at all, but used the unused addresses in Upper Memory, and swapped or paged data to the expanded memory boards with the use of these addresses. They also used proprietary drivers that came with the memory boards for this. |
| | Later, when 80386 or later processors appeared in computers, the built-in capabilities of those processors provided for memory management without specialized memory boards. You only had to add megabytes of memory to a system. Then we could use two DOS drivers: HIMEM.SYS and EMM386.EXE to configure memory the way we wanted. EMM386.EXE allowed us to provide expanded memory for applications that could use expanded memory but, more importantly, it allowed us to load device drivers (that would previously have taken up conventional memory) into unused portions of the upper memory where the memory manager had mapped RAM. We called these portions of upper memory with mapped RAM Upper Memory Blocks (UMBs). To do this both HIMEM.SYS and EMM386.EXE had to be loaded in CONFIG.SYS. |
| | The lines that would load these memory managers, load DOS into the HMA, and create UMBs were: |
| | ```
DEVICE=C:\DOS\HIMEM.SYS
DEVICE=C:\DOS\EMM386.EXE
DOS=HIGH,UMB
``` |
| | In addition, the LOADHIGH command had to be used to load each device driver into UMBs. |
| | Wow! It has been a long time since we had to even think about all that nonsense, but we had to do this for several years in order to have all the device drivers and network support files in memory and still have room for a program and its data. This was necessary for DOS, and later for Windows 3.x (which depended on DOS). Windows 95 changed this for most of us. |
| Virtual Memory | Virtual memory is actually a scheme for expanding the address space of an operating system by using disk space to store program code and data that is loaded into memory, but not (at the moment) active. The operating system's memory manager handles all this, bringing code and data back into physical RAM when needed, and swapping it out to the swap file when it is not active. |
```

## Lab Solution 8.04

### Step I.

    a. NTVDM should not appear in Task Manager as a result of running CMD.EXE.

    b. The new process CMD.EXE should be listed under Processes in Task Manager.

    c. After opening up a command prompt using COMMAND.COM, the NTVDM process appears in Task Manager.

**Steps 2, 3, and 4.**    No response is required for these steps.

**Step 5.**    No response is required for this step.

If you had trouble with the last part of this step—turning off the Read-only and Hidden attributes—check this illustration:

The rule is that if the Read-only, System, and/or Hidden attributes are set, the ATTRIB command cannot remove them individually; they must all be removed at the same time. The archive attribute is not constrained by this rule because it has a special function used by backup programs.

**Step 6.**    Attempting to run the command EDIT.EXE from the command prompt in Windows 2000 rendered the message, "'Edit.exe' is not recognized as an internal or external command, operable program or batch file." This message may vary depending on the operating system you are running.

**Step 7.** Attempting to run the command EDIT.COM from the command prompt in Windows 2000 causes the DOS editor EDIT to load. For extra credit, look at processes in Task Manager and you will see that NTVDM, the NT Virtual DOS Machine, is loaded.

**Step 8.** No response is required for Step 8.

## Lab Solution 8.05

**Step 1** How you accomplish these steps will vary because there are many ways to create shortcuts. The following was accomplished in Windows 2000 but works very similarly in all versions of Windows since Windows 95.

a. In order to create a shortcut on the desktop to WordPad, first determine the name of the executable program for WordPad. In Windows 2000 right-click on the Start Menu, select Explore All Users, then browse through Start Menu | Programs | Accessories. The shortcut for WordPad is located in this folder. Right-click on the WordPad shortcut and select Properties. The text box labeled "Target" provides the path to the executable program for WordPad. On the test machine, this location was C:\Program Files\Windows NT\ Accessories\wordpad.exe. Use Windows Explorer to browse to this location. Once there, right-click on the file wordpad.exe and select Create Shortcut. A shortcut is created in that folder. Now, simply copy or move the shortcut to the Desktop. Test the shortcut on the Desktop by double-clicking it. If it works, you are nearly done! The shortcut will have the default name of "Shortcut to wordpad.exe." Rename the shortcut to "WordPad" (without the quotes). Congratulations, you have just done a very simple task that will probably impress a user more than the very sophisticated things you may have done to configure the hardware of their computer! That is because this is a very visible thing that will make that user's life a little easier.

b. Before you can create a shortcut to the Calculator program, you must first discover the executable filename for it. You can use the early part of the previous step to do this, then write down this location; you will need it soon. In order to create a shortcut on the Start Menu click the **Start** button, point to *Settings*, click **Taskbar & Start Menu**. This opens the Taskbar and Start

Menu Properties dialog box, which can also be opened by right-clicking on an empty area of the Taskbar and clicking **Properties**. From the Properties dialog box, click the **Advanced** tab and click the **Add** button. This invokes the Create Shortcut wizard that guides you through the process. You can even use a Browse button to find the executable file, but we prefer to know the location of the executable before getting into this wizard—the Browse button does not have a search function. Enter the full path and executable filename in the location text box such as C:\WINNT\System32\CALC.EXE. Click the **Next** button. Select a folder to place the shortcut in. You can even select *Start Menu*, which will place the shortcut directly on the Start Menu. When you click **Next**, you are prompted for a name for the shortcut. The default name is the executable filename. Name your shortcut then click **Finish**. Verify that the shortcut is on your Start Menu and test the shortcut.

c. For this step to work, another computer on the network must have a shared folder to which you have permission. Once that is done, the exact steps to create a shortcut on your desktop to a mapped drive can vary. Here is one way to do it with Windows 2000. First right-click on **My Computer** and select either *Open* or *Explore* (the one in bold is the action that is used whenever you double-click My Computer). Open displays My Computer in Folder View, while Explore opens up a Windows Explorer window focused on My Computer. No matter which you choose, the next step is to click Tools | Map Network Drive. In the Map Network Drive dialog box, the Drive box will display the next available drive letter. You may use the arrow button to select another available drive letter. In the folder box, you can enter the full Universal Naming Convention (UNC) name for the network share you wish to map to. This will be in the form of \\*servername*\*sharename* where *servername* is the name of the server containing the shared folder, and *sharename* is the name of the share. Figure 8-4 shows the Map Network Drive wizard in Windows 2000.

In this example, when this wizard completes, drive F: will map to the company share on the server Htc1. This mapping will be recreated every time the user who created the mapping logs onto this computer. Notice that this wizard also allows you to create a shortcut to a web folder or FTP site. Click the Finish button to cause your computer to attempt to connect to the share. If it fails, redo the mapping, verifying that you used the correct syntax of \\*servername*\*sharename* and that you spelled the names of the server and share

**FIGURE 8-4**

The Map Network
Drive Wizard

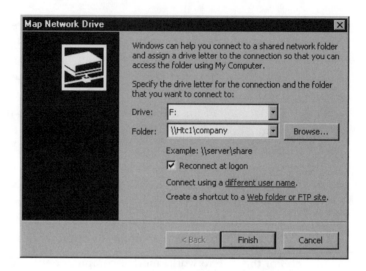

correctly. If it still does not work, ask your instructor to verify that you have
permission to connect to the share on the other computer. Once the drive is
successfully mapped, you will see the drive mapping under My Computer. In
order to create a shortcut to this mapped drive on your desktop, right-click
the icon for the mapped drive in My Computer and drag it to your desktop.
When you release the right button on the desktop, a shortcut menu will
display with appropriate choices. Select Create Shortcut(s) Here. You now
have a shortcut on your desktop to the mapped drive.

**Step 2.** The lab gives most of the steps. In Windows Explorer, if you click on the
Drive C: icon in the Folders pane then right-click in the contents pane, the shortcut
menu will appear. Select New | Folder. Replace the name New Folder with your first
name and press the Enter key.

**Step 3.** Open MYFOLDER and select two files—try using CTRL-click on each
file. Right-click on one of the selected files and select Copy from the shortcut menu.
Now browse to the new folder you created, right-click on the folder, or in the
contents pane of the folder. Select Paste from the shortcut menu.

lab

ⓗint    *The key-mouse combination of CTRL-click enables you to select
non-contiguous files, the combination of SHIFT-click, enables you to select
only contiguous files.*

**Steps 4, 5, 6, and 7.**   The instructions for these steps are complete.

**Step 8.**   The Open With dialog box appears with a list of programs to choose from. If you select Notepad from the list and click the OK button, the file will load in Notepad, even though it did not have the TXT extension.

## Lab Solution 8.06

**Step 1.**   The program or management tool you would use to partition a disk and prepare it for use with each of the following operating systems are:

- a. DOS: FDISK
- b. Windows 9x: FDISK
- c. Windows 2000: Disk Management (in the Computer Management console) or during installation of the operating system.
- d. Windows XP: Disk Management (in the Computer Management console) or during installation of the operating system.

**Step 2.**   Open Windows Explorer or My Computer and right-click on an icon for a hard drive. It will be labeled with a drive letter such as C: and may have a descriptive volume name. From the shortcut menu, select Properties. On the General properties tab, note the File system field. On our test computer there are two hard drive volumes: C and D. They both have the NTFS file system.

**Step 3.**   The main difference in the properties dialog box between a FAT drive and an NTFS drive is the Security tab. File and folder security is available only on an NTFS drive, therefore this tab will appear only on the properties dialog of an NTFS drive.

**Step 4.**   If you diligently searched Microsoft TechNet (www.microsoft.com/technet) you discovered that NTFS5 compatibility, sometimes called "support," (but it is not truly full support) was added to NT 4.0 in Service Pack 4.

**Step 5.**   The syntax to convert drive D: from fat to NTFS is:

```
CONVERT D: /FS:NTFS
```

# ANSWERS TO LAB ANALYSIS TEST

1. Tell Alexis of Algonquin Antique Auctions that Windows 2000 Professional and Windows XP are both good choices for their new desktop computers because they have local security, which was lacking in Windows 9x.

2. Help by telling him that he did no harm because Windows 2000 does not require IO.SYS. Then help him by explaining that BOOT.INI is very important to his operating system, and that he should never delete files just because he is not personally aware of why they are on his computer. Finally, help him to change the View settings in Folder Options so that he can not see these hidden files. What he can't see won't hurt him (or something like that). Resist using the words "break" and "fingers" in the same sentence!

3. Since the computer does actually boot up to Windows 98, you can use the MSCONFIG utility and test various modifications to the configuration files before making changes to the actual files. Neat trick!

4. You can suggest that she open her folders with Explore, which opens them in an Explorer window with two panes. The pane on the left contains the folders, and the pane on the right contains the contents of the currently selected folder.

5. It sounds like either they do not have NTFS on their drive, or they simply have not placed restrictive permissions on the files and folders they want to protect. If they do not have NTFS on the drive they can use the CONVERT program. If they did not place restrictive permissions on their drive, they or you will have to research how to do this.

# ANSWERS TO KEY TERM QUIZ

1. REGEDIT

2. BOOT.INI

3. attribute

4. conventional

5. virtual memory

**EXERCISES • QUESTIONS • ANSWERS**

# 9

# Installation, Configuration, and Upgrade

## LAB EXERCISES

Your job at Nerd Matrix certainly provides you with a great deal of variety. At first you spent most of your time working on the bench and assembling computers for customers. Then you did a great deal of hardware configuration and troubleshooting for customers, and now you have been assigned to the Desktop Team, which does the software installation, upgrades, testing, and troubleshooting for client desktop computers. So now you have two big reasons to study operating system installation, configuration, and upgrade: becoming competent at your new assignment and taking and completing the A+ Operating System Technologies exam—now just 5 weeks away.

In this chapter you will learn the steps to go through to prepare for installing an operating system, you will upgrade a Windows 98 installation to Windows 2000, and you will do a clean install of Windows 2000 Professional. After the Windows 2000 install, you will create an emergency repair disk (ERD).

## LAB EXERCISE 9.01

# Preparing to Install—Compatibility

**60 Minutes**

Before you install an operating system for any Nerd Matrix client you need to ensure that all the hardware is compatible with the new operating system. You do this by checking out the compatibility information at the Microsoft web site. You can also run compatibility software for Windows 2000 and Windows XP that will alert you to any incompatibility. This software will check out the hardware and software on a computer that has a previous version of Windows. If you find that a piece of hardware is not compatible, you can check at the manufacturer's site to see if they have created a driver that has not been included on the Microsoft site. You also need to check that the application software that you plan to install into the new operating system is compatible.

## Learning Objectives

By the end of this lab, you'll be able to:

■ Test a computer for compatibility with Windows 2000

## Lab Materials and Setup

The materials you need for this lab are:

- A PC with Windows 95 or Windows 98
- The Windows 2000 CD
- An Internet connection and a browser

## Getting Down to Business

There are tasks you need to perform before you install a new operating system on a computer. No matter what operating system you are installing, you need to verify that the computer on which you plan to install it is compatible with that operating system. That is, ensure the operating system has drivers and components that will install and run on the computer without problem. Of course, you might have hardware that did not exist when the operating system was being developed. In this case, new drivers may have been developed for that hardware, but not included on the distribution CD of the operating system. You may need to find the drivers at Microsoft's site or at the site of the hardware manufacturer. A search of Microsoft's web site, and that of the manufacturer, will yield the most up-to-date information and driver for the hardware. The following steps walk you through these pre-installation processes.

**cross**
**Reference**

*To prepare for this lab, read the section "Certification Objective 9.01" in Chapter 9 in the A+ Certification Study Guide. Be sure to read the two exercises and study the tables and figures.*

**Step 1.**  To find out if the computer on which you want to install the operating system is suitable, you can go to Microsoft's web site for each operating system and search for the Hardware Compatibility List (HCL) for that OS. You should also check the web site of the hardware manufacturer to see if they have posted new drivers or a new set of instructions.

A closely related issue is the capacity of the hardware—as in how much hard drive space, how much memory, and (if you stretch the meaning) which processor. For this, go to the Microsoft site and search for the Hardware Requirements. This is often stated as both Minimum Hardware Requirements (the OS will run, but nothing else will fit on disk or in memory), and the Recommended Hardware

Requirements (you can actually install and run some applications after the OS is installed). The *A+ Certification Study Guide* very nicely combines minimum and recommended hardware requirements for Windows 95, 98, and 2000 in Table 9-1. You can also find updates to this information at the Microsoft web site (www.microsoft.com). Follow the instructions below and provide your responses.

a. Go to the Windows 2000 Professional site at www.microsoft.com/windows2000/professional and click on the Compatibility link. What are the categories you can search for compatibility?

_____

_____

b. Go to www.microsoft.com/windowsxp and search for the Hardware Requirements Overview. Read through this document. Who is the target audience of this document?

_____

_____

## Step 2.

In this step you will use the Windows 2000 setup upgrade command (WINNT32.EXE) with a command line switch that runs the Readiness Analyzer. This program checks your computer hardware and applications for compatibility with Windows 2000.

To begin, insert the Windows 2000 CD in the drive and click No to close the resulting message box. Click Exit to close the Microsoft Windows 2000 CD dialog box. Open a Command Prompt and enter the following command (Repace D: with the CD-ROM drive letter.):

```
D:\I386\WINNT32  /CHECKUPGRADEONLY
```

When the procedure is complete, click the Finish button.

If Readiness Analyzer finds no incompatibilities or problems, you will see that information in the Report system compatibility page; if it does find incompatibilities or problems, you will see a screen like the one in Figure 9-1.

To complete the job, close all windows and remove the Windows 2000 CD from the drive.

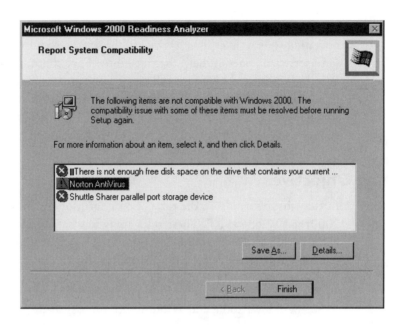

**FIGURE 9-1**

Readiness Analyzer
Report with
incompatibilities

lab
**Hint** *Microsoft formerly had a separate Readiness Analyzer executable file that was available for download from their Windows 2000 site (www.microsoft.com/ windows2000). However, it is no longer available, per a message posted October 23, 2000, on their site. Unless you downloaded it previously and saved it, the only way to run this analyzer is to use the WINNT32 command from the Windows 2000 CD. They now recommend that you use their Search for Compatible Hardware Devices page at www.microsoft.com/windows2000/ server/howtobuy/upgrading/compat/search/devices.asp.*

**LAB EXERCISE 9.02**

# Preparing to Install—Partitioning

**I Hour**

Another pre-installation task is to determine how best to partition the hard disk on which you are installing the operating system. The partitioning of disks, which was addressed briefly in the last chapter, often seems to be more art than science. This is because, as far as disk partitions are concerned, the various versions of Microsoft operating systems have different capabilities that have improved with each new operating system. Ever since DOS 2.0, the first version to work with hard drives (and very small ones at that), the capabilities have continually increased. Now Windows 2000 and Windows XP break many of the old rules of disk partitioning, including the limit on the number of partitions per disk. They use a new optional storage type, *dynamic disk*, in addition to the basic disks that earlier operating systems use. The partitions they create during install are basic disks.

## Learning Objectives

In this lab, you will learn the rules of disk partitioning for Windows 9x, Windows 2000, and Windows XP. These rules apply to what Windows 2000 and Windows XP call basic disks, not to the new (optional) way that these operating systems can partition disks, referred to as dynamic disks. By the end of this lab, you'll be able to:

- Determine the number and type of partitions supported by Windows 9x, Windows 2000, and Windows XP on basic disks.
- Understand disk partitioning of basic disks

## Lab Materials and Setup

The materials you need for this lab are:

- A PC With Windows 95 or Windows 98 installed

## Getting Down to Business

In the last chapter, disk partitioning was defined, and you researched the programs or utilities needed to partition a disk using Windows 9x, Windows 2000, and Windows XP. When preparing to install any operating system, you must think about disk partitioning, especially on a new computer. If the disk is already partitioned, and you are satisfied with how it is done, you will not repartition the disk. During the install process Windows 98, Windows NT, Windows 2000, and Windows XP can partition a disk. However, no matter what operating system you are preparing to install, you need some basic knowledge of disk partitioning before you can even decide whether you are satisfied with the existing partitioning scheme.

*To prepare for this lab, read the section "Certification Objective 9.01" in Chapter 9 in the A+ Certification Study Guide. Be sure to read the two exercises and study the tables and figures.*

**Step 1.** Because there is so much confusion about disk partitioning, we provide a summary of the rules of disk partitioning:

- Before it can be formatted for use by any file system, a disk must be divided into one or more areas called partitions. Each partition must then be formatted by the operating system that will use it.

- Partitioning information is written to the Partition Table, which resides in the Master Boot Record (MBR). There is only one MBR (and therefore only one partition table) per hard disk system.

- The Partition Table can hold information for four partitions, *but* only advanced operating systems such as Windows NT, Windows 2000, and Windows XP can create or access more than two partitions.

- Each of the four partitions defined in a partition table can be one of two different types: primary and extended.

- Although there can be up to four partitions per disk, DOS and Windows 9x operating systems can see only one primary partition and one extended partition per disk.

- Advanced operating systems can create four partitions in the following combinations: up to four primary partitions, or up to three primary partitions and one extended partition.

- Each primary partition has a single drive letter assigned to it, beginning with C:.

- DOS and Windows 9x get around their partition limits with the use of a special partition type called an extended partition. These operating systems can create (using FDISK) one primary partition and one extended partition. Within an extended partition you may define multiple logical drives.

- The partition from which the operating system boots is the primary partition that is marked as Active on the first hard disk. This is done with partitioning software. DOS and Windows 9x use their respective versions of FDISK, Windows NT uses Disk Administrator, and Windows 2000 and Windows XP use Disk Management, which is a tool in the Computer Management console.

- Only one primary partition can be marked as active.

- Once formatted with FAT16, FAT32, NTFS4, or NTFS5, each partition has a boot sector—sometimes also called a boot record—which must never be confused (Ha!) with the one and only master boot record on the disk. The master boot record is the first sector on the entire hard disk, while the boot sector or boot record is the first sector within each formatted partition. The boot sector contains the bootstrap code and information on the format of the partition.

If you can master this set of rules, you will understand something few technicians fully understand, but absolutely should. That is your entire lab—a list of rules to memorize. And you really should have these rules memorized! If you are feeling unfulfilled, use your Internet resources to research some of the points made above.

**lab**
**Hint** *For more information on disk partitions, read the following articles at www.microsoft.com/technet: "Create a Partition or Logical Drive," "Creating Volumes During Windows XP Professional Setup," "Windows NT Partitioning Rules During Setup" (includes Windows 2000), "Order in Which MS-DOS and Windows Assign Drive Letters," "Basic Disks and Volumes," "Windows 2000 Setup Does Not Allow Selection of Partition Type" (this article includes Windows 2000 setup partitioning rules), "Basic Volumes."*

*One of the many things you will learn from these articles is that Windows 2000 and Windows XP have a more advanced, optional way to partition disks that goes beyond the limits of the MBR.*

Since there are now two ways to partition disks, you must distinguish between these two storage types. You can have only one storage type per disk. A disk that uses the master boot record (MBR) to store partition information is called a basic disk, while a disk that has been converted from a basic disk to the newer method by Windows 2000 or Windows XP is called a dynamic disk. On a basic disk the areas are called partitions, but on dynamic disks the areas are called volumes. At present you are not expected to know about this new partitioning technology for the A+ exams, but you will certainly want to learn more about it for your career! Whether you are working with basic or dynamic disks, remember that this is all about storage type. File systems are another issue entirely. Either disk type can have a FAT or NTFS file system format, and the individual partitions or volumes on a single disk can have either file system.

## LAB EXERCISE 9.03

# Upgrading Windows 98 to Windows 2000

**2 Hours**

In the next few days at Nerd Matrix you are scheduled to upgrade operating systems for a client company. At Palomar Plumbing Supplies you will upgrade ten desktop computers from Windows 98 to Windows 2000 Professional. In this lab you will explore your options for upgrading previous versions of Windows to Windows 2000.

***To prepare for this lab, read the section "Certification Objective 9.02" in Chapter 9 in the A+ Certification Study Guide.***

## Learning Objectives

After you complete this lab you will be able to:

■ Upgrade earlier versions of Windows to Windows 2000

## Lab Materials and Setup

For this lab exercise, you'll need:

■ A PC with Windows 98 that can be upgraded to Windows 2000 (It must have compatible hardware.)

■ The Windows 2000 CD

■ The Windows 2000 product key

## Getting Down to Business

In this lab you will upgrade a Windows 98 computer to Windows 2000.

**Step 1.** To begin the upgrade, start and log onto your Windows 98 computer and insert the Windows 2000 Professional CD. A Microsoft Windows 2000 CD message box should appear with this message:

Click Yes to continue the upgrade. When the Windows 2000 Setup Wizard appears, select Upgrade To Windows 2000, and click Next. The common legalese concerning the License Agreement appears. Read the agreement and select I Accept This Agreement, then click Next. If you don't agree, you won't be able to continue the installation. When prompted, enter the Product Key on the Product Key page and click Next.

**Step 2.** Read the Preparing to Upgrade to Windows 2000 page. If you have an Internet connection and want to verify that your hardware is compatible, you may select Click Here To Connect To The Windows Compatibility Web Site Now. Do this only if necessary, and/or if you have time.

After you click Next, the Provide Upgrade Paths page appears. Select No, I Don't Have Any Upgrade Packs and click Next. These upgrade packs are used to make modifications for programs that are not entirely compatible with Windows 2000.

**Step 3.** To convert your system to the NTFS file system, select Yes, Upgrade My Drive on the Upgrading to the Windows 2000 NTFS File System page, then click Next.

**lab**
**(Ⓗint**

*If Windows 2000 install detects a FAT16 or FAT32 file system it will offer to upgrade to NTFS. This is actually the new version, NTFS5. If you upgrade an NT computer with NTFS4, it will not ask, but will upgrade to NTFS5 automatically. It will also do this if you are installing Windows 2000 as a separate install on a computer with NT installed. This can be a problem if you want to dual-boot between the two operating systems, because only NT 4.0 Service Pack 4 or later can run on an NTFS5 volume. Even then, it cannot take advantage of the new features of NTFS5, such as Encrypted File System.*

**Step 4.**   After a very brief wait, the Preparing An Upgrade Report page will appear showing a progress bar. If Setup detects PnP devices for which Windows 2000 does not have drivers, it will display them in a list. If you have these drivers, click the Provide Files button and point to the location of the driver files in the Browse for Folders dialog box. Proceed with the installation of any device drivers that you can install at this point. You may also choose to skip this step and add the drivers later. Click Next.

**Step 5.**   Read the Upgrade Report page, then click Next. If the upgrade report found a problem, and you choose to skip it rather than install a driver at this time, you will see this message:

If you receive this message, click Continue. It is possible that Windows 2000 cannot run without the new patch or driver, but you may find that you can do without it until after installation.

**Step 6.**   Read the Ready to Install page shown in Figure 9-2. Note the time it will take to install, then click Next. Be sure to remove any disks from the drives. Setup will now reboot your computer.

The text-mode operating system selection screen will boot with the choice of Microsoft Windows 2000 Professional Setup or Microsoft Windows. Setup will start automatically if you do not make a selection within 5 seconds. You will briefly see Inspecting Your Hardware, then the blue Windows 2000 Setup screen will appear while it loads the files needed to run the Windows 2000 Setup.

If you removed the Windows 2000 Professional CD, replace it in the drive now. From this point on, Setup will proceed much as a new install (see Lab 9.04), performing an examination of your disks and copying files to the installation folders. Then it will initialize your Windows 2000 configuration and reboot the computer.

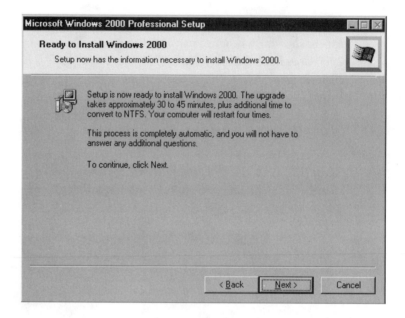

After the reboot, Windows will start, and you will see the Windows 2000 Professional splash screen. If you opted to convert a FAT volume to NTFS5, you will see the screen shown in Figure 9-3, a text-based screen within the graphics border displaying the progress of first running a disk check, then performing the file system conversion.

If a file system conversion was performed, the system will again reboot. After the reboot, Windows will start, and once again you will see the Windows 2000 Professional splash screen. A message will appear about the file system, then, after a brief delay, Windows 2000 Setup will load the Windows 2000 Setup wizard.

**Step 7.**   The Installing Devices page will display with a progress bar. This may take several minutes. Afterward, Setup will proceed to install networking components. Notice that the Workgroup vs. Domain page appears briefly, but the choices are greyed out. This is, after all, an upgrade, and it will use your Windows 98 settings. Remember, Windows 98 can be only a member of a Workgroup, never a member of a domain, although a user at a Windows 98 computer can be a member of a domain and log on to an NT or Windows 2000 domain. Setup will proceed to the Installing Components page, also basing its installation on your Windows settings.

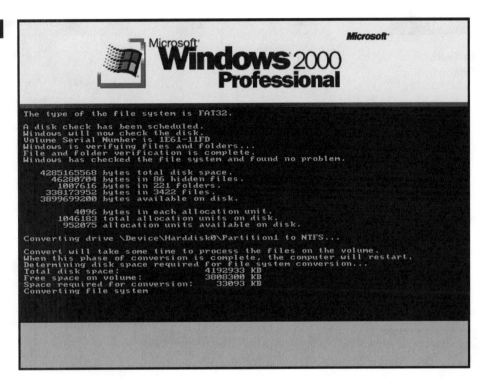

**FIGURE 9-3**

NTFS conversion screen

Installation is almost complete; the next phase displays the Performing Final Tasks page while Setup installs Start Menu items and performs other tasks, such as upgrading program and system settings, saving settings, and removing temporary files used for setup.

When Setup is finished, it will restart your computer. After the computer restarts, the Password Creation dialog box appears as shown in Figure 9-4, requesting passwords for all new Windows 2000 accounts. It instructs you to type a *single* password that will be used for all the listed accounts. You will have to use Users and Passwords in Control Panel to change this after you log on.

**Step 8.** Log on to your new Windows installation with your user name and new password when the Log Onto Windows dialog box appears. Click OK to watch the desktop begin loading,  displaying the Getting Started with Windows 2000 screen. Clear the check box next to Show This Screen At Startup, then click Exit.

Congratulations, you have successfully upgraded Windows 98 to Windows 2000.

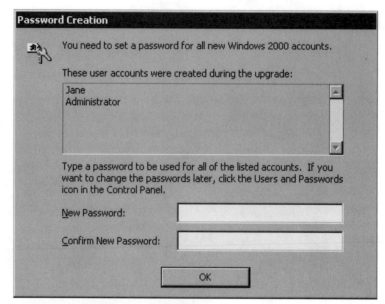

**FIGURE 9-4**

Password
Creation dialog
box

## LAB EXERCISE 9.04

# Installing Windows 2000

**1.5 Hours**

In this lab you will install Windows 2000 as you would on a new computer.
Depending on the purchasing practices where you work, systems may arrive with
an operating system preinstalled by the vendor, or you may install the standard
operating system the organization uses on new computers when they arrive. How
you perform an install will also depend on the practices of the organization. One
method is to manually install the operating system. This is what you will practice
in this lab. You will perform this labonly  if you have the Windows 2000 CD.
The lab is also written for use on a computer that is configured to boot from the
CD-ROM drive.

**lab**

**Warning**

*This installation will wipe out the previous contents of the hard disk.*

## Learning Objectives

After you've completed this lab, you will be able to:

■ Install Windows 2000 on a new computer

## Lab Materials and Setup

The materials you need for this lab are:

■ The Windows 2000 CD

■ The Windows 2000 product key

■ A PC configured to boot from CD-ROM, with no partitions defined, and with Windows 2000-compatible hardware

## Getting Down to Business

Now you are ready to run the Windows 2000 Setup program. A general description of this process is given in the section "Windows 2000" in Chapter 9 of the *A+ Certification Study Guide.* For more details on Windows 2000 Setup, see Chapter 2 of the *Windows 2000 Professional Getting Started Manual* This can be found at the Microsoft TechNet web site.

Before you begin, find the Windows 2000 Product Key which should be on the back of the CD container. Write it down and keep it handy because you will need it during the setup. General instructions are as follows:

lab
ⓗint

*CDs and their containers get separated. Sometimes Microsoft prints the product key on the CD itself. If that is not the case, use a fine-tipped permanent marker to write the product key on the label side of the CD.*

**Step 1.** Boot from the Windows 2000 CD then press Enter at the Windows 2000 Professional Setup screen (a text-mode-screen with a blue background).

At this point the setup program loads. This includes all the drivers needed to run setup on your computer. Just like NT before it, Windows 2000 Setup loads and tries out many drivers until it finds the correct combination that will allow Setup to run on your computer. Do not confuse this process with loading the actual drivers Windows will use once it is installed.

When all the setup and driver files are loaded, a message states that Windows 2000 is starting. At this point, this is just the Windows 2000 setup program, which is, at first, still in text-mode.

**Step 2.** The Welcome to Setup screen displays with three choices. Press Enter to Setup Windows 2000 Now. If your hard disk has no partitions, you will see the message shown here. Press C to continue.

```
Windows 2000 Professional Setup

    Setup has determined that your computer's startup hard disk is new
    or has been erased, or that your computer is running an operating
    system that is incompatible with Windows 2000.

    If the hard disk is new or has been erased, or if you want to discard
    its current contents, you can choose to continue Setup.

    If your computer is running an operating system that is incompatible
    with Windows 2000, continuing Setup may damage or destroy the existing
    operating system.

    •  To continue Setup, press C.
       CAUTION: Any data currently on your computer's startup hard disk
       will be lost.

    •  To quit Setup, press F3.




    C=Continue Setup   F3=Quit
```

**lab**
**Hint**

*If the hard disk was partitioned and formatted before install began, this screen will not display, and Setup searches for a previous version of Windows. If it detects a previous version of Windows 2000, it will prompt you to Repair, or to press Esc to install a fresh version of Windows 2000.*

On the Windows 2000 License Agreement screen press F8 (after reading the entire agreement). There will be a slight delay while setup checks the status of the hard disk(s), then a screen displays the result of this search.

Create a partition of at least 2GB. You will have to do this by carefully reading the screens and making the appropriate selections. When prompted to format the new partition, select NTFS. Formatting will take several minutes, after which Setup proceeds to copy files to the newly formatted partition. These are the actual source files copied from the CD. You can see the names of the files being copied on the status bar at the bottom of the screen.

**Step 3.** Next, Setup initializes the Windows configuration, prompts you to remove any floppy disk from drive A:, and reboots.

After the reboot, Windows 2000 Setup loads as a GUI and the Windows 2000 Professional Setup Wizard loads and quickly moves to the Installing Devices page. It will detect and install devices, displaying a status bar as it does so. This can take several minutes.

**Step 4.** On the Regional Settings page, leave all settings at the default if US English numeric, currency, and date and time settings are appropriate. Otherwise, select the correct settings for your locale then click Next.

On the next few screens, you will enter Your Name and Company Name in the Personalize Your Software page, and the Product Key, clicking Next after each.

**Step 5.** Enter a Computer Name on the Computer Name and Administrator Password page. As you can see in Figure 9-5, you will not want to use the suggested name, which is a concatenation of the company name and a randomly generated string.

Assign an administrator password in the Administrator Password and Confirm Password boxes. Click Next to enter the current date and time and select the correct time zone on the Date and Time Settings page. When complete, click Next.

Setup continues through the next steps, stopping at the Network Settings page for you to select between Typical and Custom settings. Select Typical, unless told by your instructor to do otherwise, then click Next.

Select Workgroup on the Workgroup or Computer Domain page. Actually, you first select No, This Computer Is Not On A Network, Or Is On A Network Without A Domain. Then you type a name for the workgroup. For this lab, use the default name "workgroup" unless otherwise instructed. If the classroom is part of a domain, the instructor will give you instructions for joining a domain. Then click Next.

Windows 2000 setup will continue through the Installing Components and Performing Final Tasks pages.

Finally, the Completing the Windows 2000 Setup Wizard page appears and you are prompted to remove the CD, and click Finish. After Windows 2000 reboots, Windows 2000 Professional starts and, if you are on a network, the Network Identification Wizard will run. Click Next.

FIGURE 9-5

Computer Name
and Administrator
Password

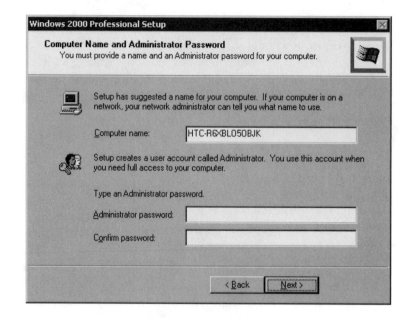

**Step 6.**   The Users Of This Computer page appears and you must choose between having users enter a user name and password to log on to the computer, or having Windows always assume that a single user has logged on (this choice will cause Windows to automatically log the user on with his local user name and password). Select User Must Enter A Username And Password To Use This Computer, then click Next.

Click Finish on the Completing the Network Identification Wizard page. Enter a username and password when the Log On to Windows dialog box appears, and click OK. When the desktop appears, it will show the Getting Started with Windows 2000 wizard.

Congratulations, you have successfully installed Windows 2000!

**LAB EXERCISE 9.05**

# Creating an Emergency Repair Disk for Windows 2000

**1 Hour**

At the conclusion of installing Windows 2000, and after each service pack or configuration change, you should create an Emergency Repair Disk (ERD). Remember that this does not take the place of regular backups. In fact, the Windows 2000 ERD is different fromthe Windows NT ERD, which contains compressed backup copies of registry files. For this reason, the Emergency Repair Diskette dialog box has a check box to back up the registry to the repair directory (C:\WINNT\REPAIR).

## Learning Objectives

After you complete this lab you will be able to:

- Create an Emergency Repair Disk for Windows 2000
- Back up the Registry to the Repair directory

## Lab Materials and Setup

The materials you need for this lab are:

- A PC with Windows 2000 Professional installed
- A blank, formatted diskette labeled "Windows 2000 Emergency Repair Disk"

## Getting Down to Business

In the following steps you will learn to create an Emergency Repair Disk for Windows 2000, and to back up the registry to the Repair directory.

cross **Reference**

*To prepare for this lab, read the section "Certification Objective 9.03" in Chapter 9 in the **A+ Certification Study Guide**. Be sure to study the Scenario and Solutions, tables, and exercises.*

**Step 1.** From the Start menu select Programs | Accessories | System Tools | Backup.

**Step 2.** In the Backup window click on the Emergency Repair Disk button. When prompted, insert a blank, formatted floppy disk into drive A: and click OK.

**lab**
**Warning**

*If your diskette is not truly a formatted, blank diskette, the emergency repair diskette creation operation will fail.*

**Step 3.** Click to place a check in the box to Backup The Registry as shown in Figure 9-6, and then click OK. When it is complete, use My Computer or Windows Explorer to examine the files on the diskette.

a. What files were copied onto the Emergency Repair Disk?

_____

_____

Open My Computer or Windows Explorer and browse to C:\WINNT\REPAIR. Notice the directory named RegBack. Open this directory, and you will see the registry files that were backed up.

| FIGURE 9-6 | |
|---|---|
| Emergency Repair Disk creation | |

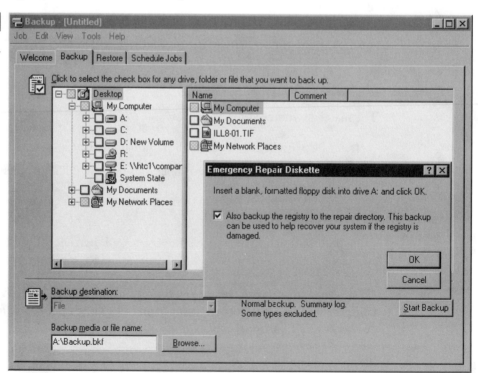

# LAB ANALYSIS TEST

**1.** Winifred has called about having her Windows 98 desktop upgraded to Windows 2000. She has tried to install Windows 2000 herself, but the installation has failed every time. Her Windows 98 computer is as powerful as many departmental servers so she does not want to replace it. What can you do to help her find the source of incompatibility?

_____

_____

**2.** Henry has ordered a new desktop computer and requires six "drives" on his computer. His company has unused licenses for Windows 98 and Windows 2000, and their present computer leasing plan includes Windows XP installed on each computer, with a 40 GB hard drive. Even if he stays with Windows XP, he will have to repartition the hard drive and reinstall the operating system for his new scheme. Which operating system will you recommend, and why?

_____

_____

**3.** Valerie at Victor's Violins has upgraded her computer from Windows 98 to Windows 2000, but she ignored screens to provide an upgrade path, and now two of her applications do not work in Windows 2000. She has called you and is desperate for help. What can you tell her?

_____

_____

**4.** You are preparing to install Windows 2000 Professional on a new computer. All the hardware components are Windows 2000-compliant, and you have all the application software (an office suite) and necessary patches that you will install after you install the operating system. However, there is only 32 MB of RAM on the computer. The rest of the hardware exceeds the recommended requirements for Windows 2000. How should you proceed?

_____

_____

**5.** Quincy supports 40 desktop computers running Windows NT Workstation but the replacement computers are coming in with Windows 2000 (and soon Windows XP). It took him ten minutes to find how to create an emergency repair disk for Windows 2000 (using NTBACKUP), and he is now confused by the option to back up the registry to the repair directory. He wants to know if this is really necessary?

_____

_____

# KEY TERM QUIZ

Use the following vocabulary terms to complete the sentences below. Not all of the terms will be used.

> FDISK
>
> partitions
>
> operating system
>
> Emergency Repair Disk
>
> upgrade
>
> Startup Disk
>
> format
>
> Readiness Analyzer
>
> WINNT32
>
> MBR

1.  To prepare a hard disk for use you must create one or more _____, which can then be formatted.

2.  During the Windows 98 Setup you are prompted to insert a diskette, which the Setup program will format and copy files to in order to make a Windows 98 _____.

3.  In Windows NT, registry files were saved to this disk, but beginning with Windows 2000, registry files are not saved to the _____.

4.  Before upgrading a computer from Windows 98 to Windows 2000, you should run the Windows 2000 _____ to determine if there are any incompatibilities or problems.

5.  On the Windows NT and Windows 2000 CD, the program _____ is known as the upgrade program.

# LAB WRAP-UP

If you did the installation and upgrade labs in this chapter, you have spent considerable time in the lab, but we hope you have learned quite a bit about how Windows installs and how upgrades work. You also studied disk partitioning and ran the Windows 2000 Readiness Analyzer. You are ready to move on to Chapter 10 where you will practice diagnosing and troubleshooting problems with Windows.

# LAB SOLUTIONS FOR CHAPTER 9

In this section, you'll find solutions to the lab exercises, Lab Analysis Test, and Key Term Quiz.

## Lab Solution 9.01

**Step 1.**

   a. At the Windows 2000 Professional web site, the three categories you can search for compatibility are Computers, Hardware Devices, and Software.

   b. The Hardware Requirements Overview document at the Windows XP Professional web site is focused on the home and small-office networking user.

**Steps 2.**   This step is complete and requires no response.

## Lab Solution 9.02

**Step 1.**   This step is complete and does not require a response.

## Lab Solution 9.03

**Steps 1-8.**   These steps are complete and do not require a response.

## Lab Solution 9.04

**Steps 1-6.**   These steps are complete and do not require a response.

## Lab Solution 9.05

**Steps 1-2.**   These steps are complete and do not require a response.

**Step 3.**

   a. The following files are copied onto the Emergency Repair Disk: AUTOEXEC.NT, CONFIG.NT, and SETUP.LOG.

# ANSWERS TO LAB ANALYSIS TEST

**1.** Advise Winifred that she can run the Windows 2000 Readiness Analyzer from the Windows 2000 CD. All she has to do is open a command prompt in Windows 98 and type: D:\i386\ WINNT /CHECKUPGRADEONLY. This will help her home in on the incompatibility. An educated guess is that the problem is with the BIOS, and that a BIOS upgrade may be the solution. Therefore, in addition to the Readiness Analyzer, she should check out the manufacturer's site to see if they have a flash BIOS upgrade available for download.

**2.** This is one of those times when the answer is not carved in granite. In fact, on the job, you would ask more questions to get more information! Windows 98 would not be a good choice. Although you can actually create six "drives" with Windows 98, they would include a single primary partition C:, and multiple logical drives on an extended partition. If you have done any further reading on this, you know that the logical drive information is not stored in the MBR, but within the logical drives on the extended partition. In other words, to find the logical drive beyond the first logical drive (D:), the operating system searches the logical drives sequentially to determine the location of the next logical drive. This is very inefficient. Both Windows 2000 and Windows XP are capable of changing the storage type of an entire hard disk system from basic to dynamic. A dynamic disk does not have a limit on the number of volumes, so either of these operating systems would work.

Either Windows XP or Windows 2000 would be a good choice. In either case, Henry should only create a single partition during setup. How big? You would really need to know more about the installation, but since this is the partition in which the operating system will reside, and the operating system grows with every component and application added, we recommend 4GB. After Windows XP is installed, convert the disk to dynamic storage type. Now you can install as many volumes as you can fit in the space.

**3.** Actually, you have some hopeful news for Valerie. She may be able to find upgrade patches for the problem programs at the Microsoft site. During the install she was given an opportunity to point to the patches, but had declined. Now she should go to the Microsoft web site, find the patches, and follow the instructions for installing them.

4. You should wait until the memory can be upgraded to at least 64MB (the recommended minimum). Technically, you can install the operating system with only 32MB of RAM, and may actually succeed in installing the applications, but that is doubtful. It is almost certain that performance will be below par, and some functionality will not be available to the user. Rather than deliver a computer that underperforms, attempt to get the RAM upgraded before completing the installation of the software.

5. If Quincy wants the same functionality from the repair process that he had with Windows NT, he will have to select the option to back up the registry to the repair directory when he creates an ERD. The ERD no longer contains registry files, so selecting this option is how he should create a backup of the registry after making a configuration change (which is stored in the registry).

## ANSWERS TO KEY TERM QUIZ

1. partitions

2. Startup Disk

3. Emergency Repair Disk

4. Readiness Analyzer

5. WINNT32

EXERCISES • QUESTIONS • ANSWERS

# 10

# Diagnosing and Troubleshooting

## LAB EXERCISES

Y ou are gaining knowledge about Windows operating systems that you will need on the job and for the A+ exam. Now you are ready to explore methods for troubleshooting problems with the operating system, especially problems that can occur at bootup. And it is just in time because your boss at Nerd Matrix is looking forward to sending you out on your own to troubleshoot some of these problems.

**LAB EXERCISE 10.01**

# Creating Setup Boot Diskettes for Windows NT, 2000, or XP

I Hour

You have noticed that most of the technicians at Nerd Matrix carry cases with disks and tools. Every day you seem to discover more CDs and diskettes that you want to have with you while working. Your disk carrier has grown from a small CD case to a briefcase-sized binder with plastic CD holders. This lab and the ones that follow will add some weight to your case because there are several diskettes that you should keep handy for working with Windows 2000—beginning with the setup boot disks. This is a set of four diskettes that can be used to boot into the Windows 2000 Setup program on a computer that cannot boot from the Windows 2000 CD. The four setup boot diskettes, along with the Windows 2000 CD, can be used together to perform a new install on a computer that has a CD-ROM drive, but that does not boot from the CD-ROM drive. These diskettes, the Windows 2000 CD, and the Emergency Repair Disk (ERD) can be used to repair an existing Windows 2000 installation.

## Learning Objectives

After you've completed this lab, you will be able to:

■ Create setup boot diskettes for Windows NT, 2000, or XP

## Lab Materials and Setup

The materials you need for this lab are:

- The Windows 2000 CD
- A PC with Windows 2000 installed
- Four blank diskettes (for Windows 2000 or NT) or five blank diskettes for Windows XP

**cross Reference** *To prepare for this lab, read the section titled "Certification Objective 10.01" in Chapter 10 of the A+ Certification Study Guide.*

## Getting Down to Business

In this lab you will create the setup boot diskettes for Windows NT, 2000, or XP. For simplicity, we describe the process for Windows 2000, with hints for doing the same task for Windows NT or Windows XP. It is easier to do this at your leisure than to wait until you are at a customer site and realize that you are being asked to install Windows on a brand new computer that does not have a CD drive, or that will not boot from the CD drive. The diskettes may not be your only option if the computer has a Windows or DOS (Yes!) operating system that can connect to a network. In that case, you can copy the CD files to a share on a server, connect from the client computer and use WINNT (from DOS or Windows 3.x), or WINNT32 (from Windows 9x or newer) to install Windows 2000. These programs are in the i386 directory on the Windows 2000 CD. That is the directory you need to copy to a server for an over-the-network install. It is still good insurance to carry the prepared setup diskettes.

**Step 1.**   Run the Windows 2000 Help program. On the Index tab enter **boot disks**. Select Creating Boot Disks from the list that appears, then click Display. Follow the instructions in the Contents pane of the Help program to create a set of Windows 2000 Setup disks. Be sure to label them carefully.

When you have completed making these diskettes, test them by booting into Windows 2000 setup, but instead of actually running it, quit the setup program and remove the diskette that is in the diskette drive.

You now have four diskettes to add to your Windows 2000 tool kit in addition to the Emergency Repair Disk you created in Chapter 9. Make sure they are clearly labeled and keep them together (rubber bands are good!).

**lab**
**ⓗint**

*If you need to create a set of setup boot diskettes for Windows NT, you can do this from any computer running Windows by opening up a command prompt and typing the command winnt /ox or winnt32 /ox from the i386 directory of the CD. The first command will run on DOS or Windows 3.X, the second command will run on Windows 9X or greater. This creates a set of three setup boot diskettes.*

*Microsoft did not include a utility to generate a set of setup boot diskettes for Windows XP, but you can download an executable file from the Microsoft web site that will create a set of six setup boot diskettes. You can find this file at Microsoft's download site www.microsoft.com/downloads.*

## LAB EXERCISE 10.02

# Creating a Boot Diskette for Windows NT, 2000, or XP

**I Hour**

Another important diskette to keep handy for any operating system is a boot diskette. Although Windows NT, 2000, and XP are each actually too big to fit on a diskette, you can prepare a diskette that can be used to boot up your computer if there is damage to the files used in the early part of startup. You will have to do this for each of these operating systems, but the procedure is the same for all of them.

## Learning Objectives

After you've completed this lab, you will be able to:

- Create a boot diskette for Windows NT, Windows 2000, or Windows XP

## Lab Materials and Setup

The materials you need for this lab are:

- A PC with Windows NT, Windows 2000, or Windows XP installed
- One diskette (it will be formatted in the Lab)

## Getting Down to Business

For simplicity, we will refer only to Windows 2000 in the steps below, but this procedure works for standard installs of Windows NT, Windows 2000, and Windows XP.

**Step 1.** Now you will create a single diskette that can be used to boot into Windows 2000 in case the hardware specific boot files are damaged.

Label a diskette "Windows 2000 Boot Diskette" and insert it into Drive A:. From My Computer or Windows Explorer, right-click on Drive A: and select Format. In the Format dialog box, click Start. A warning message will appear; click OK to close it and continue. When the format is complete, click OK and close the Format dialog box.

Next, copy the following files from the root of Drive C: to the root of drive A:

NTLDR

NTDETECT.COM

BOOT.INI

NTBOOTDD.SYS (If it exists.)

**lab**
**Hint** *These files have the hidden attribute turned on, so you will have to adjust the View setting of Windows Explorer in order to see them.*

Leaving the boot diskette in the drive, restart Windows 2000. It should start up normally, but you should notice that the diskette drive is used early in the bootup process.

Remove the diskette; be sure that this diskette is labeled properly. Put it away. You will use it in Lab Exercise 10.03

In this lab, you created a boot diskette. Although this method can be used for Windows NT, Windows 2000, and Windows XP, the boot diskette is not exactly generic. It works best if you are using a boot diskette you created on the machine that you later must boot up from a diskette. (Where is that crystal ball when you need it?) At minimum, if you want to boot into Windows NT, Windows 2000, or Windows XP from diskette, you must use a boot diskette created on a computer with the same version of Windows as the computer on which you plan to use the boot diskette. Also, there can be other variations on computers of the same operating system that may keep a boot diskette from working. Research the details of using this boot diskette further by doing the next lab and by searching Microsoft TechNet for more information.

**lab**
**Hint** *Windows XP also enables you to create a DOS boot disk. This can be a valuable disk to keep on hand.*

**I Hour**

**LAB EXERCISE 10.03**

# Troubleshooting Windows NT, 2000, or XP Boot Problems

Since Windows 3.0 (the first interesting version of Windows) was introduced over a decade ago, we have accepted the fact that there seems to be at least five ways of doing any task. That is also true of problem resolution. One bootup problem that you may encounter is a computer that successfully completes the Power on Self Test (POST) and BIOS bootup, but fails to load the operating system. If you watch carefully, you will see clues in the error messages. Several of these operating system startup problems can be resolved by using the Emergency Repair Process in Windows NT, Windows 2000, and Windows XP. Some of the same problems can also be corrected using the Recovery Console that is available beginning with Windows 2000. However, a few of these same problems have yet another, easier resolution—using a boot diskette like the one you created in the previous lab.

## Learning Objectives

After you've completed this lab, you will be able to:

■   Troubleshoot and resolve boot problems with Windows NT, Windows 2000, and Windows XP

## Lab Materials and Setup

The materials you need for this lab are:

■   A PC with Windows NT, Windows 2000, or Windows XP installed

■   The boot diskette created for that operating system in Lab 10.02

## Getting Down to Business

Some of the troubleshooting labs in the earlier chapters of this book, particularly in Chapter 3, had you sabotage your own computer, observe the symptoms generated by the problem, then resolve the problem. You will go through that process in the following steps. This lab will be the same for Windows NT, Windows 2000, and Windows XP. However, for simplicity's sake, the lab will refer only to Windows 2000.

**lab**
**Warning**

*Before you begin, be sure that you have the appropriate boot diskette for the operating system you are using.*

**Step 1.** Boot up your operating system, observing the messages you see on the screen during a successful bootup. Do not insert the boot diskette yet! After logging on, open My Computer or Windows Explorer and ensure that the view options will enable you to see hidden files.

**lab**
**Hint**

*If you are unsure of how to do this, go back to Chapter 8 and review lab 8-03.*

Locate the file NTLDR in the root of drive C: and rename it NTLDRX. Click Yes on the following message box:

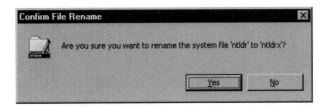

Reboot your computer, observing the messages you see. What error message appears that is related to this problem?

_____

Insert your operating system boot diskette into drive A and reboot the computer. After logging on, open My Computer or Windows Explorer and copy the NTLDR file from your diskette to the root of drive C:. Remove the diskette and reboot the computer. The problem should be resolved, and your computer should boot up from the hard drive.

**Step 2.** Boot up your operating system, observing the messages you see on the screen during a successful bootup. After logging on, open My Computer or Windows Explorer and locate the BOOT.INI file in the root of drive C:. Right click on BOOT.INI and use the properties dialog box to remove the read-only attribute (if it is set).

Using Notepad, open the BOOT.INI file for editing. Modify two lines in the file as described below:

- Edit the line that begins with the word **default=** and ends with **\winnt**. Add an **x** so it appears as **\winntx**.

- Edit the line that contains the name of the operating system in quotes on the right so that **\winnt** to the left of the equals (=) sign also has an **x** at the end. For instance, if a line appears as:

```
multi(0)disk(0)rdisk(0)partition(1)\WINNT="Microsoft Windows
2000 Professional" /fastdetect
```

Modify it by just adding an **x** after WINNT so that it reads:

```
multi(0)disk(0)rdisk(0)partition(1)\WINNTX="Microsoft Windows
2000 Professional" /fastdetect.
```

Save BOOT.INI and reboot the computer.

a. What message appears at bootup?

_____

_____

b. It is said that this message is deceiving. Do you agree? Why is it deceiving?

_____

_____

Insert your operating system boot diskette into drive A: and reboot the computer. After logging on, open My Computer or Windows Explorer and edit the BOOT.INI file, removing the **x** from the end of the string **winnt** in both lines. Remove the diskette and reboot the computer.

The problem should be resolved, and your computer should boot up from the hard drive.

In this lab you repaired a bootup problem using the boot diskette you created in the previous lab. Another way to solve this problem would have been to run the repair process, which is more involved. We have found this boot diskette method to be easier than the repair process, but it will work only on the boot files residing on the root of drive C:. It will not help you recover from a corrupted NTOSKRNL.EXE, corrupted component or driver, or damaged registry, all of which can be repaired with the repair process.

**LAB EXERCISE 10.04**

# Using a Windows 98 Boot Diskette to Resolve Problems

**30 Minutes**

Larry's Laundromatic is a chain of launderetts in Arizona. Their computing needs, beyond their business offices, are very modest. At each facility they have a Windows 98 computer used by the day and night managers. The day manager of the Goodyear, AZ facility, Louisa, has called you and described a problem. When the computer boots up, all that displays is a black screen with the words Invalid System Disk. Replace The Disk, And Then Press Any Key." You immediately asked if there was a diskette in the floppy drive, because you have seen this error occur when a floppy disk has been left in the drive accidentally and the system is trying to boot from the floppy drive with a non-bootable diskette. Louisa assured you that no diskette was in the drive, so you are going to walk her through the process of determining if the hard drive has a missing or damaged IO.SYS, and then fixing the problem.

## Learning Objectives

After you've completed this lab, you will be able to:

■ Use Windows 98 startup diskette to resolve bootup problems

## Lab Materials and Setup

The materials you need for this lab are:

■ A PC with Windows 98 installed

■ The Windows 98 startup diskette created during the Windows 98 installation

## Getting Down to Business

Fortunately, when you shipped the computer to Goodyear, you included a Windows 98 startup diskette—the one created during the installation, but with a small modification. The creation and modification of this disk is described in Step 1 below. In Step 2 you will sabotage your classroom lab computer to simulate the problem. Step 3 describes the procedure that you will describe for Louisa.

**Step 1.** In Add/Remove Programs in Control Panel, click the Startup Disk tab. Then click Create Disk, and follow the instructions on the screen. Look at the contents of the disk using My Computer or Explorer and rename the three files as shown in Table 10-1.

| TABLE 10-1 | Old Filename | Renamed Filename |
|---|---|---|
| Renaming Startup diskette files | MSDOS.SYS | MSDOS.SET |
| | AUTOEXEC.BAT | AUTOEXEC.SET |
| | CONFIG.SYS | CONFIG.SET |

Copy the MSDOS.SYS file from the root of C: to the root of A:. This file tells IO.SYS where to find the Windows 98 system files to load during bootup. Without these instructions, Windows 98 will boot only to the DOS prompt. Test this diskette by restarting the computer. It should boot into Windows 98.

**lab**
**Hint**

*By renaming these files on A:, you are preventing the startup disk from booting into Windows 98 DOS mode from the diskette. You are also preventing the performance of several other tasks, such as offering you a menu of choices, loading DOS-based CD-ROM drivers, creating a RAM disk in memory, and expanding and copying additional DOS-based utilities that are handy for troubleshooting from DOS. If you ever need to use the diskette for this purpose, rename these files to their original names, using the table above. Or, better yet, create two diskettes—one left as a normal startup diskette and another modified as above to allow you to boot into Windows 98.*

**Step 2** Now sabotage your computer. Remove the diskette from drive A:. Rename the IO.SYS file in the root of C: to IO.BAD and reboot the computer.

It should display the error message that Louisa reported. Stay at this screen and move on to the next step.

**Step 3**    Insert the Windows 98 startup diskette into drive A: and reboot the computer. It should boot normally into Windows 98. Copy the IO.SYS file from the diskette to the root of C:, or rename IO.BAD back to IO.SYS on drive C: (But that is cheating!). Reboot the computer. It should now boot normally.

In this lab you simulated a problem that can be resolved using a modified Windows 98 startup diskette. You will now want to add such a diskette to your tool kit if you expect to work with Windows 98 computers.

**lab**
**Warning**

*The boot disk that ships with Windows 98 is different from the one you can create during setup or after setup (from the Add Programs icon in Control Panel). It does not have all the utilities needed for problem solving. It is missing many important utilities such as FORMAT and ATTRIB. Always create a new boot disk by one of these last two methods so you have the extra utilities that are loaded onto the RAM disk. In this lab you actually disabled the RAM disk and copying of the utilities by renaming the CONFIG.SYS and AUTOEXEC.BAT files.*

**LAB EXERCISE 10.05**

# Using the Repair Process in Windows NT, 2000, and XP

**30 Minutes**

There are several problems that prevent Windows from booting up that can best be solved with the Emergency Repair Process. These include damage to the boot sector on the system partition, and damage to the registry or system files. It is important to have an up-to-date Emergency Repair Disk (ERD) to use during this process. You can still elect to perform the Emergency Repair Process without an ERD, but the process may not work, although the ERD is not as critical to the process with Windows 2000 and Windows XP as it was with Windows NT. This is because the ERD no longer contains registry files.

## Learning Objectives

After you complete this lab you will be able to:

- Run the Emergency Repair Process in Windows NT, Windows 2000, and Windows XP

## Lab Materials and Setup

The materials you'll need for this lab are:

- The Windows NT, 2000 or XP CD
- A PC configured to boot from CD-ROM and with Windows NT, 2000, or XP installed

## Getting Down to Business

For simplicity, the steps below describe using Windows 2000, but this procedure works for Windows NT, Windows 2000, and Windows XP. Some differences will be seen. For instance, Windows NT does not offer the Recovery Console option, nor does it have Fast Repair.

**Step 1.**  Boot from the Windows 2000 CD. After the Windows setup files load, a text-mode screen will display. From the three choices on the menu, press R to repair a Windows 2000 installation.

The next menu displays the Windows 2000 Repair Options. Notice that you can run either the Recovery Console or the Emergency Repair Process. Press R again to run the Windows 2000 Emergency Repair Process.

From the next menu you can select between Manual Repair and Fast Repair. Fast Repair does not appear in Windows NT. Press M for Manual Repair.

The next menu allows you to select any combination of up to three options: Inspect Startup Environment, Verify Windows 2000 System Files (this will repair damaged registry files, and others), and Inspect Boot Sector.

Leave all choices checked and, with the highlight on *Continue*, press Enter. The next screen prompts you for your Emergency Repair Disk. If you have an Emergency Repair Disk created on this computer, press Enter. If you do not have an appropriate

Emergency Repair Disk, press L. Another screen appears requesting that you insert the Emergency Repair Disk into drive A:. Insert the disk and press Enter.

If you are using an ERD, the Emergency Repair Process will load the SETUP.LOG files from the ERD and proceed with the process. This is a very important file that should never be manually modified. It records activity from running Windows setup, which includes the initial setup and service packs.

If you are not using an ERD, the Emergency Repair Process searches for your installation of Windows 2000. It will display the installation that it found, and give you the choice to repair that installation, go back to the previous screen, or to quit setup. Press Enter to repair that installation.

**lab**

**Warning**

*If the Emergency Repair Process finds file discrepancies between the information in the SETUP.LOG and the files it finds on disk, it will prompt you to choose between skipping the file, repairing the file, or repairing the file and all others that were not originally installed with Windows 2000. When performing an emergency repair on a client desktop PC, be very cautious about having any of these files repaired by this process. For instance, if you have made manual changes to driver files, they would show up as files that were installed during Windows setup, but have been modified since then. If you allow the repair process to take these files back to their status at install, you may affect any program relying on the newer driver files.*

When Setup completes the Emergency Repair Process, it will prompt you to remove your disk, and it will reboot the computer.

In this lab you went through the steps of performing an emergency repair on Windows NT, Windows 2000, or Windows XP. The steps were written for Windows 2000, but are similar in all three operating systems.

**lab**

**Hint**

*Fast Repair is new beginning with Windows 2000. To learn more about the emergency repair process in general and the differences between Manual and Fast Repair, search for the article titled "Differences between Manual and Fast Repair in Windows" at the Microsoft TechNet site.*

**LAB EXERCISE 10.06**

# Discovering Advanced Startup Options

**30 Minutes**

Nerd Matrix has received a call from a customer whose computer will not boot up after he installed a new video capture card driver. The technician who responded said he was able to fix it using Last Known Good. You are curious about the advanced startup options, especially Last Known Good and Safe Mode. You have decided to experiment with it so you too can have success stories like his.

## Learning Objectives

In this lab you will explore the Windows advanced startup options. Once you've completed this lab, you will be able to:

- Use the Safe Mode options
- Use Device Manager in Safe Mode
- Select a Last Known Good Configuration

## Lab Materials and Setup

The materials you'll need for this lab are:

- A PC with Windows 9X, Windows 2000, or Windows XP installed

## Getting Down to Business

Every version of Windows since Windows 95, except Windows NT 4.0, offers a great tool for troubleshooting and resolving problems at boot up—Safe Mode. All but Windows 9x offer the Last Known Good option.

You will see that you actually have several Safe Mode options. You should use Safe Mode before you use more drastic measures, such as the Recovery Console (Windows 2000 and Windows XP) and the Emergency Repair Process (Windows NT, Windows 2000, and Windows XP). In the following steps, you will explore these startup options using Windows 2000. If you are using Windows 9x or Windows XP, you may see slightly different operations and screens. You use the Help program in this lab, and it may provide slightly different information in these various versions of Windows.

**Step 1.**    Restart your lab computer. At the operating system selection menu, press F8 to access the Advanced Options menu. If this menu does not appear, press F8 when you see the splash screen (the graphic that displays while Windows starts up). You should see the following menu:

```
Windows 2000 Advanced Options Menu
Please select an option:

    Safe Mode
    Safe Mode with Networking
    Safe Mode with Command Prompt

    Enable Boot Logging
    Enable VGA Mode
    Last Known Good Configuration
    Directory Services Restore Mode (Windows 2000 domain controllers
    Debugging Mode

    Boot Normally

Use ↑ and ↓ to move the highlight to your choice.
Press Enter to choose.
```

Select Safe Mode and press Enter. Windows will load in Safe Mode without network support.

**Step 2.**    Open Device Manager. If a problem with a device driver is preventing the operating system from starting normally, you can look here for yellow question mark warning icons that indicate an unknown device, or yellow exclamation mark icons that indicate conflicts with existing devices.

If you are troubleshooting a non-plug-and-play driver, click the View menu, and then click Show Hidden Devices. A new device type, Non-Plug and Play Drivers, will display. The number of non-plug and play drivers may surprise you. Many of these are not associated directly with hardware, but are special system-level drivers associated with services on your computers. We recommend that you work only with drivers for the device you are troubleshooting. The actions available to you vary based on the driver.

After you locate the problem device, you may stop or disable it, or remove the driver and replace it with a new driver. To learn more about Device Manager, check out the online Help, using the Help button (the question mark) in the Device Manager console.

**Step 3.** Use the Help program to research problems that can be corrected in Safe Mode. Read the articles you find when you search on "Safe Mode."

**Step 4.** Restart your computer again. At the operating system selection menu, press F8 to access the Advanced Options Menu. If this menu does not appear, press F8 when you see the splash screen (the graphic that displays while Windows starts up).

**Step 5.** At the Advanced Options menu move the cursor to Last Known Good Configuration and press Enter.

Quickly read the next screen, which is the Hardware Profile/Last Known Good Configuration screen. It will time out and continue without your decision if you don't make one.

Press L to select Last Known Good. The operating system will continue to load. If you had loaded a device driver before you restarted the operating system, selecting Last Known Good *before* a successful log on would cause Windows to select the configuration that existed the last time you logged on (before you installed the new device driver) and the driver would no longer be installed.

**lab**
**Warning**

*Last Known Good can fix configuration problems only if you use it before a successful reboot and log on after the change. Last Known Good cannot correct problems that are not related to configuration changes in the operating system. This includes problems caused by hardware failure, and corrupted files not related to a recent configuration change.*

In this lab you explored and used the startup options of Safe Mode and Last Known Good to repair problems that keep Windows from successfully starting up. You also used Device Manager in Safe Mode to view the status of device drivers.

**LAB EXERCISE 10.07**

# Exploring Event Viewer

**1 Hour**

The Windows Event Viewer, available in Windows NT, Windows 2000, and Windows XP, is a valuable tool to anyone who must administer or troubleshoot these systems. Any administrator soon learns that monitoring various log files is an important part of the job. This gives the administrator a feel for the health of the operating system, its services, and applications. Such consistent monitoring is normally done only on servers. On desktop computers we are less proactive, and depend on the log files to help determine the cause of a problem. The Event Viewer allows you to view three (or more in Windows 2000 and XP servers) important log files on a computer.

## Learning Objectives

After you complete this lab you will be able to:

- Identify the log files available in Windows NT, Windows 2000 Professional, and Windows XP Professional
- Adjust the log file options
- Clear a log file
- Archive a log file

## Lab Materials and Setup

For this lab exercise, you'll need:

- A PC with Windows NT, Windows 2000, or Windows XP

## Getting Down to Business

In the following steps you will use event viewer to determine the types of messages logged in the event logs. Then you will customize it.

**Step 1.** Click Start | Run and type EVENTVWR.MSC and click OK. (Windows NT uses EVENTVWR.EXE.) The Event Viewer will display events from three log files, as seen in Figure 10-1.

**FIGURE 10-1**

Windows 2000
Event Viewer

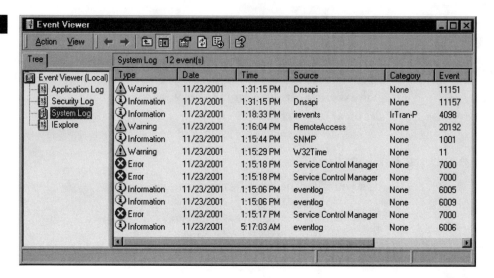

**lab**
**(i)int**

*Although the Event Viewer is available through the Start Menu, this shortcut may be located in a couple of different places, based on how the user has customized the desktop. It is common for technicians and administrators to learn the names of the files or commands that call up frequently used utilities. Then, rather than sorting through the client's Start Menu, and being annoyed by the custom cursor or sounds they have installed, you can quickly run commands from Start | Run. It is even quicker if you use the keyboard rather than the mouse to access the run command: Ctrl/Esc opens the Start Menu, and pressing the R key opens the Run box.*

**Step 2.** On the Event Viewer menu bar click Action | Help. Find the answers to the following question in the Event Viewer Help.

    a. Who can view Event Viewer logs?

    _____

    _____

    b. What are the five types of events that Event Viewer displays?

    _____

    _____

Browse through the Event Viewer Help console. When you are done, close Help.

**Step 3.** In Event Viewer, right-click on the System Log and select Properties. In Properties look at the Log Size box, which defines how large a log file may grow and what action should be taken when the log file reaches the maximum size. The defaults are 512KB and Overwrite Events Older Than 7 Days. Change this to 1MB and Overwrite Events As Needed. Then click on Filter. These settings filter what is displayed so that when you are viewing a large log file, but have a preference for what you want to see, you can filter out events based on type, source, category, ID, user, and computer. You can also choose to filter based on date. This controls only the viewer, all events will still be logged to the file.

Click OK to close the Properties dialog box.

**Step 4.** Clear the System Log by right-clicking on System Log and selecting Clear All Events. You will be prompted to save the System Log; click Yes.

You can archive a log file that you want to be able to view later by saving it to a different filename. Save the file in the My Documents folder using the first four letters of your name and the number 1. If you were at a client's site, you might save the log files to a network file server, or you might save them to a diskette to be viewed later (if they are not bigger than 1.44MB).

**Step 5.** To open the file you just saved, click on the Action menu, select Open Log File, select the file, select the log type of System and then click Open. Your saved log file will open. Notice how it appears in the Tree pane of Event Viewer.

In this lab you examined Event Viewer, a tool that allows you to view certain log files. Depending on the services and applications installed on a computer, there may be other log files that you need to check for troubleshooting purposes. Watch for these other log files on the job, but don't expect to have to know them for the A+ exam.

# LAB ANALYSIS TEST

1. Don, another technician at Nerd Matrix has called you from Delwood's Delicious Donuts. He was sent there to do a clean install of Windows XP on a new computer. The computer is one that Delwood purchased himself, and while it has a CD drive and the BIOS appears to enable him to configure it to boot from CD, he has not been successful in booting from the CD. He remembered that Windows NT came with boot diskettes that you could use in a case like this, but none were packed with Windows XP. What can you tell Don to help him?

   _____

   _____

2. You carefully formatted a diskette in Windows 2000 to use as a boot diskette. When you attempted to boot from the diskette you received the message NTLDR Missing. Press Any Key To Restart. What could be wrong with the diskette?

   _____

   _____

3. True or False? The boot diskette that comes packaged with Windows 98 is identical to the startup disk you create during a Windows 98 install.

   _____

   _____

4. You have determined that you need to do an emergency repair on a Windows 2000 computer. However, there is no recent repair disk available. What should you do?

   _____

   _____

5. You have been called to the corporate offices of Chuck's Chocolates because Cyril in customer service reported seeing an error message about a service. This message appeared before he logged on, but he continued with the logon. Cyril's computer is running Windows 2000 Professional. How can you determine what the error message was?

   _____

   _____

# KEY TERM QUIZ

Use the following vocabulary terms to complete the sentences below. Not all of the terms will be used.

>
> NTLDR
>
> Safe Mode
>
> setup
>
> NTDETECT.COM
>
> MSDOS.SYS
>
> ATTRIB
>
> Last Known Good Configuration
>
> Recovery Console
>
> Event Viewer
>
> system log

1. After you installed a new device driver, Windows 2000 stopped responding. You restart the computer, use the F8 menu and select the _____ from the Advanced Startup Options menu.

2. On a Windows NT, Windows 2000, or Windows XP computer the _____ file is in the root of the system partition, and is the first operating system file loaded during bootup.

3. After installing Windows 2000 on a computer you are preparing for a client, there is a message that a service failed to start at the first restart, but the startup was otherwise normal. You run _____ to look at the system log.

4. A Windows 98 computer fails to start normally. You restart the computer, press F8, and select _____ to troubleshoot the problem.

5. _____ is the file that directs a Windows 98 startup to the correct directory.

# LAB WRAP-UP

In other chapters you gathered knowledge and visited web sites to find more, but in this lab you accumulated something extra—lots of diskettes. You created setup boot diskettes and one or more system boot diskettes to add to the Emergency Repair Disk (ERD) you created in Chapter 9. Then you put these diskettes to use resolving problems. You also looked at the Advanced Startup Options of Windows 98, Windows 2000, and Windows XP. Finally, you worked with Event Viewer, which is available in Windows NT, Windows 2000, and Windows XP.

# LAB SOLUTIONS FOR CHAPTER 10

In this section, you'll find solutions to the lab exercises, Lab Analysis Test, and Key Term Quiz.

## Lab Solution 10.01

**Step 1.**    This step is complete and does not require a response.

## Lab Solution 10.02

**Step 1.**    This step is complete and does not require a response.

## Lab Solution 10.03

**Step 1.**    The message that will appear is "NTLDR is missing".

**Step 2.**

a. On a Windows 2000 computer, the message that will appear is: Windows 2000 Could Not Start Because The Following File Is Missing Or Corrupt: Windows 2000 root\system32\ntoskrnl.exe. Please Re-install A Copy Of The Above File.

b. You will probably agree that this message is deceiving in that it suggests that the file NTOSKRNL.EXE is missing. Since the days of Windows NT, technicians have learned that this message is more likely pointing to a missing or incorrectly configured BOOT.INI file. The line that you edited tells NTLDR where to find the NTOSKRNL, a central component (kernel) of the operating system. The strange syntax used in the BOOT.INI files is referred to as an ARC path. Search Microsoft's Technet site to learn more about ARC paths.

## Lab Solution 10.04

**Steps 1, 2 and 3.**    These steps are complete and do not require a response.

## Lab Solution 10.05

**Step 1.** This step is complete and does not require a response.

## Lab Solution 10.06

**Steps 1, 2, 3, 4, and 5.** These steps are complete and do not require a response.

## Lab Solution 10.07

**Step 1.** This step is complete and does not require a response.

**Step 2.**

  a. All users can view the system and application logs. This is important when you are doing phone support, because you can have the user look for errors in these logs. However, only administrators can view the security log, which is actually a security audit log.

  b. Event Viewer displays error, warning, information, success audit, and failure audit events.

**Steps 3, 4, and 5.** These steps are complete and do not require a response.

# ANSWERS TO LAB ANALYSIS TEST

1. You can tell Don that Microsoft has a utility available at their download site that will enable him to generate the diskettes to use to boot into the setup program when he cannot boot from the Windows XP CD, and does not have an operating system on the computer.

2. It sounds like you failed to copy the NTLDR file to the diskette. This file, along with NTDETECT.COM and BOOT.INI are required. In addition, you may need the NTBOOTDD.SYS file for a SCSI controller with the BIOS disabled.

3. False. The boot diskette that comes with Windows 98 is not identical to the one you create during the Windows 98 install. They both load CD drivers, but the one you create also

configures a RAM disk which it expands and to which it copies additional files that are useful for troubleshooting.

4. It is always best to have a recent ERD. However, in the absence of an ERD, just proceed with the emergency repair. The program will attempt to find repair information on the hard drive.

5. To see the error message that Cyril saw before he logged on, you can use Event Viewer to look at the System log. The system log contains information about events logged by system components. The actual message that was displayed is normally stored in the event viewer. From there, you can troubleshoot the problem. For instance, you can search the Microsoft Technet site using the event ID.

## ANSWERS TO KEY TERM QUIZ

1. Last Known Good Configuration
2. NTLDR
3. Event Viewer
4. Safe Mode
5. MSDOS.SYS

EXERCISES • QUESTIONS • ANSWERS

# 11

# Networks

This is the home stretch! If you have gone through the previous chapters in this lab manual, and completed all the labs for the A+ Hardware exam, you only have to go through this last chapter of labs to complete your preparation for the A+ Operating System Technologies exam. These labs are designed to help you prepare for the network portion of the exam. However, these are just the minimum skills needed by a hardware technician who also performs troubleshooting of basic network problems. After you complete these labs and take the exam, continue to explore the capabilities of TCP/IP. You will find that all you learn will be useful on the job.

---

## LAB EXERCISE 11.01

# Configuring TCP/IP Settings in Windows Manually

**30 Minutes**

In most organizations, desktop computers receive their IP configuration automatically from a Dynamic Host Configuration Protocol (DHCP) server. This is the most efficient way to configure IP hosts if the DHCP servers in an organization are well managed. However, because you work for Nerd Matrix, a company with many client organizations, you will undoubtedly encounter situations in which you must configure a host manually. Therefore, your boss requires you to know how to do it.

Manual configuration (also called static configuration) of TCP/IP settings may be needed in some small organizations, or in organizations of any size that either do not use DHCP or that make exceptions for certain computers. For instance, most servers are manually configured, even when there is a DHCP server available.

## Learning Objectives

In this lab, you will manually configure the IP settings on your lab computer. By the end of this lab, you'll be able to:

■ Manually configure IP settings when provided with the parameters to use

## Lab Materials and Setup

The materials you need for this lab are:

- A PC with Windows 95 or greater.
- All necessary IP settings, including IP address, subnet mask, and the addresses for default gateway, DNS server, and WINS server.
- If you are running a Windows operating system other than Windows 95 or 98, you will need to be logged on with local administrator privileges to complete this lab.

## Getting Down to Business

In the following steps you manually configure IP in Windows. If you are unsure of how to perform any steps, search Windows Help for static IP configuration. These steps use Windows 2000, but the process is very similar for Windows 9x, NT, or XP.

**Step 1.**   Using the IP settings provided by your instructor, enter the IP Address, subnet mask, default gateway, DNS, and WINS settings in the Internet Protocol (TCP/IP) Properties dialog box.

**Step 2.**   If you are using Windows 9x or Windows NT you will need to reboot after configuring TCP/IP. If you are using Windows 2000 or Windows XP you will not need to reboot after configuring TCP/IP.

**Step 3.**   Verify the IP configuration by using the IPCONFIG or WINIPCFG command. The WINIPCFG utility is a graphical utility, as seen in Chapter 11 of the *A+ Certification Study Guide.* IPCONFIG /ALL will result in output similar to that shown in Figure 11-1.

**Step 4.**   If necessary, return the computer to its original IP settings, reboot (if necessary), and verify that the IP configuration has been returned to its previous state.

```
C:\WINNT\System32\cmd.exe                                                  _ □ X

C:\>ipconfig /all

Windows 2000 IP Configuration

        Host Name . . . . . . . . . . . . : sierra
        Primary DNS Suffix  . . . . . . . :
        Node Type . . . . . . . . . . . . : Hybrid
        IP Routing Enabled. . . . . . . . : No
        WINS Proxy Enabled. . . . . . . . : No

Ethernet adapter Local Area Connection:

        Connection-specific DNS Suffix  . :
        Description . . . . . . . . . . . : AMD PCNET Family PCI Ethernet Adapter

        Physical Address. . . . . . . . . : 00-50-56-40-03-97
        DHCP Enabled. . . . . . . . . . . : No
        IP Address. . . . . . . . . . . . : 10.0.0.4
        Subnet Mask . . . . . . . . . . . : 255.255.255.0
        Default Gateway . . . . . . . . . : 10.0.0.1
        DNS Servers . . . . . . . . . . . : 10.163.82.4
                                            10.161.110.79
        Primary WINS Server . . . . . . . : 10.0.0.2

C:\>
```

**LAB EXERCISE 11.02**

# Creating a Dial-Up Connection in Windows

**45 Minutes**

Nerd Matrix technicians are often called upon to configure dial-up connections for clients. You have decided to practice this so that you will be familiar with the steps required. You realize that a dial-up connection first requires a properly configured device to use for the connection. You have often installed plug and play modems and have found that process to be extremely simple. However, other technicians have told you about their terrible experiences with modems that were not automatically detected. Therefore, you want to go through the steps of a manual modem driver installation, as well as the dial-up connection configuration.

## Learning Objectives

After you've completed this lab, you will be able to:

■ Manually install a modem driver

■ Create a dial-up connection

## Lab Materials and Setup

The materials you need for this lab are:

- A PC with Windows 95 or later version of Windows installed.
- If you are running a Windows operating system other than Windows 95 or 98, you will need to be logged on with local administrator privileges to complete this lab.

## Getting Down to Business

Before you can configure a dial-up connection, it must have a device to use for dial-up. This will usually be done during the installation of the operating system, if a modem is attached to the computer, or later, if the modem is added. In both cases, it is a simple operation if the computer and modem are all plug and play, but sometimes that is not the case. Therefore, in step one, you will go through the steps of manually installing a modem that was not detected. This can be done on a computer running Windows 98, Windows NT Workstation, Windows 2000 Professional, or Windows XP Professional. If you are uncertain about how to perform these steps, check out the Windows Help program.

**lab**
**Hint**
*We assume lab computers will not have a modem installed into Windows. Step one, therefore, gives you a fictitious modem to use for the later part of the class. If you have a modem, Step 1 is optional.*

**Step 1.**   Use the Windows Help program to find the instructions for installing a modem. Follow the instruction with one variation: in the Install New Modem wizard, select Don't Detect My Modem; I Will Select It From A List, then select a manufacturer and model.

After your modem is installed, you are ready for the next steps in which you will configure a dial-up connection in Windows 2000.

**cross**
**Reference**
*To create a dial-up connection in Windows 9x, see Exercise 11-5 in Chapter 11 of the* **A+ Certification Study Guide***.*

**Step 2**   Configure a dial-up connection. If you are unsure of how to do this, use the Windows Help program to find the steps. You will use your previously installed, "fictitious" modem, any phone number, and configure the connection so that it is not shared with other users on your network.

**Step 3**   If you configure dial-up networking on laptop computers for mobile users, they will need different settings, called Dialing Rules, if they are making calls from different locations. Experiment with creating a new location, such as "Hotel." Configure this location to dial 9 to access an outside line. When you are done, close all dialog boxes.

## LAB EXERCISE 11.03

# Troubleshooting with Network Utilities

**30 Minutes**

As a Nerd Matrix technician, you received a phone call from a manager at Tacony Trucking who is unable to connect to the server hosting their dispatch program and database. You expect that you will need to use the command line network utilities that come with TCP/IP so, before you leave your office, you try out some of the utilities you plan to use to help resolve the customer's connection problems.

## Learning Objectives

After you complete this lab you will be able to:

- Use the IPCONFIG or WINIPCFG command to verify the configuration of a connection
- Use the PING utility to verify connectivity to other host computers

## Lab Materials and Setup

For this lab exercise, you'll need:

- A PC with Windows 95 or later version of Windows.
- The IP address of another computer on your LAN.
- The IP address of your default gateway.
- If you are running a Windows operating system other than Windows 95 or 98, you will need to be logged on with local administrator privileges to complete this lab.

## Getting Down to Business

After you have gathered information about the symptoms that the client is experiencing, you will use a variety of utilities to research the problem. You will begin by looking at the TCP/IP configuration. If that checks out, then you will use the PING command to check for connectivity between the client's computer and other computers.

lab
ⓘint

*If your Internet connection has a firewall that restricts the types of traffic that flows between your network and the Internet, some of these steps may not succeed.*

**Step 1.** First view the TCP/IP properties to determine if there are any manual settings that may be causing a problem.

What are you looking for? You should check that the settings are consistent with the standards required for this computer by the network administrator. If those standards require that all desktop computers be DHCP clients, then confirm exactly how the client should be configured. It turns out that you have some flexibility in this matter, and if the users are allowed to have administrative access to their computers they can alter the company standards. So, check that both Obtain An IP Address Automatically and Obtain DNS Server Address Automatically are selected.

It is still possible to manually configure some settings through the Advanced button. Click that button now and check that no manual settings have been added, unless the network administrator has authorized them. In the four tab sheets on the Advanced TCP/IP Setting dialog box, there should be the defaults displayed in Table 11-1.

If you find any discrepancies, consult with the network administrator.

**TABLE 11-1**   Advanced TCP/IP Setting dialog box defaults for DHCP clients

| Tab Sheet | Option | Setting |
|---|---|---|
| IP Settings | IP Addresses | DHCP Enabled |
| IP Settings | Default gateways | Empty (even if DHCP configures the client with a default gateway) |
| IP Settings | Interface metric | 1 |
| DNS Settings | DNS server addresses, in order of use | Empty (even if DHCP configures the client with one or more DNS server address) |

| TABLE 11-1 | Advanced TCP/IP Setting dialog box defaults for DHCP clients *(continued)* |

| Tab Sheet | Option | Setting |
|---|---|---|
| DNS Settings | Append primary and connection-specific DNS suffixes. | Selected |
| DNS Settings | Append parent suffixes of the primary DNS suffix | Selected |
| DNS Settings | Append these DNS suffixes (in order) | Empty |
| DNS Settings | DNS suffix for this connection | Empty |
| DNS Settings | Register this connection's addresses in DNS | Selected |
| DNS Settings | Use this connection's DNS suffix in DNS registration | Empty |
| WINS Settings | WINS addresses, in order of use | Empty |
| WINS Settings | Enable LMHOSTS lookup | Enabled |
| WINS Settings | Enable NetBIOS over TCP/IP | Enabled |
| WINS Settings | Disable NetBIOS over TCP/IP | Not selected |
| WINS Settings | Use NetBIOS setting from the DHCP server<br><br>Use DHCP for WINS Resolution (Windows 9x only) | Not selected<br><br>Selected |
| Options | The only optional settings listed should be IP security and TCP/IP filtering. | However, if you view the settings for these two components, the default is for neither to be configured. |

lab
**ⓘint**  *If you make any changes to these settings on a Windows 9x or Windows NT computer, you must reboot. The newer operating systems do not normally require a reboot for these settings.*

**Step 2.**  Once you have confirmed that the IP configuration is correct or made any necessary changes to the configuration, and rebooted the computer (if required), then move on to verify that the configuration changes have taken effect by using IPCONFIG or WINIPCFG.

If your network card shows an empty IP address (0.0.0.0), you may need to reboot. Or if it is a DHCP client, it may have failed to receive an address from the DHCP server.

If you have already rebooted, but still have an empty IP address, or an address beginning with 169 (see Lab Hint below), and if the client is a DHCP client, enter one of the following commands:

```
WINIPCFG /RENEW_ALL (in Windows 95)
IPCONFIG /RENEW
```

If this still does not provide the correct settings, check with the instructor or DHCP administrator. If you use the second command, and it is successful, you should see a short message similar to the following:

```
C:\>ipconfig /renew

Windows 2000 IP Configuration

Ethernet adapter Local Area Connection:

        Connection-specific DNS Suffix  . :
        IP Address. . . . . . . . . . . . : 10.0.0.20
        Subnet Mask . . . . . . . . . . . : 255.255.255.0
        Default Gateway . . . . . . . . . : 10.0.0.1

C:\>
```

lab Hint

*Windows 98, Windows 2000, and Windows XP have a new default behavior for DHCP clients that do not get a response from a DHCP server, or if lease configuration fails. These DHCP clients will use an address in a special range reserved by Microsoft for use with Automatic Private IP Addressing (APIPA) — 169.254.0.1 to 169.254.255.254 with a subnet mask of 255.255.0.0. The client selects a number from this range, broadcasts it on the subnet to verify that it is not already in use, and uses it (if not in use) until a DHCP server can be located and a new address leased. This all happens on the client side. The client continues to attempt to locate a DHCP server at regular intervals. This feature is intended to make network configuration very simple in a small office/ home office (SOHO) environment, but it can be annoying in a corporate environment. Learn more about APIPA at www.microsoft.com/technet.*

**Step 3.** Once you have confirmed that the configuration actually took effect, test the computer's connectivity with other computers on the network. Open a command prompt and PING the IP address of another host on your local network segment. If this is successful, PING the IP address of the default gateway (router). If this is successful, PING the IP address of a host computer beyond your router. Figure 11-2 shows the result of running these three commands successfully.

**Step 4** If you cannot PING another host computer on your network, try to PING that same computer from another computer. If you can PING it from another computer, but not from yours, reverify your configuration. The most common reason for this type of behavior is an incorrect network subnet mask setting made when the IP settings were configured manually. Verify that you are using the same network subnet mask as other computers on your network segment. This requires examining the output from your IPCONFIG command, then making any necessary changes in the TCP/IP properties.

```
Command Prompt                                              _ □ X
C:\>ping 10.0.0.11

Pinging 10.0.0.11 with 32 bytes of data:

Reply from 10.0.0.11: bytes=32 time<10ms TTL=128
Reply from 10.0.0.11: bytes=32 time<10ms TTL=128
Reply from 10.0.0.11: bytes=32 time<10ms TTL=128
Reply from 10.0.0.11: bytes=32 time=30ms TTL=128

Ping statistics for 10.0.0.11:
    Packets: Sent = 4, Received = 4, Lost = 0 (0% loss),
Approximate round trip times in milli-seconds:
    Minimum = 0ms, Maximum =  30ms, Average =   7ms

C:\>ping 10.0.0.1

Pinging 10.0.0.1 with 32 bytes of data:

Reply from 10.0.0.1: bytes=32 time<10ms TTL=64
Reply from 10.0.0.1: bytes=32 time<10ms TTL=64
Reply from 10.0.0.1: bytes=32 time<10ms TTL=64
Reply from 10.0.0.1: bytes=32 time<10ms TTL=64

Ping statistics for 10.0.0.1:
    Packets: Sent = 4, Received = 4, Lost = 0 (0% loss),
Approximate round trip times in milli-seconds:
    Minimum = 0ms, Maximum =  0ms, Average =   0ms

C:\>ping 206.163.82.4

Pinging 206.163.82.4 with 32 bytes of data:

Reply from 206.163.82.4: bytes=32 time=101ms TTL=234
Reply from 206.163.82.4: bytes=32 time=100ms TTL=234
Reply from 206.163.82.4: bytes=32 time=100ms TTL=234
Reply from 206.163.82.4: bytes=32 time=100ms TTL=234

Ping statistics for 206.163.82.4:
    Packets: Sent = 4, Received = 4, Lost = 0 (0% loss),
Approximate round trip times in milli-seconds:
    Minimum = 100ms, Maximum =  101ms, Average =   100ms

C:\>
```

Once you have resolved any settings errors, and rebooted (if required), test again. If you can now PING the local host, try pinging your gateway. Troubleshoot this if it does not work. PING the gateway from another computer. Reverify the gateway settings.

**Step 5**　Once you have resolved any settings errors, and rebooted (if required), test yet again by PINGing a remote host (beyond your router) that can be PINGed from other computers on your network.

If you and others on your network cannot PING a remote host, then check with your router administrator (this may be your ISP). They may have a problem at their end, or they may tell you that the host you are trying to ping is not available.

## LAB EXERCISE 11.04

# Troubleshooting DNS Errors

**I Hour**

Patrick, the operations manager at Palmyra Painting, has called and said that he cannot connect to any web pages with Internet Explorer (IE). When he attempts to connect, he receives an error in IE stating The Page Cannot Display. Because you aren't sure how to handle this situation, a senior Nerd Matrix technician has advised you on how to proceed.

He suggests that this may be a name resolution problem, since the fully qualified domain name (FQDN) (e.g., www.osborne.com), must be resolved to an IP address before a single packet will be sent to the web site. You will first test by either PINGing (using the PING command) the IP address of the web site, or using the IP address in place of the FQDN in the universal resource locator (URL). If you can reach the web site using its IP address, then it is a name resolution problem.

lab
ⓗint
*For a more thorough treatment of this topic, search the Microsoft TechNet site for the article "How to Troubleshoot Basic TCP/IP Problems."*

## Learning Objectives

Once you've completed this lab, you will be able to:

■ Troubleshoot common DNS errors

## Lab Materials and Setup

The materials you'll need for this lab are:

- A PC with Windows 95 or greater.
- An Internet connection and the URL of a site to which you have previously connected.
- An IP address to use as a bogus DNS server.
- If you are running a Windows operating system other than Windows 95 or 98, you will need to be logged on with local administrator privileges to complete this lab.

## Getting Down to Business

The first two steps get your computer set up for the troubleshooting steps that follow. First you will connect to a web site. Then you will open a command prompt and PING the fully qualified domain name (FQDN) of the web site to obtain the IP address (sometimes you can pick it up by watching the status bar of your browser, but we are rarely fast enough to do that). After you have obtained this IP address, you will then "break" DNS on your lab computer. Then you will look for the behavior that indicates that DNS is not functioning. Finally, you will resolve the DNS Problem.

**Step 1.** Using your Internet browser, connect to the Osborne/McGraw-Hill web site at www.osborne.com. Then open a command prompt and enter the following command: PING www.osborne.com. Write down the IP address.

---

**Step 2.** In your TCP/IP properties dialog box enter a bogus DNS server address and close out of the dialog box.

**Step 3.** Now you will view the symptoms of a DNS error.

Open your Internet browser and try to access www.osborne.com. If you are using Internet Explorer, scroll down to the bottom of the message. You should see a line that says Cannot Find Server or DNS Error.

**Step 4.**   There are several ways to verify that this is a DNS error, rather than a problem with the server not being available. Use your Internet browser and substitute the IP address of this site that you wrote down in Step 1. If you can connect with the IP address, it is a DNS problem.

A second way to verify that this is a DNS error is to open a command prompt and use the PING command to test the connection to the web site, using the address you used above. You should be able PING the server, even though you were not able to connect with your web browser.

A third method that does not require knowing the address of the web site involves using the NSLOOKUP command. Open a command prompt and enter NSLOOKUP. If the DNS name server is not available, you will see this message:

```
C:\WINNT\System32\cmd.exe - nslookup                        _ □ ×

C:\>nslookup
*** Can't find server name for address 10.0.0.2: No response from server

*** Default servers are not available
Default Server:  UnKnown
Address:  10.0.0.2

>
```

In the command prompt, type EXIT to exit from NSLOOKUP, and type EXIT again to close the command prompt window.

lab

**ⓗint**   *For the A+ exam it is important for you to be able to recognize a DNS error, but you are not required to understand the NSLOOKUP command. However, you will want further knowledge of this command. You can begin by searching for NSLOOKUP in the Windows 2000 Help program, or at the Microsoft TechNet site.*

**Step 5.**   OK, you have had your fun, now you must fix DNS. Open the Advanced properties for Internet Protocol and remove the bogus DNS address you added. If you removed addresses from here earlier, reenter the correct addresses now, and use the OK buttons to exit first from the Advanced, and then from the Internet Protocol properties dialog boxes. Then close all windows except your Internet browser.

**Step 6.**   Using your Internet browser, attempt to connect to the site again, using the URL. If this is not successful, retrace your steps and verify all of your IP settings, especially the DNS settings. When you have successfully connected to the site, close all windows.

## LAB EXERCISE 11.05

# Configuring a Windows Mail Client

**1 Hour**

In the installations of Windows that you have done since coming to work at Nerd Matrix, you have noticed that a typical installation of Windows now includes Outlook Express. This application includes both an e-mail client and a newsreader. E-mail is a phenomenally popular way to communicate. Clients often ask for help in getting access to their e-mail and (less often) to news groups. You want to be prepared to do these tasks. You will configure Outlook Express as an e-mail client in this lab. In the lab that follows, you will configure Outlook Express as a newsreader because as a service technician you may be called upon to set up both of these components for a customer.

**lab Hint**

*New to e-mail concepts? Check out the Hot Flash animation of how e-mail works at www.learnthenet.com/english/index.html.*

## Learning Objectives

After you complete this lab you will be able to:

■ Configure an Internet mail client

## Lab Materials and Setup

In order to complete this lab you will need to know some specific information. If you do not have this information, ask your ISP (if this is your private account) or network administrator (if your mail server is a corporate mail server). The materials and information you need for this lab are:

■ A PC with Windows 95 or later

■ Outlook Express installed into Windows

- An Internet e-mail address
- Your account name and password
- The DNS name or IP address of an incoming mail server for POP3, IMAP, or HTTP
- The DNS name or IP address of an outgoing mail server (SMTP)
- The HTTP mail service provider (if needed)

## Getting Down to Business

After acquiring the correct information from the customer, their ISP, or their network administrator, you are ready to configure Outlook Express as an e-mail client. This may not be the software you use for every client, but the type of information you need is the same for any e-mail client. The following steps describe how this is done using Outlook Express running in Windows 2000, but the tasks will be similar in any version of Outlook Express, and with any e-mail client.

**Step 1.**   Open Outlook Express. If this is the first time you have run Outlook Express, and if you have not configured an Internet connection, the Internet Connection Wizard will appear. Cancel out of the screen requesting phone information, unless you are using a local modem to connect to the Internet. Complete the Internet connection information, based on information provided by your instructor, or provided by your ISP if you are doing this lab independent of a classroom environment.

**Step 2.**   On the Your Name page on the Internet Connection Wizard, enter the name you would like to display when you respond to e-mail messages, then click Next.

**Step 3.**   On the Internet E-mail Address page, enter your e-mail address, and then click Next.

**Step 4.**   On the E-mail Server Names page, select the protocol of your incoming mail server (POP3, IMAP, HTTP). If you select POP3, IMAP, or HTTP you will enter the DNS name of your incoming mail server on this page. With all but HTTP, you will also enter the DNS name of your outgoing mail server. The E-mail Server

Names page appears as shown in Figure 11-3, when you select POP3 or IMAP. POP3 is shown, but the choices are the same.

If you select HTTP as the protocol for your incoming mail server, the E-mail Server Names page displays an additional option: HTTP Mail Service Provider. Your choices are Hotmail or Other. Figure 11-4 shows this page with the additional option, and you can see that outgoing SMTP server is no longer available, but greyed out. When you enter the incoming mail server for an HTTP mail server, be sure to include the complete URL for the mail server, including the prefix for the HTTP protocol (http) and a file name. If you select Hotmail, as shown in Figure 11-4, notice that it uses an ASP file.

After you have configured the E-mail Server Names page, click Next.

**Step 5.**   On the Internet Mail Logon page, enter your account name and password, and leave the check box next to Log On Using Secure Password Authentication (SPA) blank unless you know that this is required. Choose Remember Password only if you are the only person who uses your username to log onto your computer. Click Next.

**Step 6.**   On the Congratulations page, click Finish, and close the Internet Accounts dialog box.

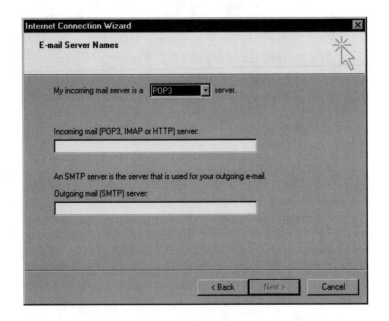

| FIGURE 11-3 |
| --- |

Setting up a
POP3 or IMAP
server

**FIGURE 11-4**

Setting up an
HTTP server

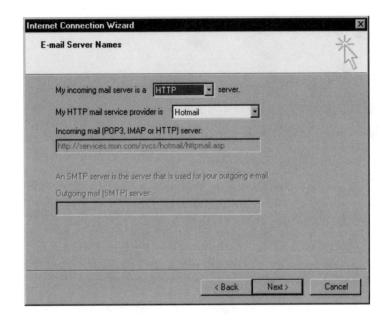

**Step 7.** To pick up your e-mail (optional), click Inbox in Outlook Express. Then on the menu bar, click Tools I Send and Receive I Receive All.

## LAB EXERCISE 11.06

# Configuring a Newsgroup Client

**30 Minutes**

Those who like to participate in a newsgroup (a discussion forum for people who share a common interest) use newsreaders. With a newsreader you can access a newsgroup to view and post messages to the newsgroup (also referred to as a "threaded discussion"). There are many newsgroups on the Internet. Network News Transfer Protocol (NNTP) is the protocol that a newsreader uses to communicate with a news server.

lab
**ⓗint**  *New to newsgroups? Check out the "How to" information on joining Newsgroups at www.learnthenet.com/english/index.html.*

## Learning Objectives

After you complete this lab you will be able to:

- Configure the Outlook Express newsreader to connect to a news server

## Lab Materials and Setup

The materials you need for this lab are:

- A PC with Windows 95 or later version of Windows
- Outlook Express installed into Windows
- An Internet e-mail address

## Getting Down to Business

The following steps were written using Outlook Express in Windows 2000. However, the steps are very similar in any version of Windows.

**lab Hint**

*In the following steps you will use the public newsgroups at Microsoft. If you would like to select a different newsgroup, use your web browser to connect to www.ii.com/internet/messaging/newsgroups/. Browse through this site and select a newsgroup. You will need to know the name of the newsgroup server (also referred to as an NNTP server), and you will need to know if you need a username and password to log on. We chose Microsoft public newsgroups because they do not require a username and password. If you select a newsgroup that requires a username and password, you will have to investigate what you will need to do to acquire them. Sometimes there is a charge, or simply a requirement that you provide them with information about yourself.*

**Step 1.**    Open Outlook Express. If this is the first time you have run Outlook Express please see Step 1 in Lab 11.05.

**Step 2.**    On the menu bar, select Tools | Accounts. Click Add, then select News. If you completed Lab 11.05, the first two pages (Your Name and Internet News E-mail Address) should already be complete, and you can click Next two times unless you wish to change one of the options.

**Step 3.** Enter the name of your Internet news server. To use the news server at Microsoft enter: news.microsoft.com. This news server does not require you to log on, therefore leave the box for this choice empty.

Click Next then click Finish on the Congratulations page.

**Step 4.** Click Close on the Internet Accounts dialog box. Click Yes on the Outlook Express message box that asks Would You Like To Download Newsgroups From The News Account You Added? Outlook Express will download the names of all the newsgroups at this news server and display a list similar to Figure 11-5.

**Step 5.** In the box labeled Display newsgroups which contain:, enter WindowsXP. When the list of newsgroups appears, scroll down until you see microsoft.public.windowsxp.network_web, and click to select this newsgroup.

**Step 6.** Click Subscribe. To see the lists that you are subscribed to, click on Subscribed below the list to display the Subscribe tab sheet. The selected newsgroup should be displayed. When you click Go To at the bottom of the box, Outlook Express will appear, as seen in Figure 11-6.

| FIGURE 11-5 | |
| --- | --- |

Newsgroup
Subscriptions

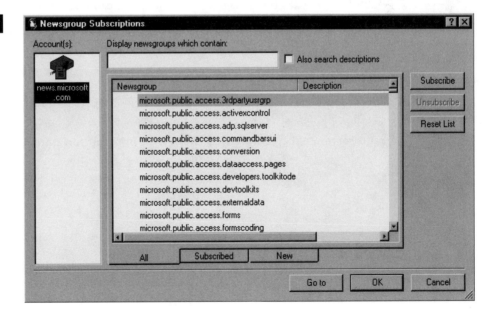

**FIGURE 11-6**

Outlook Express
with the news
client

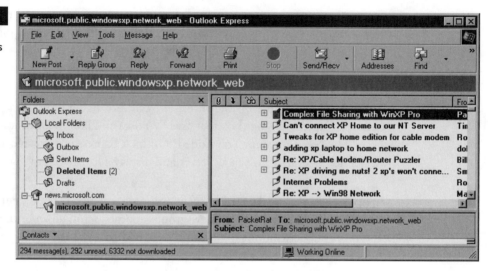

Congratulations, you are now connected to the Windows XP newsgroup. Browse
through the messages. A message with a plus-in-a-box is the initial message of a thread.
A thread contains all the responses to an initial message.

Optionally, select other newsgroups from this server. The list in the Subscribed
tab will grow with the newsgroups you add. You can unsubscribe to a newsgroup by
selecting it and clicking Unsubscribe.

# LAB ANALYSIS TEST

**I.** A DHCP server was configured on your network with computers on your subnet having an address range of 10.0.1.100 to 10.0.1.200, a subnet mask of 255.255.255.0, and the following settings:

- Gateway: 10.0.0.1
- Preferred DNS: 10.161.220.79
- Alternate DNS: 10.161.220.80
- WINS: 10.163.82.4

You can locate DNS resources from your computer, but cannot locate the NT file and printer server on another subnet. You have been told this server is located using WINS because it is registered with the WINS servers as a NetBIOS resource. Running the IPCONFIG /ALL command shows your computer is a DHCP client and all information matches except the WINS, which is an entirely different IP address. If your computer is a DHCP client, how can it have an entirely different setting for WINS than that which the DHCP server assigns to the client?

---

**2.** You have changed a manually configured client to be a DHCP client by selecting the correct two radio buttons in Internet Protocol Properties for your local area network on a Windows XP client computer. How can you ensure that the computer requests an address immediately?

---

**3.** A client opened his web browser but was unable to connect to any URLs that have worked in the past. You successfully PING the IP address of another computer on the network, the gateway, and a remote computer on the Internet. You checked your IP configuration, and nothing has changed. You PING the addresses of the preferred and alternate DNS servers and receive replies. What do you do next to discover the solution to the problem?

---

**4.** You have been called to configure Outlook Express on five desktop computers to connect to a POP3 mail server. You have been told that the IP configuration is correct on these computers, and you will have to work only in Outlook Express. What information is needed to configure each client?

---

**5.** You have been called to configure Outlook Express on ten desktop computers to connect to a news server. You have been told that the IP configuration is correct on these computers, and you will have to work only in Outlook Express. What information is needed to configure each client?

---

# KEY TERM QUIZ

Use the following vocabulary terms to complete the sentences below. Not all of the terms will be used.

> PING
>
> NNTP
>
> Dial-up connection
>
> SMTP
>
> HTTP
>
> POP3
>
> DNS
>
> WINS2
>
> IPCONFIG
>
> NSLOOKUP

1. When you configure an Internet news client you must enter the name of a/an _____ server.

2. _____ is a utility that allows you to test a computer for connectivity on a TCP/IP network.

3. When troubleshooting DNS, you will want to learn more about the _____ utility.

4. _____ is a protocol used by outgoing Internet mail servers.

5. _____ is a protocol used by incoming Internet mail servers.

# LAB WRAP-UP

In this chapter of the lab manual you configured a computer with a static IP and other settings, because you will encounter occasions to manually do this job that is often accomplished by DHCP. Similarly, you manually configured a modem driver on your lab computer, then configured a dial-up client. You worked through some troubleshooting procedures using GUI configuration properties dialog boxes, as well as command line tools, IPCONFIG, PING, and NSLOOKUP. Finally, you configured Outlook Express as an e-mail client and a news client.

This chapter wraps up operating system tasks for the A+ Operating System exam. It is also the final chapter in the entire book that guided you through your study and preparation for both the hardware and operating system exam. We hope you take the exam soon, and we wish you great success on the exams and with your career. GOOD LUCK!

# LAB SOLUTIONS FOR CHAPTER 11

In this section, you'll find solutions to the lab exercises, Lab Analysis Test, and Key Term Quiz.

## Lab Solution 11.01

**Step 1.** In Network and Dial-up Connections, open the Properties of Local Area Connection, then in the Properties dialog box double-click Internet Protocol (TCP/IP).

Click the radio button to select Use The Following IP Address. Enter the IP address, subnet mask, and default gateway addresses you have received from your instructor.

Click the radio button to select Use The Following DNS Server Addresses, and enter any DNS server addresses you have received from your instructor.

Click the Advanced button, and then click the WINS tab. On the WINS page, click Add and enter the IP address of the WINS server given to you by your instructor. Click Add. Leave the default settings for the other options on this page.

Click OK on the Advanced dialog box.

Click OK on the Internet Protocol (TCP/IP) Properties page, and click OK on the Local Area Connection Properties dialog box.

**Step 2.** This step is complete, and no response is necessary.

**Step 3.** Open a command prompt and enter the correct command for running the IP Configuration utility:

- In Windows 9x the command is WINIPCFG

- In Windows NT, Windows 2000, and Windows XP the command is IPCONFIG /ALL

- Windows 98 can use either command

**Step 4.** If you need to configure your lab computer as a DHCP client, open the properties of the Local Area Connection, select Obtain An IP Address Automatically, and select Obtain DNS Server Address Automatically. If you configured WINS in Step 1 above, use the Advanced button to access the WINS tab and remove the WINS server(s) you added. Be sure to click OK on the Advanced dialog box and also again on the Internet Protocol (TCP/IP) Properties.

If you changed back to automatic (DHCP) settings, open a command prompt and do one of the following:

a. In Windows 9x, reboot the computer.

b. In Windows 2000 or Windows XP, enter IPCONFIG /RELEASE. When this command completes, enter IPCONFIG /RENEW.

## Lab Solution 11.02

**Step 1.**   Start the Phone and Modem Options from the Control Panel in Windows 2000 and Windows XP. The Add/Remove Hardware Wizard runs and the Install New Modem page appears.

Select Don't Detect My Modem; I Will Select It From A List and then click Next.

Select Standard Modem Types in the list of manufacturers, select a model from the list of models, and click Next.

Select a Port and click Next.

Click Finish.

Click OK to close the Phone and Modem Options dialog box.

**Step 2.**   Open Network and Dial-up Connections and select Make New Connection.

On the Welcome page of the network Connection Wizard click Next.

On the Network Connection Type page (see Figure 11-7) select Dial-Up To Private Network and click Next.

On the Phone Numbers to Dial page, enter a phone number and click Next.

On the Connection Availability page select Only For Myself and click Next.

On the Completing the Network Connection Wizard page click Finish.

**Step 3.**   In the properties dialog box of your dial-up connection, select Properties. On the General tab, select Use Dialing Rules, then select Rules. This screen is useful for laptop users who travel and make calls from different area codes. Experiment with creating a new location, such as "Hotel" that would require dialing 9 to access an outside line.

Cancel from the Dialing Rules page, then Cancel to exit from the Dial-up Connection.

**FIGURE 11-7**

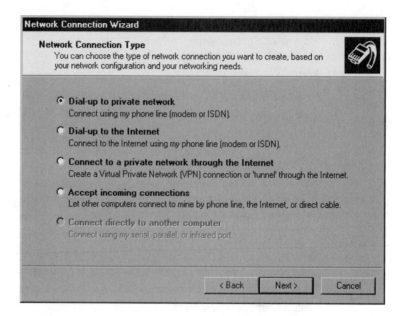

**Network Connection Wizard**

**Network Connection Type**
You can choose the type of network connection you want to create, based on your network configuration and your networking needs.

- **Dial-up to private network**
  Connect using my phone line (modem or ISDN).

- **Dial-up to the Internet**
  Connect to the Internet using my phone line (modem or ISDN).

- **Connect to a private network through the Internet**
  Create a Virtual Private Network (VPN) connection or 'tunnel' through the Internet.

- **Accept incoming connections**
  Let other computers connect to mine by phone line, the Internet, or direct cable.

- **Connect directly to another computer**
  Connect using my serial, parallel, or infrared port.

< Back | Next > | Cancel

## Lab Solution 11.03

**Step 1.** When using the Windows 2000 GUI, TCP/IP properties must be viewed by connection. Therefore you must open Network and Dial-up Connections and view the properties of your Local Area Connection, then double-click Internet Protocol (TCP/IP) to open its properties.

**Step 2.** Open a command prompt. Run the IPCONFIG /ALL command (WINIPCFG /ALL in Windows 95). The output of this command should be similar to that shown earlier in Figure 11-1.

**Steps 3, 4, and 5.** The instructions for these steps are complete.

## Lab Solution 11.04

**Step 1.** The IP address of www.osborne.com is 198.45.24.130.

### Step 2.

1. In the Properties for your Local Area Connection, open the Properties Of Internet Protocol.
2. Click on the Advanced button in the Internet Protocol Properties dialog box.
3. Select the DNS tab, and click Add below the DNS server addresses box.
4. Enter a bogus DNS server address. Use 10.0.0.2 (or an IP address provided by your instructor).
5. If there are any other IP addresses in this box, write them down now, and then remove them with the remove button.
6. When your bogus DNS server address is the only address in this list, click OK on the Advanced Properties.
7. Click OK on the Internet Properties box.
8. Close all open windows. (If you are using Windows 9x you will have to restart.)

**Steps 3, 4, 5, and 6.** These steps are complete and no response is necessary.

## Lab Solution 11.05

**Steps 1 through 7.** These steps are complete and no response is necessary.

## Lab Solution 11.06

**Steps 1 through 6.** These steps are complete and no response is necessary.

# ANSWERS TO LAB ANALYSIS TEST

1. Settings that can be entered through the Advanced button on the Internet Protocol Properties will override the settings from the DHCP server. When troubleshooting, be sure to check the Advanced settings. If you are logged on as an administrator, and you have modified these settings, they can cause problems like this. Never manually change settings unless the network administrator has explicitly told you to do so.

2. To ensure that the computer immediately requests an IP address after converting from static to manual, open a command prompt and enter the following command: IPCONFIG /RENEW.

3. It looks like a DNS problem. Although the DNS servers respond, they may not be functioning properly. Try one more thing: NSLOOKUP. If you receive a message that it cannot find the server, it is time to contact a network administrator. Tell the administrator exactly what you have done so far, and the results of your tests. If there are two DNS servers configured, and you received a response from both, the first one might be on the network, and responding, but it could not resolve the problem. A DNS client queries the alternate DNS server only when it receives NO response, not when it receives a negative response. Your network administrator (or ISP) may need to check the DNS server for problems and configuration changes.

4. You will need the display name, e-mail address, user account name, and password for each user, as well as the IP address or DNS names for the POP3 (incoming) server and the SMTP (outgoing) server. You will also need to know whether the mail server requires Secure Password Authentication (SPA).

5. If the e-mail has not already been set up in Outlook Express, you will need the display name, e-mail address, user account name, and password for each user, as well as the IP address or DNS names for the POP3 (incoming) server and the SMTP (outgoing) server. You will also need to know whether the mail server requires a user name and password, and you will need the name of the Internet News (NNTP) server.

## ANSWERS TO KEY TERM QUIZ

1. NNTP

2. PING

3. NSLOOKUP

4. SMTP

5. POP3

# INDEX

**J**

**K**

**L**

## M

**N**

## P

# INTERNATIONAL CONTACT INFORMATION

**AUSTRALIA**
McGraw-Hill Book Company Australia Pty. Ltd.
TEL +61-2-9417-9899
FAX +61-2-9417-5687
http://www.mcgraw-hill.com.au
books-it_sydney@mcgraw-hill.com

**CANADA**
McGraw-Hill Ryerson Ltd.
TEL +905-430-5000
FAX +905-430-5020
http://www.mcgrawhill.ca

**GREECE, MIDDLE EAST,
NORTHERN AFRICA**
McGraw-Hill Hellas
TEL +30-1-656-0990-3-4
FAX +30-1-654-5525

**MEXICO (Also serving Latin America)**
McGraw-Hill Interamericana Editores S.A. de C.V.
TEL +525-117-1583
FAX +525-117-1589
http://www.mcgraw-hill.com.mx
fernando_castellanos@mcgraw-hill.com

**SINGAPORE (Serving Asia)**
McGraw-Hill Book Company
TEL +65-863-1580
FAX +65-862-3354
http://www.mcgraw-hill.com.sg
mghasia@mcgraw-hill.com

**SOUTH AFRICA**
McGraw-Hill South Africa
TEL +27-11-622-7512
FAX +27-11-622-9045
robyn_swanepoel@mcgraw-hill.com

**UNITED KINGDOM & EUROPE
(Excluding Southern Europe)**
McGraw-Hill Education Europe
TEL +44-1-628-502500
FAX +44-1-628-770224
http://www.mcgraw-hill.co.uk
computing_neurope@mcgraw-hill.com

**ALL OTHER INQUIRIES Contact:**
Osborne/McGraw-Hill
TEL +1-510-549-6600
FAX +1-510-883-7600
http://www.osborne.com
omg_international@mcgraw-hill.com